Subject to Death

Subject to Death

Life and Loss in a Buddhist World

Robert Desjarlais

The University of Chicago Press
Chicago and London

Robert Desjarlais is professor of anthropology at Sarah Lawrence College. He is the author of several books, including *Shelter Blues: Sanity and Selfhood among the Homeless* and *Counterplay: An Anthropologist at the Chessboard*.

The University of Chicago Press, Chicago 60637
The University of Chicago Press, Ltd., London
© 2016 by The University of Chicago
All rights reserved. Published 2016.
Printed in the United States of America

25 24 23 22 21 20 19 18 17 16   1 2 3 4 5

ISBN-13: 978–0-226–35573–3 (cloth)
ISBN-13: 978–0-226–35587–0 (paper)
ISBN-13: 978–0-226–35590–0 (e-book)
DOI: 10.7208/chicago/9780226355900.001.0001

Library of Congress Cataloging-in-Publication Data
Names: Desjarlais, Robert R., author.
Title: Subject to death : life and loss in a Buddhist world / Robert Desjarlais.
Description: Chicago ; London : University of Chicago Press, 2016. | ?2016 |
    Includes bibliographical references and index.
Identifiers: LCCN 2015039597| ISBN 9780226355733 (cloth : alkaline paper) |
    ISBN 9780226355870 (paperback : alkaline paper) | ISBN 9780226355900
    (e-book)
Subjects: LCSH: Death—Religious aspects—Buddhism. | Death—Social
    aspects—Nepal—Helmu. | Helambu Sherpa (Nepalese people)—Religion.
Classification: LCC BQ4487 .D47 2016 | DDC 294.3/423—dc23 LC record
    available at http://lccn.loc.gov/2015039597

♾ This paper meets the requirements of ANSI/NISO Z39.48–1992 (Permanence of Paper).

Death, like the sun, cannot be looked at steadily.
François de La Rochefoucauld

Contents

Note on Transliteration

Most Hyolmo people, or "Hyolmo wa" (Hyolmo wa is nowadays usually pronounced as "yhol-mo wa," with an aspirated *y* leading into "ol-mo"), speak their national language, Nepali, as well as a distinct Tibetan-derived language known to them today as Hyolmo. In recent years people have tended to spell the name in English as "Yolmo" (drawing from how the word would be transliterated from Tibetan into English), or as "Hyolmo" (drawing from how the word can be transliterated from Nepali into English). Earlier anthropological writings of mine used the "Yolmo" spelling, as did other scholarly writings. But given that the majority by far of people who identify as "Hyolmo" presently use that spelling for their names and for formal social organizations, and given that this lettering has been registered with the Nepali government as the formal name of Hyolmo people, I have adopted that spelling in the current text, as have other anthropologists in their texts recently.

The grammar, syntax, and lexicons of the Hyolmo language are quite similar to those of many Tibetan dialects, especially classical Tibetan. A majority of Hyolmo people rely on both Hyolmo and Nepali in everyday conversations, and talk in one language is often interspersed with phrases from the other. Hyolmo people have no standard method of writing Hyolmo. When people write out Hyolmo words, they usually use Tibetan or Nepali (Devanagari) scripts, each of which poses obstacles to perfect transliteration. English letters are less accommodating still.

Hyolmo words cited in this book are spelled phonetically, as they might sound to the English ear; I determined these spellings in consultation with

Hyolmo colleagues. Since many Hyolmo words, especially religious terms, have direct correlates in the Tibetan language, the correlates are often noted, spelled as they are in written Tibetan. They are transcribed according to Wylie's system of Tibetan orthography (1959). The spelling of Nepali words follows the method of R. L. Turner (1966). Non-English words that are set in parentheses and are prefaced by *N.* are words in Nepali. Foreign terms that are not designated as being either Tibetan or Nepali are most often Hyolmo words.

Prelude

"Āmā, Khoi?"

That's the tricky thing about consciousness, yours or mine. It can get hooked on one moment or another or swoop into flights of fancy. Shape-shifting consciousness can get stuck on a wound, dissolve into emptiness, or channel into new forms of life altogether. It's soon elsewhere, tarries a while, skirts here or there. A soul can find itself lonely and bereft, unsure of the right way. Or, others can reach out and change how we think with the sudden force of a word or gesture, such that our lives are never the same. As for my own consciousness, it keeps going back to that wintry day, which took place a good decade ago. There's much that has been lost and much that recurs.

What I do recall is that on a brisk Sunday morning in late January I drove from my home in Westchester County to Queens, New York, to attend the Hyolmo New Year's festivities held that weekend. I began the day by visiting friends in an apartment in Sunnyside, a diverse and bustling neighborhood, in anticipation of attending a community gathering taking place that afternoon at a banquet hall a few streets away. Talking some and sipping salt butter tea, I watched a young boy about two years old and sporting white running shoes play with a cousin's bracelet. His mother, cousins, aunts, and uncles stepped about a busy, crowded living room, locating coats and dress shirts and hosting their guests. The boy's mother left the room and walked down a hallway into a friend's apartment, where I could hear the sizzle of potatoes and onions frying in oiled skillets. The boy did not notice his mother leaving the room. He tinkered with some toys.

1

An uncle of his, around thirty years old, took to jesting with the boy. He held out his hand in front of the boy, moved it slightly about, and said, "Eh, eh." The boy looked at the hand, and his uncle said "*āmā*"—"mother"—and waved his hand smoothly to his right as the boy's eyes followed. The man snapped his hand upwards while saying "Khoi?" and then moved the hand away and hid it by his side.

Khoi is a Nepali interrogative that can be translated here as "Where is _____?" or "What has happened to _____?" When uttered in itself, the word can signal the speaker's confusion or uncertainty. People often say "khoi?" when something once close by has been misplaced or lost track of, as in the sentence "Where is my pen?" ("*Mero kalam khoi?*") The implication is that the pen was once there, or is known to be somewhere, but now cannot be found.

Awareness of this absence can throw off a person. A befuddled search for the lost object works to recover what was just there. The word is often sounded in combination with a rapid upturning of both hands or of a single hand, as though that gesture confirmed the sudden turn of events and the uncertain, open-endedness of the situation. The Nepali phrase "*Āmā khoi?*" accordingly can mean, "What has happened to your mother?" or "Where did your mother go?" It can suggest, "Your mother was with you, but now she is not here. She left you and went somewhere."[1] The soft, labial warmth of *āmā*, one of the most intimate and incorporative of sounds, is set against the harsher, outward-reaching consonant of *khoi*: "*Āmā, khoi?*"

Your mother was right here, but now she is not, so what happened?

The boy looked at the vacant space where the hand had just been. He turned to a toy car.

The uncle again held out his hand to the boy and said, "Eh, eh." When the boy's eyes set anew upon it, the man said "*Āmā.*" The boy gazed at the floating hand, which disappeared to the sound of "*Khoi?*"

"Eh, eh. Āmā. Khoi?"

Hey, hey. Your mother, what happened to her? The boy looked for a few seconds. He turned his eyes away and went for the toy car. He picked it up and started to walk away. As he passed his uncle, the man again held out his hand.

"Eh, Eh, Āmā, khoi?"

This is so much like the funeral rites, I thought. *Image after image of an absent person for others to perceive and to recognize, only to vanish in a moment's immolation.*

The boy stood, holding the toy.

Where is she?

He scanned the faces in the room. His mother wasn't there. Distress swelled onto his face. He dropped the car onto the floor and ventured out into the hallway. I followed him. He walked toward familiar voices and the scent of fried potatoes. He banged with both palms on a closed door, crying slightly. His mother appeared. She spoke to him and brought him into the room.

My memory of this passing event has grown stronger in time as other details of that day have faded. Lost to the past is an understanding of whose apartment we were in or the identities of the uncle and nephew. Forever in question will be the intentions behind the man's gestures, whether he meant, for instance, to tease the child, teach him a moral lesson about the impermanence of life, allow him to master absence, or something else. Also unfathomed is what the boy thought of these actions and how they might have tied into any emerging sense of image, personhood, or relationality. Yet none of these uncertainties has kept me from spinning strands of interpretation. I have come to perceive a world where people learn from an early age that life is characterized by a tense and ever-shifting play between presence and absence, fullness and emptiness. This realization has led me to consider the ways in which ritual and imaginative forms tie into procedures of life, death, and mourning.

A few years back I ventured on weekend trips to Queens, every month or so, by steering a Ford Focus alongside highways that ran alongside the eastern edge of Manhattan and then traversing the vast expanse of the Triborough Bridge as it spilled out onto the many neighborhoods of Queens. Once in Woodside or Sunnyside, where Hyolmo families had set up homes, I visited friends and, at times, talked with them about research efforts of mine. I came to rely on these dialogues; I would be reluctant to write about Hyolmo lives without them. Outside of generating recorded conversations with people about themes relevant to their lives, I often consulted with these interlocutors—they were colleagues, really—about the ethnographic portraits I was trying just then to get right. These conversations often led me to conclude that I was on the right track, though just as often the introduction of new ideas or perspectives disrupted any secure sense I might have established about how life proceeds for Hyolmo people: "Well, maybe it's more like this . . . ," "We wouldn't necessarily see it that way. . . ." Comments like these could spark moments of befuddled understanding. *Khoi?* I then found myself trying to recover a sense of cognitive and personal coherence as I headed back home on Interstate 84, cresting the Triborough around sunset, passing between boroughs in the heady exhilaration of a necessary bewilderment. Only in the days that followed, once I listened to the recordings and worked through my notes, would

I come to adequate terms with the jolt of that weekend's conversations and go on from there.

During one such visit, to the Sunnyside home of Karma Gyaltsen Lama, an artist and thinker I've known for over twenty years, I asked Karma and Temba Dongba Hyolmo, a similarly thoughtful friend now in his thirties, if the interaction was reminiscent of a social script familiar to them. They explained that adults sometimes tease children by asking them where their mothers are if they happen to be out of sight but close by, such as in another room. "Sometimes we play with kids by saying, '*Āmā, khoi?*' Just to get their attention," the two told me. But they could not recall interactions as full-blown as I had observed. "In this situation, it looks like teasing as well," they said when discussing the above narration of the event. "If the man wanted to convey something to the boy's mother, and didn't know where she was, he might have asked the boy about her whereabouts. But it doesn't look like that was the case here. The man might have been trying to provoke something in the boy, to see what his reaction would be when he didn't find his mother."

It's likely that the boy and the man soon put their interaction behind them. Yet it's often the case that small, easily unnoticed moments can say much about how lives are put together.

What stands out for me is that in a modest span of social life a sensate set of images—an unsettled hand and a tandem of words—came to note the recurrent presence, then absence, of a person. The man named the presence of someone, and he gave a name to her absence. The man's hand served as a substitute body for the mother, one that signaled her appearance and disappearance. The substitution implies her absence and disappearance, much as a name intimates the potential absence of the person or object named. The hand became an effigy of sorts, much like the simulations of deities, ghosts, and lost loved ones found in healing and funeral rites. The hand's disappearance is not what unsettled the boy, but what it signified. *Your mother, who was just here, should be here, but she is not.* The sequence, at a minimum, is one of presence; representation of presence; presence becoming absence; representation of that presence-having-become-absence; recognition of that absence; the implications of that absence and its recognition; and responses to them. The gestures, at once summoning and undermining a sense of graspable, reliable realities, echo Buddhist ideas that all life and composite forms—people, objects, boddhisattvas—are empty of inherent existence. They speak to "the form of no form."[2]

There is no hand, no mother, no self.

Conceivably, the boy is learning about the vicissitudes of self and other, life and its shadows. He is coming to form, as we all do, a relation to death. The mother-child bond, psychodynamic thought tells us, is often the first and most pure example of oneness, completion, bonding, and accompaniment in a person's life. To learn that one's mother can disappear or be taken away is to learn that one's world can disappear, that nothing is certain or stable, including the formations of one's own self and family. Everything is composed, with one form dissolving into another. The surrogate hand and the sounds "a-ma" are aggregates of form that signify a certain presence (and absence). Yet doesn't the figure of the "mother" proceed along similar lines? The boy's mother is, like any other person or object, a constellation of forces, forever mutable and fleeting, at once full and empty of existence, here and not here. And anyone else, too, including the boy himself, or anyone observing the scene, is just as virtual and transient. The hand while in motion, gliding through space, ever shifting, arising and abiding for a while before trailing off, figures well these themes.

The gestures had a ritual quality to them, in that a series of actions took on a stable form through time. This was a spontaneous, fleeting rite of fullness and emptiness. *Here, now gone.* Form flows into formlessness and then tides back to form and formlessness again, with neither of these ever fully complete. In this intricate economy of vision and sound, the images invoked worked with the boy's consciousness, presumably tripping sentiments of awareness, distress, loss, longing, connection, and comfort. Each conjuring up of the mother's image was similar in form but different as well, as each new conjuration took on new implications and resonances within that chain of repetitions. As Gilles Deleuze writes of repetition in general, "Repetition changes nothing in the object repeated, but does change something in the mind which contemplates it."[3] The boy was different after he considered the recurrent play of sound and body, speech and image. Significantly, he initiated actions of his own. He did not wallow passively in his distress, hovering in a space of tears and absence, but did something about it.

"*Khoi?*" itself implies a grammar of uncertainty. Open-ended, the interrogative looks onto an unclear present and unknown future. The question implies a grammar of life, for so often people are faced with situations of uncertainty, if not downright bewilderment, in which they have to find their way. *Khoi?* speaks to the hard questions that come with a death: what happens in death, what happens to life in death? What has happened to the consciousness, the self, of the person once there? How might one respond to a loss? With any death, secure and clear knowledge is missing, thrown off, and those involved have to find their way within the subversion of certain existence.

When I first noted to Karma and Temba my interest in the interaction between the man and the boy, they did not make much of it themselves. It was only after reading the written narration and exegesis of the event, spelled out here, that their attention was piqued. Two weeks earlier I had sent by mail to Karma and Temba a version of this Prelude and what I had written to date of part 1 of this book. We met up together in Karma's home in Sunnyside that day, a sweltering Sunday in July, to discuss their thoughts on these materials. "The hand movement itself is interesting to me," said Karma, as his wife and two daughters, newly arrived in the States, stepped into and out of the room where we spoke, cups of tea graciously refilled. Karma explained that the way an outsider had noticed something of significance in a routine social interaction in his cultural world, one that he or others would not make much of on their own, reminded him of what he had learned about art therapy in his work as an artist, that when a person draws or paints something, it can say so much about her situation, even if she's unaware of what she's doing or communicating through those expressions. (A person asked to draw a picture of a tree, for instance, might include ruptures in the tree's design which correspond to painful events in that person's life.) "But then, for the therapist, who is making the analysis, it makes so much sense," Karma noted. "And this situation works the same way. It's not really something we would be aware of, but you're looking at it and you're finding meaning. It really is speaking to a lot of things, particularly the balance between the here and the not-here. It constantly provoked thought in me."

Embedded in everyday efforts are rich strands of sense that often go unnoticed. And yet while the interaction between the man and boy might speak "to a lot of things," it's forever difficult to articulate in any clearly definable way what those are. Nothing is certain here, as we're dealing with a shadow realm of fleeting imaginings and cultural formations, few of which come with obvious meanings or explanations. Yet perhaps it's safe to say that the man's ritual play of presence and absence and the boy's efforts to lessen his distress hint at the ways people respond to the demands of life and loss. We rely on words, images, objects, bodies, sensory textures, memories, and virtual imaginings to relate to loved ones while they are alongside us, and to mourn them when they

Figure 1. Repairing a drum. Thodong, 2011.

are no longer here. We do so hesitantly, tentatively, finding our way, alongside others, unsure of our actions.

Poiesis in Life and Death

This book is concerned with understandings and experiences of death and mourning among Hyolmo Buddhists, an ethnically Tibetan Buddhist people who locate their historical and cultural home in the Hyolmo region of north central Nepal. It draws from my comprehension of these themes, as that tentative understanding has emerged and is emerging still, through stints of ethnographic fieldwork conducted in the Hyolmo region (often called "Helambu" in the Nepali language); in Kathmandu, Nepal; and in Queens, New York, dating back to the late 1980s. One reason the man's sleight of hand caught my attention is that its sequence of presence-then-absence of substitute bodies is reminiscent of an analogous theater of form that transpires during the funeral rites sponsored by Hyolmo families when a loved one dies. Here, a series of tangible images of the deceased—the corpse, a bundle of clothes, a set of name cards, and a life-size effigy—simulate the deceased's identity as it changes through time. Like the man's hand, coming and going, each of these images is first invoked and then taken away, either by being burned or dismantled, in spiraling rounds of simulated presence and absence. How that series of transmuting images might relate to the changing condition of the deceased and the grief of mourners is of abiding concern here. Yet there's more to the story than that, for deeply in question are the shifting circumstances of consciousness, memory, and longing in moments of life and death.

In what ways is a "self"—or a "subject" or "person," if you will—constituted in life? In what way does a self come undone at the end of a life? What are the interrelated social, political, linguistic, cultural, sensorial, and existential forces that contribute to processes of constitution and dissolution? These questions are simple in form but highly important for an anthropologically informed philosophy of life.

In considering how Hyolmo people die and mourn the loss of those who have died, we need to give thought in particular to the two continuums of selfhood most involved here: the concerns and efforts of the dying and the dead, as well as the concerns and efforts of those who care for the dying and mourn their loss. What can the processes associated with living, dying, and death tell us about how certain features of human existence—such as consciousness, identity, memory, agency, desire, longing, and bodiliness—are enacted and dissolved through a gamut of social and communicative practices?

Given the rich and complicated ties that take form among the living and the dead, we need to attend just as often to questions of intersubjectivity: about how, that is, people relate to—care for, imagine, remember, part from, long for, wound, haunt—important others in their lives. The two strands of selfhood are connected in situations of radical interrelationality; they are caught up with one another and easily influence each other with their respective circuits of sensed thought and action. All of this points to the recurrent social connections fundamental to Hyolmo lives. Think of two weavings of selfhood coursing through time, intersecting with and flowing into each other through a varied terrain of life, loss, and transformation, and we are close to an idea of what is involved.

Those two currents of selfhood, in constant confluence with one another, are distinct in their pathways. Hyolmo Buddhists are often concerned with a good death, one that helps them to achieve liberation or a good rebirth. Undertaking a quiet apprenticeship on the matter, they often adopt a number of techniques that help them to die well, from preparing for their deaths, to giving a last testament in their final days, to forging a calm and peaceful state of mind in the hours of their demise. Family and friends often help in these endeavors; they try to calm and support the fading loved one, help him to sever his attachments to his life, and accompany him in the process of dying up to the "mouth" of death itself. After a person dies, as Hyolmo people know it, his consciousness departs from his body and enters into a phantasmagoric liminal realm between one life and the next, which can last up to forty-nine days after the death. Bereft of a tangible body, that spectral subject lacks the capacity for personal action, while needing to find the right route to a good rebirth.[4] He must depend on the aid of the living, who should perform a number of rituals on his behalf. Mourners need to deliver the consciousness from the body, cremate the corpse, and undertake a series of funeral rites, which usually conclude some seven weeks after the death.

"The dead are attached to the living, and the living are attached to the dead," runs one Hyolmo saying. The task of the living is to cut off the deceased from his world to the point of a zero-degree desire. They have to put an end to the busy confluence and tightly knit relations between them and their deceased loved ones. They must render the deceased no longer a living, fully human, flesh-and-body person. If the funeral rites go well, the personhood of the deceased fades in time; his persona becomes increasingly nameless, apersonal, and distant from the world of the living. Family members sponsor and participate in these rituals in a spirit of care and responsibility while attending to wounding grief which diminishes but never fully expires in time.

The living and the recently dead are engaged in delicate technologies of cessation and transformation. A strong sense of creative making and fashioning runs through these efforts. Dying calls for an active patterning of self and other, as do the funerary rites. An element of *poiesis* rips through Hyolmo responses to death. There is a creative making, a generative fashioning of sense and consciousness that serves to aid the deceased's plight, while tending to the ache of grief and longing.

The concept of poiesis first took form in Greek philosophy, most significantly in the writings of Plato and Aristotle. It has subsequently been adopted by modern philosophers such as Martin Heidegger and Hannah Arendt, as well as by some anthropologists.[5] Derived etymologically from the Greek *poiein*, "to act, to do, or to make," and related to the words "poetics" and "poetry," the term poiesis has come to designate any making or doing beyond purely practical efforts. Poiesis is involved in the crafting of poems and the art of shipbuilding. It implies a begetting, a fabrication and bringing forth, of some new form or actuality; something that was not present is made present. Biologists, in turn, have come to use the phrase as a suffix in terms like hematopoiesis, the formation of blood cells. Some biologists also speak of "autopoiesis," a coinage which means self-making and which refers to dynamics through which "realities" come into existence "only through interactive processes determined solely by the organism's own organization."[6]

Ideas of poiesis skirt dichotomies problematically common to Western thought, such as art and deed, virtuality and actuality, and idea and matter. As anthropologist Michael Lambek remarks in his discussion of poiesis and narrative history among the Sakalava people of Madagascar, "Poiesis—making, creative production, craft, artistry—is useful because it grasps the creative quality of so much of Sakalava practice and because it avoids the rift between ideal and material that has characterized so much thought since Plato. . . . Not distinguishing 'art' from 'work,' poiesis provides a framework in which neither concept must be given priority."[7] Imaginative visualizations are as much a matter of poiesis as religious statues. Such begetting is central to procedures of dying, death, and mourning in Hyolmo communities. Consciousnesses are transformed, ceremonies enacted, substitute bodies made and unmade, and memories revised—all in ways that entail techniques of fabricating, bringing forth, and transmutation. The concept of poiesis developed here is an attempt to redescribe certain processes of social life and existential form, particularly as they occur in situations of death, mourning, and ritual. My aim is not so much to apply Western models of poiesis to Hyolmo lives as it is to grasp how Buddhist orientations to generative fashioning and creative subtraction shed light on processes at work in all of our lives.

The idea of poiesis in life and death accords well with Hyolmo ways of thinking of and engaging in the world.[8] When I introduced to Karma the idea of relating Hyolmo lives and deaths to the concept of poiesis, he immediately warmed to the idea and its implications, and he grasped, more than I did then, its pervasive relevance for Hyolmo lives. "It fits into so much of what people are concerned with," he said. "There is a focus on creating things in a more beautiful way. *Fashioning*. That's a good word. Whatever someone is doing, he is doing it in a very fashioning manner. That's important for us. Even when we're presenting ourselves to our guests, to our people, there's a manner, there's a fashioning to it. We're not very aware of it, people are not usually aware of that. But they are working toward it. People are driven by how they have to look good. It's really guided by this idea of poiesis. There is a sense of aesthetics, too, of doing things in a good way, and of looking good. . . . So

Figure 2. Cham dance during Losar celebrations. Takpakharka, 1989.

much is about composing and creating. Something that is not there, you are creating it out of what's not there."

Perhaps a straightforward way to phrase the sentiment invested in the last sentence of Karma's quoted above might be, "You are creating something out of what was not there to begin with." But the Buddhist glint to Karma's phrasing could serve as a lingering refrain here, particular when it comes to mourning and funerary rituals in Hyolmo lives: something that is not fully there, to begin with or later on, something which is empty of inherent existence, is created out of what is not there, or from what was once here, but is no longer here.

While ideas and doings of poiesis are central to many Hyolmo lives, they involve only one particular cultural rendering of something at work in the lives of peoples throughout the world. Poiesis is found in the strivings of all peoples—and, perhaps, of all life forms more generally. Poiesis is there in the urge we have to make something of, and in, our lives, both individually and collectively. It ties into Spinoza's idea that "each thing, as far as it can by its own power, strives to persevere in its being," and it has resonance with Deleuze's philosophy of becoming. It echoes Kathleen Stewart's considerations of "cultural poesis," which she richly locates in "the generativity of emergent things." It relates to Tim Ingold's inquiries into "making" and the "form-giving" principles of creation. And it parallels a theme in Michael D. Jackson's writings on the generative capacities of human beings.[9] People fashion something out of the elements of their lives, even if those elements are bone bare, at times. We go beyond what is given to us, in one way or another. There is a creative tendency in life itself. Poiesis is found in moments of joy and suffering, and of life and death. It is inscribed in the very fact of rituals. Peoples throughout the world turn to ritual and symbolic forms in the wake of death and absence. Form comes of loss. Something is made present when something else is no longer present. "That's it. Weave, weave."[10]

The catch to all of this, however, is that those weavings often run up against the strivings of others similarly intent on making something of their lives. We all know of moments of counter-poiesis; a boy at play crosses creations with a man at play. Or, more harshly, our efforts hit up against the world at large, blind and inert to human strivings; a man respected by his community for his inspired, generative contributions to their lives falls ill of a sudden fever, and dies. A "coefficient of resistance" is involved in any human strivings in life, to use a term of Sartre's.[11] We create and fashion most often within situations of struggle, denial, want, and the wastages of time. One form of resistance relates to the fact that what is done usually cannot be undone, much as the *Rubaiyat* of Omar Khayyam casts it:

> The Moving Finger writes: and, having writ,
> Moves on: nor all thy Piety nor Wit
> Shall lure it back to cancel half a Line,
> Nor all thy Tears wash out a Word of it.[12]

And yet people can and do work with what has been "written"—be it historically, economically, socially, discursively, fatally, genetically—in "writing" something of their own. We fashion a world with the resources and constraints given by that world. There is a recurrent tension between what people aspire to in their lives and the forces that shape and constrain those lives.

One significant way that this tension takes form in Hyolmo lives ties into ideas of karma (or *le*, "work" or "deeds"). The principle of karma, in which, quite simply, any moral act, good or bad, brings about a correspondingly positive or negative result, either in this or in a future lifetime, is as basic and commonsensical to Buddhist peoples as the law of gravity is to others. Karma involves a kind of natural poiesis, in that a person's deeds, positive and negative, bear "fruit" down the road. It's a matter of karmic "cause and effect" (*rgyu 'bras*, in Tibetan), wherein a person reaps what he has sowed, even if that sowing occurred in previous lifetimes of his. Karmic forces bring forth certain situations, be it a stretch of happiness or a lifetime of hardship, and there's not much that a person can do to change that. He or she can strive to generate positive karma, however, by undertaking virtuous deeds and "cutting" negative ones. Many a Hyolmo life—and death—is founded on an intricate, indeterminable play between the generative designs of karma in a person's life and that person's attempts to steer the consequential flow of karmic actions. While a person might strive for a good death, he and others know well that his karmic heritage will play a large role in the ease or suffering of that death. It's a matter of what is karmically "written on the forehead," as many phrase it, and what a person endeavors to contribute to what is written. Those who are written write anew, as they add to, and sometimes revise, what has been inscribed.

Poiesis can assume many forms. Among them are inclinations, in no particular or purely distinct or finite order,

> to make new things, more or less concrete or virtual,
> to alter or fashion the appearances of the world,

to shape or change the consciousness of someone or something,
to construct memories,
to change the form or someone or something,
to teach someone something significant or lasting,
to create relations between forces in the world,
to alter the ways in which relations take form or proceed in the world,
to forge a path, a line, or a trajectory in the world,
to bring forth something previously dormant, hidden, or germinating,
to play with the forms and formations of life,
to unmake something; to dissolve something or take it apart,
to withhold from acting in the world

Each of these efforts plays a central role in how Hyolmo peoples go about their lives, as well as how they tend to moments of death and loss. Houses, songs, and meditative visualizations are made. Rituals are performed. Consciousnesses and memories are fashioned and refashioned. Selves are made.

And selves are unmade. The procedures of dying and death often entail a poiesis of cessation, in the seemingly paradoxical sense that a dying self endeavors to dissolve its self. In effect, a person strives, often with the help of others, to create the conditions whereby she can contribute to the surcease of her place within, and longing for, the world. Mourners in turn try to facilitate these endeavors on behalf of lost loved ones, while trying to abate their own attachments to them. Much of the dying process and the cremation and funeral rites orbits around an intricate making of unmaking, a calm forging of undoing, dissolving, and stillness. In many respects, these efforts fit well with the intent of Buddhist teachings and practices, which tirelessly work toward the idea of letting go of ego, attachments, sensory dependencies, and the sense of a solid and unchanging self in the world. Dissolving, taking away, releasing, removing, until all is emptiness, until the self itself is stilled: these hard-gained endeavors apply both to Buddhist practices and Hyolmo methods of dying and post-life transformations. In thinking of how people engage constructively in the world, we need to entertain Buddhist ideas of "taking away" and consequential "nondoing" as much as we do Western philosophical ideas of poiesis as entailing a directly active "bringing forth." Stable ideas of active and passive break down here. Something present is rendered less present. At the same time, poiesis here implies a *tentative* making and fashioning, one couched in the virtuality and impermanence of its own constructedness.

Given that people usually do not engage in these efforts on their own, it's clear that much of the "bringing forth" that takes place in situations of dying and death, as in those of life, have a decidedly social cast to them. We are speaking most often of a kind of co-poiesis, of a collaborative fashioning and unfashioning of self and other, as well as of a poiesis-on-behalf-of-another. People often bring forth, or dissolve, on behalf of others. This is particularly crucial after a person dies, as the dead can accomplish little on their own. Roaming a "land without power," a domain where they no longer have powers to act, they have little recourse to generative action. They cannot effectively "act" or "produce" anymore, or alter their karmic heritage, in any forthright way. They must rely on the living to do this. The call for the living to labor on behalf of the deceased makes such efforts a matter of care, responsibility, respect, and honor, implying an ethics of mourning. The ritual assistance is a welcome responsibility, as the living long to act in ways that can benefit lost loved ones. These efforts at cooperative making and assisted cessation trip up prevalent ideas of agency in Western social and political thought, which often paint "personal agency" as being a question of actions undertaken by individuals, often while under the constraining weight of political forces. Here, the operations involved are more like those apparent in the artwork "Drawing Hands," by M. C. Escher, in which two hands are busy drawing one another.

And yet we can also envision a scene where one hand strives to erase another, or itself. We draw the lines and shadings of a life, and then those lines are erased.

Also rendered complicated in ideas of human poiesis are notions of intentionality. One way to think of people's efforts in the world is that a conscious mind or set of minds is purposefully doing what it intends to do. But such a model of action runs aground of such involved arrangements as a person's memories or the centuries-long development of a set of funerary rites. Where do we name intentionality in the flow of a conversation or the haunting of a household? How do we locate it in the images that come to a poet or a spirit medium or a child's excursions in play? The narrator of *Tristram Shandy*, when asked about the design of his book, said, "Ask my pen; it governs me; I govern not it."[13] Given that human efforts seldom arise from a single author or subject in the world, alone, there is a need to de-individualize ideas of making and creating. As conscious subjects and actors in our lives, we are "made"—by words, social relations, cultural formations, and life circumstances—as much as we produce words, relations, and forms. While any phrasings stumble in depicting the operations involved here, it's clear that designs altogether remarkable lay within the subtle, curious ways that life proceeds.

Figure 3. Drawing Buddhist icons in a gompa, Sermathang, 1989.

The designs most in circuit here involve social and ritual practices whose effects are to transform people or situations in some way. If we were to string out a lexicon of change involved in Hyolmo scenes of dying and funeral rituals, it would include such active verbs as generate, provoke, transform; visualize, imagine, remember, forget; transfer, invoke, dislodge; clarify, instruct; quiet, console, soothe; purify, extinguish, dismantle, release; connect and disconnect; build, destroy, and reconstitute. What are being changed in an evolving charge of relations are perceptions, karmic statuses, moods and longings, forms of attachment, social and sensual relations, and ways of knowing and being in the world. The actualities and virtualities generated in these moments, in line with a world familiar with tantric energies and transformative intensities, are without any single author or known agent to their name. They have powerful effects in and on life.

This book endeavors to trace the terrain of these effects. In tracking them myself I have come to consider the dynamic and ever-shifting dimensions of selfhood, consciousness, and relationships in life, and how all of this changes in time. I have also come to appreciate the stunningly potent, transformative forces invested in certain words, images, and ritual moments.

Theorizing Death

These pages have their origins in ethnographic fieldwork conducted in Nepal in the late 1990s and early 2000s. While immersed in research on the life histories of two respected Hyolmo elders, Kisang Omu and Ghang Lama, I found that my separate conversations with them in their homes in Kathmandu often turned to thoughts on dying and death, in part because both of them were finding that, now that they were in their mid-eighties, they were approaching the "time of dying." The hard-gained ease with which Ghang Lama and Kisang Omu spoke of their increasing frailty and what they expected to happen once they died led me to feel more comfortable broaching the topic with them and others. These conversations led to more general reflections on death and mourning in Hyolmo communities.

When I returned to Nepal in the summer of 2001 I set out to study these themes in more systematic ways. The thought occurred that there might be some value in writing about death and mourning among Hyolmo people in a direct and comprehensive way, much as one might tell a meaningful story— though, like most stories, the current one is far from simple or straightforward. In talking with a number of Hyolmo friends and acquaintances on the topic, and tagging along in their everyday lives, I gained a better sense of what occurred for Hyolmo people in times of death and mourning. Many people have contributed to this understanding in important ways, making for a collaborative fashioning of its own. Some conversations centered on the ways in which people have died and understandings of good and bad ways to pass on. Other dialogues explored the rites that follow a death. Yet others touched painfully on recollections of grief and mourning. Subsequent conversations took place in Queens, New York, in 2009–11, and sporadically since then. Karma and Temba have had a particularly helpful hand in all stages of this work. They have been colleagues of the best sort, attesting to the idea that friendship is a "primary site of thinking."[14] Deep gratitude is what I feel for the ways friends and acquaintances have talked about themes difficult to talk about.

These pages would be different if I had penned them when I was younger. I did not know as much about loss then, about the end of lives and relationships, or of how the pain of parting can sear long after its first burning. Nor did I appreciate as much the value and power of connection. When I was conducting fieldwork with Hyolmo people for the first time while in my mid-twenties, in years that now seem eager and youthful to me, I came across the social restriction against saying the names of the dead. I asked people about this and took it principally as a social taboo, something that is not done, for reasons more cultural than anything else: saying the names of the dead can summon up their ghostly presence in unwelcome ways or lead someone to be drawn incurably to the past. "Dead people have no need for names," one man told me, an edge to his voice. Back then, I took the reluctance to be impatience with an inquisitive researcher pressing on a touchy subject. I understand better now how invoking the names of the lost or any reminder shot out of the past—a photograph in a desk drawer, the ring of a telephone—can ignite painful memories best not summoned.

Considerations such as these complicate any writings we might gather about memory, about the kind of memories that people live with, named or not. I continue to feel ambivalent about theorizing the losses of others or mentioning them in print. But I have been reassured by friends who remind me that it's important for us to know better how people throughout the world make sense of these most inescapable of events. I have come to realize that Hyolmo peoples themselves theorize death, in a kind of ordinary death philosophy, and that my efforts through this book echo their attempts to gain a handle on death, to anticipate or know it better than we might otherwise. A theory of death implies a theory of life. "What is more intimate to life, more a part of it than death, or rather dying? . . . What is more cultural than how people represent death?"[15]

Thoughts about the book have seeped into thoughts about life, while the eventualities of life continue to inform ideas in the material. I have come to notice that the permutations of loss, what haunts people and what soothes them, is something we all get a strong taste of, one time or another. Sometimes these situations take form in ways stunningly reminiscent of one another: a person close to me tells me of how the presence of a friend who moved on to another city continues to linger in her life, as though he was still there, right beside her, walking about with her, sharing thoughts, and yet he is not quite there; and then I come upon a passage in Proust in which the narrator remarks that "people do not die for us immediately, but remain bathed in a sort of aura of life which bears no relation to true immortality but through which they continue to occupy our thoughts in the same way as when they were alive. It is as though they were traveling abroad";[16] and these strands of life bring to mind how the faint nearness of the deceased continues to be felt, viscerally, in Hyolmo households, for weeks after the death. As there is no sharp divide between how loss and consolation proceed in Nepal, in France, and in the United States, there is no reason to maintain such a divide here and write about Hyolmo lives as though they occurred in a world apart from my own. Loss nicks at all of us. While it is important to note its cultural patternings, it is equally necessary to note the similarities in the wounds and in our efforts to mend them. A language of "they" easily slides into one of "we."

Sensible to me are these words of the artist Francis Bacon: "If life excites you, its opposite, like a shadow, death, must excite you. Perhaps not excite you, but you are aware of it in the same way as you are aware of life, you're aware of it like the turn of a coin between life and death."[17] We need, as we thrive on life, to keep company with its shadow, without getting too excited about it. For me, a balance has arisen between a felt sympathy for the losses involved and an appreciation for the idea that, by attending to those misfortunes, we might gain a richer, more informed sense of what it means to be alive.

"To philosophize is to learn how to die," or so wrote Cicero, echoing a sentiment axiomatic to ancient philosophy, recurrent from Plato on. As Simon Critchley explains the abiding idea, "The main task of philosophy in this view, is to prepare us for death, to provide a kind of training for death, the cultivation of an attitude towards our finitude that faces — and faces down — the terror of annihilation without offering promises of an afterlife."[18]

Might anthropologizing also help one to learn how to die? And would the means and lessons of that education be distinct from those common to philosophical reasoning? That is, can a careful attentiveness to how others die, near and far, to ways of living and dying in human communities, to the all-too-human responses to a loss, to the limits of knowledge and action, to the profound and ubiquitous role of rituals, to the affective force of images, to the stark depths of grief, to the spectral play of memory, to generative making and unmaking, to a sense of vitalities echoing on — can all of this enable one to cultivate an expansive grasp of the actualities of death? Can an anthropology of dying teach a consciousness, yours or mine, how to dissolve into emptiness, and thus how to live?

PART I

The Impermanence of Life

A Good Death, Recorded

Try to die in a good way, peacefully, at home, without pain, in the presence of loved ones. Try to cultivate appropriate states of mind while dying. Avoid a bad death, one marked by thoughtlessness or terrible pain or distorted bodies and speech. Avoid hospitals, if possible.

In August of 2001 I watched a video recording that documented the passing of an elderly man we will refer to as "Sange's father." The man cast on the screen was on the margins of death, and then beyond.

Sange Lama, the man's third and youngest son, is related to Karma Gyaltsen Lama. Sange married Karma Gyaltsen's sister Pemba Dolma when in his late twenties, and since then the couple has had three daughters. Sange's father was a well-respected head of family in Norbugang, one of the older villages in northeastern Hyolmo. Late in life he had moved with his wife to Kathmandu, and they lived in a three-story house in the neighborhood of Mahankhal, on the outskirts of Boudhanath. The house was built and owned by Sange's eldest brother. This eldest brother had since moved with his wife to India, where he thrived as a contractor. While he and his wife lived chiefly in India, they maintained a home on the top floor of the house on the outskirts of Boudhanath, where their daughter Tshering, Sange's niece, and their youngest son resided. The family felt that at least one person should be at home at all times.

Sange's family and his mother and father shared the second floor with an unmarried sister and aunt, both of whom identified as *Ani*, Buddhist "nuns." In the mid-1990s Sange obtained a visa to travel to the United States. He arrived in New York City, and he has lived and worked there since, phoning home often to speak with family. His wife joined him in Queens in late 2001, after receiving a visa of her own, and she soon gave birth to their third daughter.

In 2001, I lived for two months in a room on the second floor of this family's house in Mahankal. I met Sange only after returning to the States. While in Nepal I ate meals with his family, tried my hand at shaping Tibetan dumplings, and anticipated with the two girls the next Bollywood extravaganza to appear on the STAR Network. People moved from one room to another in the well-kept home. Relatives visited for tea and conversation. Evenings, I retreated to the quiet of my room, marked off another day on a hand-drawn calendar, and faded to dense sleep. The room was set off from the main area of the second floor by a solid wooden door, which I bolted shut when we all retired at day's end. Most dawns I awoke to the sounds of a karate class taking place in the grassy clearing below my window. The athletes umphed into the imagery of my dreams until I fully woke to their muscled shouts. Between the house and the gate leading to the neighborhood's streets stood a neighbor's home, guarded by a snarly black dog tied to a long chain. I learned to stay an inch beyond the dog's bite.

I came to know the members of the extended family, and they came to know me. Anyone's absence was sensed in the house. It filled the quiet of conversation and the stillness of rooms. The father had died in 1999, after a lengthy illness.

It was Sange's niece Tshering, the young woman who lived on the top floor, who alerted me to the video's existence. When I asked Tshering if it would be possible for me to see this video, she said that would be fine, but noted that it was at her aunt's house. "It will be good to watch it there, anyway," she said. "Because when it's shown among close family members, they cry. It's difficult for them to watch it."

A few days later, early on a sunny Saturday afternoon, Temba and I met Tshering at the home of her father's sister and the three of us watched the video together on a large color television set. We sat in a tidy room with family photographs on a mantel, *thangku* paintings on the walls, and a portrait of the Dalai Lama close to the altar. I felt uncomfortable watching the video, voyeuristic. I had never observed recorded images of someone's death before. *This man, whom I never met in life, was dying.* I was watching the events of that death, now past, play out in an intimate visual record. The man who was there was no longer here. Temba and Tshering appeared to be fine with the viewing, perhaps because they had seen videos of this sort before. They commented on the events glimpsed on the screen, and I took notes.

Filmed with a borrowed camcorder by Binod Lama Hyolmo, the husband of Pemba Dolma's and Karma Gyaltsen's sister, the video held a series of unedited segments, recorded on successive days. The first segments showed scenes of relatives and friends visiting to sit with the dying man, in the home's main room. The man sat, and rested, in his bed. He appeared gaunt and weak, with tired eyes. He looked at his guests when they spoke and nodded at what they said. At times he contributed to the conversations in a faint, measured voice. His wife sat on the floor in the room amid a group of women. She was quiet, looking on and listening to the conversations. I later asked Karma if he thought the wife's composed demeanor was typical. It was not, he said. "There's a lot of crying and grieving in many cases. Here she also understood that it was his time."

In one scene of the video the father, smiling, with his eldest son by his side, handed an envelope to another man while others looked on approving. Temba told me that the son had given his father a significant amount of money, which he donated to a temple in Norbugang. Images followed of people visiting and family members preparing food in the kitchen. The video cut to a scene at night, when the man was dying. Several men talked quietly among themselves in the room with him, as though to help him die peacefully.

A lama leaned over the man to check his breathing. He determined that he had died. He draped a white cloth over the body.

People whispered and stepped silently about the room.

It was strange to see this person, this old man, who was close to dying, and the people gathered around him, I wrote later that day.

He looked quite alive, but also weak, and somewhat vacant. What must it be like to know you're dying, and these people have come because they know you're dying? Later on he was lying down, then sitting up, then he was as though dead, and then he was dead. He was also talking a bit, at times. . . . He didn't look especially sad or frightened. He knew what was happening, and he seemed to be accepting of it. There was a sunken look around his eyes, as though he had been sick for quite some time and he was already on the margins of death.

He was as though dead, as though alive. Later segment of the video showed two Tibetan lamas performing a rite beside the body. People returned to the

house on the day of the cremation, three days after the death. The final frames
depicted the cremation rites and several funeral rites.

I was tempted to ask if I might make a copy of the video, but thought better
of it. Several weeks after watching the recording I asked Pemba Dolma if she
would be willing to relate to me how her father-in-law had died. She agreed to
this. Accompanied by Tshering, we sat in their home late one afternoon and
Pemba spoke in Nepali into a tape recorder.[1]

When he went once to Swayambhunath [a sacred Buddhist and Hindu site
in the Kathmandu Valley], he met with an accident. He broke one of his legs,
and his leg remained fractured for three months. Due to his leg, he wasn't
able to go for *khora* [circumambulations around the *chhorten* in Boudhan-
ath], but he was in good health at that time. But after a year he got sick and
weak, and when we took him to the hospital the doctors there told us that he
had tuberculosis, and they gave him lots of medicine.

But when those medicines didn't show any improvement in his health,
we again took him to the hospital for a check-up, and there the doctor told
us that he wasn't suffering from T.B. Because my father-in-law used to drink
a lot, the internal parts of his body got damaged. The doctor didn't say all
these things in front of him; he told us later that his inner parts were now
damaged. "So now it's useless to treat him. Now the only thing you can do is
take care of him as properly as you can until he dies."

The doctor said all these things to us. But we didn't lose our hope and we
kept giving him vitamins and Tibetan medicines. But still his health did not
improve. Slowly his condition worsened. The main problem was in his stomach. There was a large, hard substance in his stomach.

But after keeping him there for some days, the doctors gave us permission to bring him home. They told us to take care of him because there was
no use of doing further treatment, as he was now in his final stage. So after
that we brought him home. He always used to read Buddhist texts and recite
lots of *mani* prayers.

He would read texts in the morning and during the day he would rest for
some time. But one thing about him was that he never put his rosary down.
He always used to pray. The doctors told us that he would only survive for
three more months, at most, but we continued giving him some good Tibetan medicines, due to which he survived for six more months. But later
he again felt sick and he used to say to me, "Now I think I'm going to die, be-

cause now my condition is getting worse day by day." We all decided then to do a big *pūjā*. But he only used to get pain at night.

Many people used to visit our house to see my father-in-law. When they did so, he would sit with them and say to them, "Now, as it is my age to die, so I have to die. But don't be upset or sad." He was not even afraid of his death. He was satisfied because all of his sons had work of their own, and they all are very responsible and can look after their families. All of these thoughts made him relaxed and satisfied.

He became sure of his death, so he called all his sons, one of whom was in India and another who was in America. The eldest one was in Nepal itself. He asked the son who was in India to come back as early as he could, because now he was about to die. He used to talk with him on the phone and he used to call him. But he himself asked Sange, who was in America, not to come because once he came here he wouldn't be able to return to America. So he told him not to come. But Sange used to call three or four times a day when he was sick and in the stage of dying.

Pemba spoke of the final hours.

A few male relatives were staying here to look after him. I gave soup to him and after taking my dinner I went to sleep. His wife was in his room, looking after him.

Suddenly he put his rosary down on the table. It made a loud noise. He never put his rosary down like that, but when his wife asked him what had happened, he told her that he wanted to go to the toilet. Then she called Pasang [a young man who stayed in the house] and a few others to take him to the toilet. After they took him to the toilet they set him on the bed, and he fell unconscious there, without any pain. After that we called the lamas, and they did a *pūjā*.

Others told of how Sange's father died a peaceful death, without fear, with little longing for the life he was leaving behind. He knew he was dying but he was at ease with that fact.

"When I saw him in those days, I saw that he was very confident," Karma told me. "He didn't appear nervous about it. 'Who knows? Tomorrow, or the day after, my breath will go.' That's what he was saying, very calmly. We felt uncomfortable, but he did not."

"He wasn't afraid at all," I proposed.

"No, he wasn't, not at all. He wanted to hear the *Liberation upon Hearing* because he knew that the time was near. And Sonam was there, explaining everything. He even stopped his son from coming from America. He said to Sange, 'You're there, and it would be very difficult for you to return. Your brothers are here. See, everything is going to be all right.'"

"To me, in seeing him on the video, it was like he was going on a trip, and he was saying goodbye to people," I said.

"Yes, to him it was just like that," Karma answered. "I could see that. To him it was just like he wasn't going to see these people anymore."

"Is it usually like that, or was that exceptional?"

"Not everyone is like that. In his case, I don't think he was in so much pain. And some people are in a lot of pain, and that's a totally different situation."

"Or if they are younger."

"Right."

Sange's father, certain of his death, had prepared for it. Content that it was his time, he was spiritually engaged until the end, his family beside him and desires fulfilled. He died at home without fear or longing.

There are good and bad ways to die. "Many years before," Temba's grandfather told Temba and me, "Uncle Bhaktu prayed every day to the deities that he might die in a good and easy way. He even used to talk in front of us about death, and about the ways of dying. He was worried about his death. He was always hoping to die in a calm, peaceful way, without any disturbances, and without giving trouble to others. Almost all of the old people do the same. They want to die in a good way."

The sentence *"Shyi lu yhabu shyisin"* might be heard in the wake of a death: "He died in a good way of dying." Alternatively, people might say, "*Shyi lu tsokpa shyisin*": "He died in a bad way of dying." The "way" or "manner" of a person's death is important for several reasons. It's better to die without pain. It's better not to be a burden upon others in one's last years. It's better to die at home, surrounded by family members. A person should not die with fear or longing; his state of mind at the moment of death can contribute to the nature of his rebirth. And the manner of dying reflects one's karma, the fact of which people commonly take note.

"What people are longing for, really, is a good death," Karma told me. "That's all. A good death. Hearing good words at the last moment, feeling comfortable, and you are dying comfortably, without any panic."

There should be little or no pain. "The best way to die," opined Gom

Dolma, "is without any pain, and in an unconscious state. Because if we don't have any pain or sensation of dying, we don't have to bear any pain and trouble with our bodies while dying." In line with these sentiments, many find that it's good to die while sleeping, in an unconscious state, without sensing the process of dying. "The best way to die is to die while sleeping, which I rank as the best," Kesang Lama posited. "I think it's good to die while sleeping," Pemba Dolma noted. "Because at that time we don't have to go through any pain or suffering, and we can die peacefully without saying 'āiya-āmā.'" Dawa Jyaba Hyolmo said much the same when I spoke with him on the subject. "Most people want to die," he said, "without any diseases, without saying 'āiya-āmā,' and after working during the day, going to sleep, and then dying while asleep at night."

Death has coordinates in a person's speech and vocalizations and in the sinews of the mouth. The Nepali phrase "āiya-āmā" is taken as an expression of pain. While the Nepali "āiya" utters something like the English "ouch!" "āmā" can be heard as plaintively echoing "mother." A self in pain seeks the first figure of warmth and protection known to it. Pragmatically, the syllables signal a knot of pain, need, urgency, disturbance, and unrest; the body is rocking back and forth between the ache of pain and the search for comfort. The utterances are sensations issued from the mouth more than they are composed statements.

Some accounts point to an absence of pain or suffering in a person's passing. The person dies "peacefully," often while unconscious, unaware that the death is occurring.

If a person dies without pain, it's much better. In Sermathang there's a man, Kesang Lama. His mother was working in the field the whole day, to harvest potatoes. Just the two of them were there, she and her husband. Everyone else was in Kathmandu—their three sons, and the sons' wives and children, were in Boudhanath. . . . And this Kesang Lama's mother was working in the fields all day. And at night, after eating dinner, they went to sleep. When it was time to wake up in the morning, the father found that his wife had died. And as she had died, they called all the lamas, to do all the ceremonies. And after doing these ceremonies, a week later, seven days, the husband also died.

After this happened, everyone began to talk, saying that this is the right way to die. This is the easiest. Because there was no pain. Just while falling asleep, then sleeping. "It would be good if I died in this way." Each and every Hyolmo person thought this. [Dawa Jyaba Hyolmo]

"So that's it: 'May we die in reaching our age, and may we die without suffering any diseases or illnesses,'" Dawa Jyaba Hyolmo once proposed after an
exposition on the topic. Elderly people in particular are known to die quickly,
without pain or illness, possibly because they have reached their proper age
or "time" of dying.

Hyolmo people find value in quick deaths, for several reasons. Outside of
the sheer suffering involved in a slow death, if a person suffers a long period of
illness or debility before his death, efforts to heal him can prove to be costly.
At the same time, a sickly, bed-ridden person can be a burden on others for
months or years at a time. When asked which way of dying was "all right, in
your opinion," Phur Gyalmu replied, "In dying, the way for me is: 'May illnesses not come. May I die while going on the road.'"

"Do you wish to die on the bedding, or while walking?"

"Walking, walking may I die. For me."

"Why?"

"Why? Let my children not have hardship. This is what I want, for me. That
would be good."

To die in great pain is to die poorly. The pain itself is hurtful, unwanted, of
no value, a sign of death going badly.

> One of my uncles died. It was from cancer. Maybe it wasn't from cancer—
> actually he was suffering from T.B. Was it T.B., or cancer?—It's difficult to
> say. The sons brought him to the hospital and he was admitted there, but in
> the end he died at the age of sixty, due to T.B.
>
> While he was dying, for him it was the most difficult death. Here and
> there he was hanging on, what to do? *Āiya-āmā*, so uncomfortable. For
> some eight, nine hours, he was very uncomfortable, the villagers had filled
> his house, after being so uncomfortable, he couldn't die, the breath couldn't
> leave. There were so many expressions of pain [*āiya-āmā*], of being seared
> [*ātau āmā*], leaping, jumping in a disordered way he died. In this way he
> died, this man. [Dawa Jyaba Hyolmo]

The disjointed, staccato rhythm of the words conveys the knotty pulse of
the death. Leaping, jumping in a disordered way he died. An absence of collected smoothness troubled the man's last hours. The contours of his plight
were far removed from the poised and skilled means of comportment that
Hyolmo people often strive for in moments of health and propriety. No balance or harmony here. "He can't die peacefully," Dawa Jyaba Hyolmo said of

such situations. "His heartmind [*sem*] is struggling, flopping about. I've seen many people die in this way."

A twisted, delirious syntax of body and speech comes with the lacerating throes of dying. When people speak of deaths that could be considered bad ones, they tend to use adjectives such as "complicated," "difficult," "unbearable," "painful," "unprepared," and "disordered." A body might be "seared" by pain, or it might be portrayed as "mispositioned," "disjointed," or "disabled." Mouths remain open. Breaths get stuck, obstructed. Bodies and beds get soiled. Blood seeps. People stutter, suffer. *Oh so tired.*

Impossibly and Intensively

Speak of death flatly, with little adornment or narrative flourish. Attend to the intensity of dying, its ruptures and unsettled openness.

Writing about dying unsettles me. If thoughts of death are unnerving, then stories of dying are doubly so. Dying tears at the self. Dying tears at the world. Tending to the actual ends of people ruptures any secure sense we might gain by thinking about death as either a null point in existence or a self-contained category of thought or experience. The abstract purity of death, as an idea or ideal in the world, stands in contrast to the jittery, open-ended tracks of dying. The wrenching sharpness of dying is forever wounding, forever cutting into the flesh of life and the cold stillness of death. "There is in death, it would seem, something stronger than death: it is dying itself—the intensity of dying," Maurice Blanchot conveys it.[2] For Blanchot death is "power and even strength—limited, therefore." Dying, in contrast, is "unpower."

> It wrests from the present, it is always a step over the edge, it rules out every conclusion and all ends, it does not free nor does it shelter. In death, one can find an illusory refuge: the grave is as far as gravity can pull, it makes the end of the fall; the mortuary is the loophole in the impasse. But dying flees and pulls indefinitely, impossibly and intensively in the flight.[3]

In my writing of this book, accounts of dying make up the ethnographic terrain that has affected me the most (the grief of friends and acquaintances comes a close second). That terrain has become a charnel ground I've stepped into warily, from which I would prefer to be soon away. Only after reading Blanchot's words have I been able to gain sense of why this might be so. Dying pulls indefinitely. It draws us away from any easy models of life and death and situates us in moments of pain and nonclosure and a terrible, unending openness. Still, that terrain must be traversed if we are going to grasp something of what life and loss mean for Hyolmo families, or for all of us. Writing ethnographically about dying is a delicate matter. How does a person relate the stories of other people's deaths without making a stylistic show of it, without words dancing on the remnants of their lives? When do we need to resist the temptation to portray death, and when is it appropriate to make something out of it?

A tension lingers between the need to respect people's deaths, leaving them as they are, and the desire to say something compelling about them. In the fall of 2001, while living and conducting fieldwork in Nepal, I asked Hyolmo friends and acquaintances to relate to me, with an audio recorder running and a notebook handy, and often with Temba's assistance, what they could recall or were willing to say about the ways in which relatives and neighbors had died. They agreed to this. Temba and I spoke with Dawa Jyaba Hyolmo in the back room of his dharma shop, and we conversed with his mother, uncle, and grandparents. Conversations also took place with Nogapu Prakash Sherpa, a longtime friend, with Karma and his cousin, and with Kānchā Lama, Kisang Omu's son. We conversed with Goser Lama, a respected lama from Sermathang then in his early forties, on several occasions in his home in Boudhanath, as Goser's young son footed about the room, his fingers once reaching for the digital recorder set between us until we lured his interest away with a ripe apple. The topic also came up in more general conversations with a number of people, young and older. Temba and I later converted into English any conversations held in Nepali or Hyolmo, with Sange's niece Tshering lending her hand. It's possible that, familiar with death and its pathways, these narrators were more -comfortable with this somber deed of archiving than I was. The stories they told—loose *récits*, really, culled from memory, with little explicit social or moral commentary—were matter-of-fact in their language and emotional tone, and sometimes point-blank, graphic even, in their terms. Perhaps one way to proceed is to adopt a similarly straightforward language while keeping aware of how tender and vulnerable the narratives are.

> I remember a man who died from tuberculosis. He was in the last stage. His death became very certain, and Ghang Mheme and I were called to his place to read the *Liberation upon Hearing in the Between*. As we were reading that

text for him his head was leaning down and his breath was not so sharp. Suddenly some liquid, lather-like substances came out of his mouth, and right then he died, leaving his mouth open. It was because of T.B. He suffered from tuberculosis for a long time. It's found that those who have fallen sick for a long period of time do not face a terrible pain or situation while dying.

Another death was that of Makpa Kami Phurpa's father. At that time I was going to my village, to build a stupa, I think. I met with him for fifteen minutes. He was also seriously ill. His breathing was very bad and uncomfortable. I put some blessed substances in his mouth, and soon after that he died. [Kāncha Lama]

: : :

One woman's husband died from falling from a tree once when he went to the forest to collect some wood. His foot slipped and he fell and died. He had no friends with him, and there was no one to help him. By the time we learned about it he was dead. . . . He went to the forest at around seven in the morning, and we found him at around one in the afternoon. As he didn't come to eat his lunch at twelve, we all went to search for him. . . . Some say that if he didn't go to the forest, then this incident would not have happened. It was all due to his bad luck.

In what ways do we come to speak about death? How, and why, do we do so? Many Hyolmo reports of death have an air of matter-of-factness to them, as though they speak of events wearisome and non-extraordinary. A man loses his footing and falls to his death. Death is often banal, dumb even, in its operations.

People spoke of death flatly.[4] The narratives are unadorned, the language spare, with little explicit emotional elaboration, and only the palest of aesthetic qualities to them. The narrators speak of what they know, no more than that. "*Shikyo mi ni shi sinsin. Chi beche?*" is something that people sometimes say in the wake of a death, often while trying to console those gripped by grief. "The one who has died has already died. So what can be done now?" The echoic redundancy of the phrasing here, *the one who has died/has already died*, nudges at the futility sensed. The verb *sinsin*, a syllabic singsong, conveys an action or event "finished," "done with," or "terminated."

The life expired is irrevocable, the death itself useless and final. Any narrations of it are redundant, ineffective. There is little to say about the ways people have died except to note how they died and the possible reasons for those deaths. Incidents of death seldom generate a robust flourish of narration.

> My grandfather didn't suffer much, but he had some pains and he died with that pain. My uncle, in seeing his father feeling uneasy with pain, thought as well that he was dying. My grandfather was in my uncle's arms, and I was sitting in a corner, just below the bed. [Goser Lama]

The precision of perspective in Goser Lama's recollection of a grandfather's death, *in a corner, just below the bed*, points to how the specifics of a death can root themselves in thoughts and memories. Vivid memories often come to be "inscribed" in Hyolmo minds. Death has a strong scriptural capacity. A remembrance often secures itself through the fact that a person has witnessed a death with his own eyes. Speaking of such a sighting conveys that the event seen has marked the viewer in a lasting way. A death is an event, and an event is a mark (as Derrida suggests).

> I have seen many people die. I have seen about seventy or eighty people dying in Sermathang itself. I can remember lots of deaths, but I can't tell you properly the reasons for the deaths. But I will tell you in what ways I have seen people dying.
>   Now, my uncle's son died. He was about forty years old. First he complained about a pain in his throat. His throat hurt. Then later he couldn't eat, he couldn't drink liquids. He couldn't sleep at night. This made him feel very uncomfortable. But later I came to know that it was nothing but cancer that caused his death. He was a very good human being. He was friendly and always cooperative with others. Everyone in Sermathang liked him. He was a bombo [a shamanic healer]. His father was also a bombo. He was only forty when he died. He smoked cigarettes. He had been in India and he picked up the habit of smoking cigarettes. After smoking cigarettes, he got cancer in the throat.
>   I also saw my mother dying. Actually she was suffering from gastric [stomach pains]. When I was a child she always complained about the problem. At that time I was very young then, and I couldn't even take her to the hospital. But if I would have taken her to the hospital, she would have survived and would still be with me now. But now I've come to know that gastric gets converted into ulcers, and after that the person suffers from cancer. That could be the reason for my mother's death.

I was only eleven years old when she was first ill. She died of that disease only. Otherwise she wouldn't have died because it wasn't her age to die. I even brought her here to Kathmandu for treatment. She drank rum and had the habit of drinking and smoking. First she suffered with gastric, then from an ulcer, and it's said in fact that if you don't treat the ulcer quickly, it turns into cancer. After going to the doctor he told us about my mother's disease, and after doing a check-up he found she was suffering with cancer in different parts of her body, due to which any treatment or operations were not possible. After that I brought her back home and later she died. [Dawa Jyaba Hyolmo]

The first steps from the banality of a death often involve eyewitnesses' accounts of how a person dies. There can be a need to talk about a death, to situate it in time and language, to relate its occurrence to others, to speak of how a person was just here and then not-here. The narrations remark on the events of the death and the apparent reasons for them—and, often, no more than that. This is a way of marking a death, to name it, take the measure of it. The words stand as an effigial aftertrace of the now absent presence and the events that occasioned that absence. Form follows emptiness. The narratives stitch over a raw wound. Perhaps it's also the case that uttering or hearing such narrations offers, for some, a modest way of continued connection with the dead.

Creative Subtraction

Learn how to die. Prepare well for death. Try to fashion good and beneficial forms of consciousness in the moments of dying, while knowing that a person can never fully control the karmic and worldly forces that shape a death.

One autumn day I visited Temba and his family in their home set alongside some rice green fields on the northeast edge of Boudhanath. Sitting within the cozy warmth of the main room, we looked through some photo albums and ate a fine lunch of rice and lentils, fruit and yogurt. I retrieved a tape recorder from my knapsack and we talked about ways of dying known to Temba's family. In time, Temba's mother related the end of a man from Sermathang.

We do not know each and every detail, but we were with him and visited him before he died. It was such a terrible pain. He died within three days of suffering. Black patches on his body started to appear after two days of suffering. As time went on, the patches increased and covered his whole body. He was having unbearable pain and he always used to say to us, "No, I'll die," "I'm dying now." He died after some time. . . . He had a terrible pain and within three days he was dead. He suffered greatly when he was in his own room, and perhaps he suffered more so in the hospital. He simply repeated, "I'll die now," and he died. . . . Such a good person. Everyone liked him. A large number of mourners gathered during his funeral.

How could a good person suffer a terrible death? As Hyolmo people know it, an unshakable principle was at work here: a person's store of karmic "deeds" determines the manner of his death. If a man dies a peaceful, painless death, others will likely assume that he acted in karmically good ways in previous and current lives of his. If, however, someone dies in a painful, difficult way, that bad death is taken to be the fruit of sinful deeds enacted in previous lives. So, even if someone lived in good and virtuous ways during his present lifetime, a tracework of bad deeds enacted in previous lifetimes might resound at the time of dying.

> Watch an evil man die;
> He is a teacher demonstrating to us the effect of actions.

Or so warns a cherished Tibetan Buddhist text, *The Words of My Perfect Teacher*.[5] The text adds a narrative sequela to this statement:

Even before he is dead, the lower realms start to close in on him. Whatever he perceives becomes menacing. All his sensations cause him to suffer. The elements of his body dissolve, his breath becomes coarse and his limbs go limp. He starts to hallucinate. His eyes roll up, and as he passes beyond the life Death comes to meet him. The apparitions of the intermediate state appear, but he has no protector or refuge.[6]

Such hardships echo previous misdeeds. Kesang Lama, a middle-aged man from Sermathang, conveyed the matter squarely when talking with Temba and me in his home in Boudhanath one Saturday morning:

It's all due to one's good or bad work done in his previous life. If you have had bad deeds in your present life, then you can suffer with some diseases, illness. It's the fruit given to you for the deeds you've done in your previous life. . . . If a person dies while suffering with some disease or illness, then it's not considered good, because it's said that if a person dies with disease it's due to his karma and due to the bad deeds he undertook in his previous life.

The impersonal poiesis of karma, of consequential deeds bearing fruit in time, takes concrete form in the moments of dying. "Every death is due to a person's karma, what they have done before," Ghang Lama observed. He went on to say that, if a person is sick and in pain while dying, especially for a long period of time, then that kind of death is clearly a punishment given by a deity. Many in fact take a death to be "fated" in the sense that a person's manner of death is already determined before she is born. "We all die in ways according to our fate," noted Lhatul Lama. "Some die while eating, some while talking, some by falling into a river. Some are murdered. So there are different ways."

Temba's grandfather invoked the idea of a fateful death when talking about how people he knew wished to die. "He was always hoping," he said of his Uncle Bhaktu, "to die in a calm, peaceful way, without any disturbances, and without giving trouble to others." He continued,

Almost all of the old people do the same. They want to die in a good way. But the prayers are not working out all the time. In my opinion, the way of dying is already determined by the deity when a person is born, and this cannot be changed. Because I've found that many people pray for a good death, yet they still get sick and have to suffer. Perhaps death is determined by one's past lives, and it's impossible to change that.

But the prayers are not working out all the time. People want a good death but there's only so much they can control, because their karma and the circumstances of life bring forth the death in a certain way.

Two deaths are consistently in play in Hyolmo lives: the death that a person anticipates and prepares for, the one that he and others imagine himself having; and the death that actually occurs. There is almost always a discrepancy between these two deaths, and a rude one at that, if only because people's imaginings about their lives (and deaths) never quite match up with how those lives (and deaths) actually proceed. A tension results between these two deaths, sometimes with jarring effects. A good man is stricken with cancer. A child dies of a fever before she is able to "blossom." As in people's lives more generally, there is often a misfit between what they expect or want to happen and what in fact happens.[7]

As the actual death is distinct from any imaginings about the death that one takes as one's own, it could be said that death "always comes from without," as Gilles Deleuze puts it in his explication of Spinoza's philosophy.[8] Deleuze means this in the sense that the actual death is not internal to the self, as certain theories of a "death drive" or of "being-towards-death" suggest; it is born of the forces of the world, which often collide with the vital strivings of the self.[9] This sentiment applies to many Hyolmo lives, for the event of death can be at odds with a person's rendering of that death, and thus the death appears to arrive from outside the sphere of the practical, creative self of everyday life.

Yet it's also the case that two domains of life are in play in many moments of living and dying. There is the sphere of everyday life, of active and willful engagements in the world, known overtly and in practical ways to the person involved; and there is the domain of karmic formations, of situations slated to occur in that person's life, with those formations opaque to the subject affected by them. Since the fact and manner of one's death are largely the product of karmic forces, there is also the sense that the death stems from the grounds of a person's karmic reverberations in the world, even if most people can never fathom well what those reverberations are. (An analogy could be made with those who live with the sense of obscure "genetic" forces shaping their biological fates.) The scene is one of intimacy within remoteness: the self of everyday life grasps, only faintly, the force of karmic reverberations.

Some try to anticipate what their fates have in store for them. "Now, in becoming old, how is it?" asked Phur Gyalmu as we spoke in her home in Thodong one afternoon in 1998. "I will die. Is it that I will die while going on the road, or is it that I will die after being sick for one or two months? I only worry about that, me. I don't have other worries."

The manner of a person's future death remains an open question. "It's good to die while doing dharma," noted one woman when polled on the subject. "If people die in an accident, it's their misfortune. How to die, now? It would be good if I died while sleeping, without any illness or hardship. But will I die like that? I think I'll have to face many hardships when I die. It's all my fate."

Though many wish and pray to die in good ways, it does not always work out that way. A person's manner of dying can be assessed and talked about in terms of what it appears to say about that person's store of karma. Reality comes out in the moment of death.

Since karma plays itself out in different ways, the suffering associated with death comes in different forms. Some people enter the stage of dying, yet while it's clear that they are soon to die, they hang on for two or three days, often in pain. Those gathered in their homes try to comfort them and wait for their passing. "Some die in a difficult way," Kesang Lama noted. "Relatives of the dead person come to see the dying man, and the whole village gathers to see him, but the man in the bed who is supposed to die stays alive for two, three days. People gather there because they think he is about to die, but he is not actually dead. There are many cases in which people do not die for two, three days."

The main problem with dying in this way, outside of the cruel waiting game it poses, is that the pain of dying is prolonged and a person's mind is not at ease. "He can't die peacefully," Dawa said of a person who had difficulty in dying. "His heartmind is struggling. I've seen many people die in this way."

"If someone dies without any pain," Temba's grandfather observed, "in one's own bed while sleeping, it's the best way to die. There is no pain in the body and the other members don't have to provide a lot of care. So if anyone dies in that way, it's the best." Temba's uncle added thoughts of his own. "If the person could achieve the death without any pain or by giving little trouble to the living ones, then that would be the best way to die."

A person dies in relation to other events, which inform the shape of dying. He dies in relation to others, who are touched by that dying. Such are the effects of actions.

Most desire to die as Pasang's father did—in their homes, among loved ones. The dying should be at ease, surrounded by family members, relatives, and friends, without fear or longing, prepared to die. While many say it's best to die while sleeping, with an absence of awareness, others, especially those familiar with Buddhist principles, find it's important to die while awake and conscious of one's death. In that way, a person can say goodbye to loved ones in good terms and embrace new situations to come.

Others are not so fortunate. Hospitals present bad places in which to die. For most Hyolmo people they entail unpleasant scenes of medical instruments, tubes, infections, contagions, unfamiliar protocols, and operations that go well or poorly. They can be costly in the long run, and far from home. It's difficult for many family members to stay with a hospitalized person for long stretches of time, which may bring about a situation where a person might die alone or with only one or two acquaintances nearby.

"When we see on television a person dying in a hospital alone," Karma told me, "we say that it's a very bad death. 'What bad karma,' we say. 'Not even a chance to say goodbye.'"

Hospitals are known as spiritually impure places. The fact that many different people, including many who might be spiritually impure, have died within their confines, perhaps in the same bed that "one's own" would be assigned, make them a place of impurity [*dhip*]. Such "death impurity" can further harm and weaken a person as well as contaminate her body or consciousness if she does die. Due to this, many resist being taken to a hospital if it looks like they might die there. "I told them that I didn't want to die in a hospital," Dawa Jyaba Hyolmo said when relating a time when he was seriously ill and his family wanted to take him to a hospital in Kathmandu. "'If I have to die, then I'll die in my own home, in front of my dear ones.'"

In recent years a few people living in the United States who have been gravely injured have been cared for in hospitals. They have been kept alive, while in comas, with the aid of life-support systems, attended to by family members.

"That is very sad," Nogapu said in speaking of these situations while conversing with me in his home in Boudhanath one evening. "If a person like this had died by now, he would have already come back [been reborn]. That kind of thing is difficult for everyone. If something like this happens in Nepal, the person would die soon after getting injured. They don't have those kinds of machines here."

Unable to die, a person is stuck between lives. The temporality of a good death is obstructed. The person is also situated between two technologies of death: the Buddhist practices his family knew best and the biomedical procedures of a big city hospital. Once these latter procedures embrace an unconscious body they establish a situation often found today in American hospitals—"a prolonged hovering at the threshold between life and death," as anthropologist Sharon Kaufman has observed. "Instead of death," Kaufman notes, "the hospital opens up an indefinite period of waiting during which patients do not cross that threshold until it is decided when it is *time* for them to die."[10] Like others in hospitals sustained through ventilators and additional life-support systems, the person enters a "zone of indistinction"—biologically alive, though only because he is "sustained by biomedical technology, and without signs of unique, purposeful life."[11]

Situations such as these throw Hyolmo families up against forms of the "new death" taking hold in many societies.[12] These emergent, technologically mediated ways of dying configure death as occurring not as it will appear "naturally" but "delayed, managed, and timed."[13] It's not that Hyolmo families are against the use of technologies: far from it, as is clear with the recurrent use of

Internet connections, cell phones, and video recordings. What concerns them are medical technologies which continue to such an interminable point that they beg the question, painfully felt, of whether or not a person whose body is sustained in such a way is still vitally alive.

The gamut of biomedical interventions often applied in hospital settings to prevent a person from dying often stand in stark contrast to forms of dying in the Hyolmo region, where there is more a sense of calm, compassionate, and patient attending to a person's cessation than any kind of radical efforts to forbid the death from happening. There is caring comfort in the face of death, but there is also a sense of quiet restraint and "practices of nondoing."[14] As Eve Sedgwick has observed, instructions for dying and for working with the dying in Buddhist traditions often "involve the most passive and minimal of performances: 'Opening to' (a person or predicament), 'opening around' or 'softening around' (a site of pain), *listening*, relaxation, spaciousness, patience in the sense of *pateor*, or lying open, shared breathing."[15] Sedgwick glosses the skilled means of laconic acceptance here: "No one fails to die; at best, one can get out of one's way."[16]

This sentiment can be compared to the combative zeal that medical practitioners in Europe and the United States often have in trying to preserve a life. Death is "an enemy that has to be overcome," notes Lydie Fialová, a physician and medical anthropologist from Czechoslovakia, of medical approaches to end of life care. "For us as doctors death means that the enemy was stronger and we have lost. The condition is considered as 'hopeless' when there is nothing we can do from the medical point of view to cure the incurable disease or to prolong life. Death is then a sign of failure and this might be one of the reasons why we hesitate to confront it and leave the dying patients alone."[17]

There is an art to holding back. A calm abiding is often wiser and a more effective way to attend to someone's passing than rushing to prevent the death at all costs.

Sange's father crafted his own death. An element of poiesis runs through Hyolmo efforts at dying. At work is a generative fashioning and bringing-forth of situations and consciousness, which serves to aid a dying person's plight. Many strive to fashion appropriate states of mind while dying. They try to dissolve their attachments to the world, visualize the forms of Buddhist deities, and contemplate the impermanent nature of all life. Through these efforts a person can maintain some control over the dying process and be conscious of his or her passing.

"Dying means a lot," Karma once noted as we sat and talked in the family room in his home in Kathmandu. "It's not just the pain it brings. It's also the preparations that need to be done, the thoughts you need to have while dying, the state of mind—all that is very important."

Such matters are crucial because a person's state of mind while dying contributes to what happens to the consciousness after death, and because a prepared and proper consciousness makes for a good death. To die suddenly, in contrast, say in an automobile collision, prevents a person from preparing well for death. "I would definitely not want to die by crashing," Karma said in slapping his hands together. "That would be the most unpleasant. Because you're not prepared to die, mentally, and it just happens."

Many try to craft certain kinds of consciousness in the moments of their dying. These efforts rest on people's abilities to shape the manner and content of their thoughts. In this Buddhist world, individuals and communities understand well that the ways in which they make sense of life accord with certain perceptual and cognitive habits, which can be modified through conscious practice. Death is no exception to this. Many try to control their thoughts and feelings in the time of dying, or steer them in certain ways. In self- and other-guided acts of what philosophers and anthropologists would call "phenomenological modification," people try to blank out some matters and visualize others.[18] They act to shape their thoughts, their memories, the tenor of their minds. All this is consistent with Buddhist practices known to Hyolmo communities, in which spiritual adepts draw on tantric and ritual techniques to form and reform their thought, modes of consciousness and perception, and moral sensibilities. People go about their lives with the idea that a person's consciousness while dying is not something utterly determined from the outside, the fate of karma, or the hardships of that moment. Consciousness can be molded, worked upon, by oneself and by others, much like life itself, such that death becomes something different than it might be otherwise.

There is a gentle art to dying. Dying is often couched as an active, conscious project in life, as the last and ultimate project of a life, as an action to be undertaken, one that can be achieved in either skillful or unskilled means. Dying can be a lengthy process undertaken with foresight and self-awareness. The stage of dying is an existential domain into which one can be initiated. If dying is to be done correctly, it calls for a set of preparatory acts and last-moment efforts that fashion the dying person's karmic condition and quality of mind and body upon dying.

A dying self endeavors to dissolve the self. A person strives to create the conditions whereby she can contribute to the creative subtraction of her place within the world. This poiesis of cessation involves a making of unmaking, a calm forging of undoing, dissolving, taking away, quiescence. A hand erases itself. In many respects these efforts fit well with the intent of Buddhist teachings and practices, which ceaselessly work toward the idea of letting go of ego, attachments, sensory dependencies, and the sense of a solid and unchanging self in the world. These hard-gained endeavors apply both to Buddhist practices and Hyolmo methods of dying, to the extent that many Hyolmo people become, arguably, most Buddhist in spirit while they lie dying.[19]

Many learn how to die. They undertake an apprenticeship on the subject, lest they approach it in an uninformed way and disturb their chances for a good rebirth. Some fail to train well. Karma once told me that people will sometime remark that certain persons in their communities do not "think" about death, their deaths in particular, and thus blunder through life in a foolish way, without giving thought to the implications of their own future ends. "We say, 'He's such an old man now, but he doesn't think about think of dying, he doesn't think of death.'"

Such considerations get at pressing questions. How should we think of death? How should we live a life, knowing that we are going to die? How does the knowledge that we are to die inform how we are to live?

Karma once offered some thoughts on how he would like to die. "I really wish," he told me, "that when I die I'll have known a lot about death, and that I can die peacefully, as my father did, without any worries coming to me, about my children or my family, and things like that. I really wish that. Maybe I could kind of teach as well to my family before I die — I mean about the attachments. But I wish that I could be in that position, not having attachments, and not really worry about anything.

"As I said, by the time I die, if I have completely taken care of these things, I'll be happy. I'd like to die peacefully, aware of everything that is happening, and just before dying say, 'Okay, this is the point where I die.' So the final experience will be this, probably."

"So, a good way to die is to die peacefully?" I asked.

"Oh yes."

"Alone, or with family members?"

"With family members around. And that would even be a test for me, you see — whether I have really managed to achieve it internally."

"Because they will be crying."

"Yes. And if I'm able to say, 'Don't cry. This is it,' and explain everything, I would like to have that situation. I want to be prepared, at least, and have my mind clear of those sorts of things. And for that I'd really like to know a lot [about Buddhist teachings]."

Karma would prefer to die while awake, and conscious of his passing. "It's important to be present at one's time of going," he told me. "Otherwise, you cannot even experience your death. You are not able to say something to your family—to say, 'This is my death. This is my last word to my family.' . . . Be thankful for this life. It's important to appreciate that we had this chance to walk together, and then, at the last moment, to say, 'It's been good.' It's important to appreciate what life has given you. So death is not scary at all. Everyone has to go through it. To realize when it's the time to die, this is important."

"So anyway, people face death quite well," said Karma in passing. Accepting of death, he and others try to approach it directly, openly.

Yet the force of karma often stands as a coefficient of resistance in any strivings for a good death. A death cannot be planned for, and a person can prepare for death all of his life. With each life lies the question of its dissolution.

There are also occasions when people are anxious about their deaths. They might be worried about the attachments they have accrued in their lives, or they are fearful of what may come next. They might also worry about the possible passing of loved ones, especially if they are living in lands far away.

Learning about death can begin at an early age. Karma told me that when he was young he and his younger brother and friends of theirs use to "play death" on the outskirts of their village, away from the looks of adults, much as they would play with any other real-life events, such as weddings, working in the fields, or selling and buying in shops. "We would play at all aspects of dying and death," he said, "even people getting sick, bombos and lamas at work, the sick recovering, dying, people crying and giving consolation, cremation, the funeral rites and processions." I recall Karma once telling me, "We used to make a small model of the dead person and build a space for the funeral rites, and then we would perform the cremation rites by setting the model and its funeral pyre on fire." Intrigued by the formations of death, Karma and his pals came to play at death. They created a simulative form of death, which was not separate from life but an integral part of it. Through this, they might have furthered their intuitive sense of death.

This Life

Notice how each death is specific and precise in its unfolding, much as any single life is. Attend to narratives that speak to the stark, unfathomable chasm between one life and the next, between the living and the dead.

"But one thing about him," said Pemba Dolma of her father-in-law, "was that he always had the *mālā* with him. He never put his rosary down."

It's true that death is cultural, that dying and cessation take on particular forms in distinct social and historical settings, and it is the case that certain "dying scripts" are often at work in such settings.[20] Yet there is a singularity to many deaths. The particulars go beyond what can be said in general about Hyolmo ways of dying, good or bad. Something in the way the details unfold makes them stand apart from the typicality of cultural discourses and representations or any general story one might want to tell about how women and men die. Dying unsettles the same, the familiar, the expected—much as life does, when it comes down to it.

> I was there when Diki's brother died. He had pain in his heart, and also headaches, but he was still talking. He himself had asked to bring either Uncle Thaila or me [to perform healing rites]. Somebody came to call me, and I went to his house. When I arrived there he was facing toward the outside and shouting, as he had a bad pain in his heart, and he turned back as I arrived.
>
> When I came there his sister Diki said, "Brother, brother. Goser has arrived," and he turned toward me. I asked him what had happened and he replied, "I don't know." But still he was having very bad pain. I was preparing for the healing, and Karma and some others had gone to Ghize to call the bombo, but after a few moments, he died, as if a radio that was playing was turned off at once. I was unable to do anything at all for his recovery. His veins were so raised because of his shouting, and then he ended at once, like when a radio is turned off. [Goser Lama]

The voices linger, hauntingly so, those of the dying and the narrators of those deaths. In these voices we hear rough-throated tones crucial to life. They speak to the ways creatures of speech strain to get on in life, not to fade quickly, calling out, talking to no end, comforting others, their words held in ours. A voice is a strong measure of a life. This voice is singular, the tones distinct, exceptional, be they strong or weak. A dying voice marks a hungry, willing, vulnerable person, sometimes scared, in need. The singularity of a death points to the pressing distinctiveness of each life, as well as how different lives link together.

A death is singular as well because it's the person alone who dies. As one popular Tibetan text, the one known in English as *The Words of My Perfect Teacher*, puts it, "Your family and friends gather around you, but there is nothing they can do to delay your departure—you are going through the suffering of death by yourself, all alone."[21] Hyolmo chronicles of death speak to the limit of what the living can know and experience of it, at least in direct and immediate ways. A stark chasm marks the gap between life and death: the dying tumble over this gulf into silence and nullity.

The narratives speak to the presence of something fundamental that reveals itself in such moments: the reverence paid, usually, to a human life, any given life, especially when that life is ending. *This life, this death.* Life itself is right there, in its singular immanence, and death is right there, in its dead-mute density.[22] It's difficult to ignore the presence of these two, most fundamental domains, especially at times when the threshold between them is such a thin and porous one. Attending to the death of another can yield a raw and exceptional hour in anyone's life. Perhaps that helps to explain why the narratives are lined with details, as if the intense realness of passing moments becomes readily "etched" or "impressed" within a person.[23]

Suddenly he put his rosary down on the table. The recognition of the passing of a life is similar to an appreciation of the sacred, in the sense that something altogether remarkable and tremorous is involved. Yet perhaps there are more than similarities involved here. Perhaps one way we gain an appreciation of what could be called the sacred is by witnessing the deaths of others.[24] Some deaths reflect little of the sacred, but, rather, dumb ugliness. Or they speak to the horror of violence.

My own encounters with the narratives run up against a sense of limits. I receive the accounts apprehensively. They are a delicate gift to be preserved and passed on. In reading and reporting them, entangled strands of identification, observation, and compassion are at work. They remind me of deaths I have observed in my family and in my life, but only partly so. In reading, I find myself identifying with the participants involved, yet that identification is always partial and tentative. My consciousness sides up not with the dying so much as it does with the narrators who accompany them. While this might be because the first-person voices of the narratives draw me into that perspective, it's also because death remains foreign to me. It's harshly difficult to take that imaginative leap into the consciousness of a dying self. No one alive knows what it is to die. The narratives remain other to me, triply so. The narrators speak of dying neighbors whose consciousnesses are distinct from their own. They speak of events in a cultural world and time other than my own. Dying itself is apart from anything I have experienced in my life to date. There's compassion and sympathy, for sure, but I cannot know these dying others. "The death of the Other: a double death, for the Other is death already, and weighs upon me like an obsession with death."[25]

Violent deaths add immeasurably to the otherness of death. Many deaths are "unexceptional" in the sense that people die in familiar circumstances, due to illness or accident. Other deaths result from situations of violence or terror, where normally available modalities of cessation and ritual mourning cannot be accessed. This was the case in Nepal for many peoples during the years of bloody conflict between Maoists insurgents and governmental military and police forces. More than fifteen thousand people were killed from 1996 to 2006, when a Comprehensive Peace Accord ended the hostilities. While the worst of the fighting occurred in regions of western and eastern Nepal, the climate of the war disturbed peoples throughout the country. News reports circulated on television and radio airways documented the battles and mapped the devastation that deaths and terror wreaked on families and communities, while videos made by Maoists detailed the ideologies of their movement and their military successes. Throughout the country death became something violent, sudden, and inconceivably brutal. Those living in the Hyolmo region did not see much of the fighting and assaults firsthand, but they did suffer from the unnerving presence of Maoist patrols that roamed the region in search of food, funds, and new "recruits" (often adolescent boys coerced into joining their cause) and military units in heated search of those patrols.

I had kept clear of the Hyolmo region through those years, not so much because of fears for my safety but because friends warned me that anyone who assisted me in traveling or working there would be pressured and coerced for "donations" of money and food to the Maoist cause. When I returned in 2011, for the first time in twelve years, I sensed the remnants of a storm that had passed. Families spoke of the hard years when bands of Maoist soldiers patrolled the area. As far as they knew, only one person who identified as Hyolmo was killed in the conflict; this was a man who lived in a village an hour's walk northwest. When I visited one family in their home, they told of how the rebels would arrive in their village, carrying rifles. They demanded food and shelter from them and other lodge owners and then trooped on. When the government's soldiers swept through town, they berated its residents, chiding, "Why did you give these people food and money?!" But how, as one woman phrased it, could you say no to strangers with guns slung on

Figure 4. Gulphubanjang, 2011.

their shoulders? The soldiers' consumption of food and drink drained this family's household. The Maoists were forcibly recruiting young men—boys, really—to "join" their cause, and so their first son left for Kathmandu when he was fourteen to study in a school there, living and cooking on his own in a small flat. He returned after the truce was established.

A few days later Pasang and his brother Sange and I were visiting their uncle Lhatul one rainy afternoon. We sat in a family room off to the side of his lodge and looked at some photographs that the family had collected through the years. Lhatul's wife, Mingmar, brought us tea and commented on a few of the images. "There are some videos we could watch," Lhatul said. We warmed to this idea, and Sange set up his uncle's netbook. Lhatul reached for a plastic bag and pulled out a number of videos and placed them on the floor. We popped in a video of Shakira and listened to her sing ecstatically as her hips swiveled. Sange laughed when I mimed a couple of lyrics. We watched a film that presented richly moving songs sung by Tamang women.

"I have a video about the Maobadi somewhere," said Lhatul. "Do you want to see that?" Yes, I said after a moment's thought.

Soon we were observing a documentary style set of interviews with Maoist leaders arguing their cause. Military leaders spoke to their troops, a loose coterie of men and women, young mostly, rifles by their sides. As we listened to the speeches Lhatul repeated certain phrases, emphatically. "'We're doing this for us. We're fighting for the people'—That's what he just said."

The film jumped to vague skirmishes between the soldiers and government forces. The camera was shaky, the editing jagged; it was difficult to follow what was happening. The soldiers were preparing to attack a camp inhabited by government forces. Their assault occurred at dawn. A jumpy camera tracked the soldiers as they advanced down a craggy hillside toward what appeared to be little more than a campsite. Through much of the deadly skirmishes Lhatul reported actions or copied voices heard. "Oh. They're up behind the rock! There's a man by the tree!"

One clip showed the sparse moments of a man getting shot. The camera came in close. A bullet wounded him. He lifted up his head in an unusual way. He was pierced again. The bullets produced something like dust around him. He fell back.

"Is he dead?" I asked.

"Yes, he's dead," said Lhatul.

Khattam. Ruined. Finished. Slaughtered.

The scenes of the death were disturbing. What can one say about such a death but note the cruel, sad fact of it? Unnerving were the ways in which certain mimetic forms—the video, the echoic utterances, and my field notes on our viewing of it—created an eerie facade around the death such that its harsh, nonchalant violence combined with intimate simulations of it. This rendered the killings at once terribly facile and overwhelmingly brutal.

There was something altogether sad and despairing in these images of the dead man; his life had been cut down in one brief, unfortunate moment. The vision of his lifeless body was horrible—in the strict sense of that word, terrible, fearful, dreadful, involving a sense of horror, literally, etymologically, "a shaking, trembling, shudder, chill." This was the horror of what had happened to this young man, and what could happen to any one of us in just a few moments. As philosopher Stanley Cavell once put it, "Horror is the title I am giving to the perception of the precariousness of human identity, to the perception that it may be lost or invaded, that we may be, or may become, something other than we are, or take ourselves for; that our origins as human beings need accounting for, and are unaccountable."[26] There is a horror in the fact of death, which might be masked over at times but is there nonetheless. In the quietest of moments, by a bedside or in a hospital room, we see the face of a parent or friend change into something unaccountably foreign to our sense of that person. We encounter a lifeless, decaying body, or a body maimed beyond recognition. We know and relate to (and care for) the increasingly fragile physiology of an aged elder. In times of illness, violence, or violent death we tremble over the recognition of the bodily basis of existence. We shudder at the precariousness of a life.

Many deaths are violent. There is nothing gentle or graceful about them. Hyolmo people know this to be the case. *Jiban esta cha.* "Life is like this," they might say. And yet this understanding does not stop them from trying to provide gentle, calming care to others, when they can, and it does not deter them from preparing for a good death.

Attachment

Reduce attachment, desire, and cravings when dying. Help the dying in this. Satiate a dead person's longings for this world. If need be, create a fiction to appease a restless mind.

Clinging, craving, grasping, releasing. How do people attach themselves to life, even in death? How might they let go when it's best to do so?

Dying well is about leaving this current life without much desire or grasping for it. A person should die without any attachment to the world. Hyolmo people usually refer to such attachment as *semjha*, as an "attachment" or "clinging" of the *sem*, or heartmind, among people or objects. The second syllable derives from the Hyolmo word *chhaba*, a verb that carries connotations of "to love," "to be attached to," "to cling to," "to desire." Semjha works through a principle of longing. Its force usually bids some kind of yearning, desire, or affection that a person has for something: a daughter or son, a valued set of clothes, wealth accumulated, the sweet taste of chocolates.

People are commonly attached to loved ones or cherished objects while alive. They're hooked on them. They crave and yearn for them. Those attachments become problematic when a person is dying, because they can make it difficult for a person to expire. Death occurs when the external breath departs the body. In situations where a person is stuck on some feature of the world, the breath can have trouble leaving the body. Semjha can also occur after a person dies, for any lingering longings or desires a consciousness has for the world might result in continued attachments. Although the person dies, he "leaves" some semjha, and that attachment remains with the desired person or object. Semjha is not a spirit of its own; it doesn't have a will or consciousness. It's more an immaterial, force, a field of intensive energy that clings to that which it is attached. When such attachments occur after a death, strange, unexpected events can happen in a household or to the family that is mourning the loss. People can fall ill, or see the *zuk*, the "visual image," of the dead person in their dreams.

Attachment is an unwanted phenomenon, both for the problem it causes in the consciousness of the dead and for the ways it affects the living. As Goser Lama put it, "If a person desires something before dying, and if it's not presented to him, then the semjha of the dying person continues to cling to the object or the person that the dying person longed for. In such cases, that attachment will disturb the life of the family. Sometimes it will bring troubles, such as causing illness among the family member that the dying person wished to see." Semjha graphs death onto life. It's true enough that attachment often impels a small death of the self, in that a person, helpless to whims and longings, flails into a loss of will and foresight and steady consciousness. Attachment can consist of too much of life, too much craving for life, until one is dying with the throes of that longing.

"Semjha is not good," one woman affirmed. "Semjha is not good. We mustn't die with attachment."

Possibilities recur when people talk about the clinging attachment at the moment of death. If a dying person cherishes a loved one, but that person is not present in the hours preceding the death, the dying self may long for the absent person.

If a person dies early in life, before his fated "time," he might feel he was unable to complete certain projects or "dreams" of his in life, such as owning a business or traveling to Tibet.

If a person dies before seeing all of his children mature and married, she might worry about what will come of those unsupported children.

If a person dies without having direct heirs to his wealth, such as a wife or children, he might worry over what will happen to his property after his death.

If a person cherishes certain possessions, such as a turquoise necklace, or has a taste for certain liquors or foods, or cigarettes, he might crave those items at the moment of death.

If someone knows little about what happens to a human being when dying, he might be anxious, fearful, or wracked with longing or desire at the moment of death.

All of these situations can readily prompt attachment. Different modes of attachment flit through people's lives, waxing and waning in degrees and inten-

sities. Any particular attachment can hinder the act of dying or trouble both
the dead and the living after the death.

Semjha, then, is a matter of longing or desire. It exists within a person's
heartmind as a lingering "interest" in some aspect of the world. Something has
gone unsatisfied, unsated. Something remains apart from the self, something
unfulfilled or incomplete in the dying person's life.

"It's better to die with one's family nearby," Ghang Lama told me in the
final years of his life.

> Then your semjha won't stay with them. If a man dies away from home,
> alone, then he thinks, "I have this property, I have that many children." Then
> the semjha gets attached to the house. So then the lamas need to tell him,
> "Don't affix your mind, don't act in this manner." If the children are not
> there, or if they're in a foreign land, then the attachment comes. If the chil-
> dren are away when the person dies, then they return after the death and say
> at the funeral, "Don't do the semjha to me. I was away before, but now I'm
> here."

Attachment does not occur when nothing is longed for; many Hyolmo
people aim for such an absence of longing when they die. There tend to be
two situations where a person has little, if any, attachment to the world when
he dies: when a person is learned in Buddhist thought and practice and has
transcended attachments to the world, and when a person dies after living a
long, fulfilling life. "It's good to die after fulfilling every dream you have which
is in your fate," Lhatul Lama affirmed. Dawa Jyaba Hyolmo spoke of the value
of dying at a ripe old age. "If a person lives up to that age," he told me, "then he
is able to do everything he wanted to do."

> If a person dies in this way, he has a feeling of satisfaction. . . . At this time,
> he knows he is dying, yet he doesn't care who takes his property, or what his
> children do, because he thinks, "I have done everything I could have done,
> whatever was possible to do, and as I am dying now, in my next life, where
> I'm going to be, please know this [I leave it to the Bodhisattvas to know and
> determine this]."

Ideally, all the narratives of a person's life should play out by the time that
person begins to die, with the final ellipsis being that of dying. Yet this is not
the case for many. A parent might worry about what is to come of a young, un-

married daughter. A young woman who dies before her time might have certain unfulfilled dreams. A childless man might fret the fate of his possessions. If attachments of this sort persist for the dying person, it's important that they be lessened significantly or extinguished altogether. There should be no clinging, no yearning for the zest of life, no itch to scratch. Nothing should still be anticipated, nothing left unfulfilled or incomplete. The fullness and completion of a life, and the absence of any regrets or longings, is one ideal. Fullness can entail a kind of emptiness. If the constitution of a self is predicated on desire, then that self can be effectively deconstituted once that desire is extinguished, like a flame that burns out in time.

The detachment ultimately occurs in the domain of thought and imagination. It's chiefly a question of what is "in" a person's mind at the moment of dying, what the heartmind desires. This is a phenomenology of the subjective: attachment is of the *sem* or "heartmind" only; a person longs only for what she thinks or feels she lacks. Given this, a dying person must do away with sentiments of craving. She needs to cultivate processes of mind founded on thoughts of contentment, satisfaction, and non-attachment, even if these thoughts are virtual or makeshift, of that transformative moment.

"While dying," Dawa Jyaba Hyolmo observed, "we shouldn't think, 'I have this property, I have these children, I have to do these tasks, I owe this much money. Now that it's certain I'm going to die, what's going to happen to these things?' If a person thinks in these ways, then after dying he's stuck in the between."

Karma put it in more positive terms. "At the last moment of your life, you try to be comfortable with everything. 'My children are grown, and they have done good things.' There are no regrets."

A hand releases its grasp on life.

The project of detachment is a dialogic, intersubjective one, for others help the dying to void their attachments to the world. If a person appears to be having trouble dying due to craving for the world, then those present try to ascertain what is causing the attachment and then act to abate it.

Goser Lama: "It's difficult for some to die—to detach the external breath, that is. Those who remain attached to something or somebody or on some kind of favorite food face difficulties in dying. If the things they wished for or the person they wanted to see or the favorite foods are presented to them, it will assist the dying person in detaching the external breath."

Desire comes and goes. It's not forever fixed in the self but arises, flows, dissolves, or curves into something else. When "presented" with the desired objects or person, the desires are satisfied and dying can occur. If a person longs for one last taste of liquor, a pinch of *raksī* will be placed on his lips. If she worries over possessions or wealth, people will place valued objects, from money to jewelry on her chest. With the objects lighting on the body the dying person will feel that these matters are close by and he will not yearn for them any longer. Relations of desire are stilled. Desire is lulled not so much by denying it, as some moral and religious traditions might have it, but by calmly satisfying the yearning—and sometimes within the virtuality of that moment only.

The gratification usually comes through direct sensorial modifications—taste, touch, sight, sound, smell, and imagining. Given that so many attachments proceed through sensuous liaisons with the world, it's fitting that the means of abetting them are sensate ones.

Close contact comes into play when a mother or father longs for a son's or a daughter's presence when dying. Often the dying person asks that someone in particular, a child or a close friend, be present. That person will be called and presented in front of him.

Dawa Jyaba Hyolmo spoke of this: "And in many cases, if the son and daughter are not present there when their father is dying, the relatives of the dead person say to him, 'Yes, your daughter and son have just arrived.' Just by saying this, the dying person's consciousness separates from its body and goes away."

The living can create a fiction to appease a dying mind. Or, more accurately, they establish a virtuality of contentment to help a person die well. A few choice words send a consciousness on its way. Then again, aren't we all living within the peaceful comfort of one fiction or another? And don't all humans die within the midst of a fiction or two?

Sange's father was detached in the end. He felt good about his family, about what his sons and daughter had accomplished in life. He had no worries or regrets in dying. "He wanted to have something for the village," Karma told me. "He long wanted to have a small community house in the village of Norbugang. So for that his sons got some money together, and gave it to him, so that he could give that as a donation."

"He was so prepared," Karma continued. "He wasn't afraid at all. 'Yes, this is my time to die.' That was the idea he had in his mind."

The family found that, because the father died without any unfulfilled longings for the world, there was no attachment after his death.

I spoke with Pemba about this.

"Did any semjha come?" I asked her. "Do you and the others [in his family] see him in your dreams?"

"No, his semjha didn't come," she said. "But we do see him often in our dreams."

People in many societies speak of how the dying sometimes hold on for hours or days on end, waiting for a family member to visit, or for an important social gathering to come and go, and then die only after those events happen. Hyolmo people have made a conscious practice of these inclinations. "Satisfaction" occurs when a desired object is presented to the dying self or when a sense of presence, completion, or repletion takes form. The elements of life are no longer absent or desired, be it in the medium of thought, speech, sight, taste, smell, or physical contact. The person becomes nondesiring, nonsensorial. With the attachment dissolved, the consciousness can leave the world in vacating the body, and semjha does not linger or haunt others after the person dies. A zero degree, unworried self can be sensed: a caesura of desire, a still point in thought and feeling.

"I won't leave any semjha on anybody, anywhere," one woman told me in 1998. "I only have thoughts about how my children can grow up and have a good life. I won't leave any attachment on anybody when I die. I'll just have my eyes shut and I'll die without any thoughts or feelings."

Dying can involve an intensified form of still nonbeing.

An Ethics of Care

Care for the dying and the bereaved, and try to provide for a good and properly social death. Accompany the dying in their last moments. Make them feel less frightened and alone. Try to make the death a calm and comfortable one.

The death of Sange's father was a keenly social one, with many present in the days before the death and a few close during it. Hyolmo deaths are commonly collective affairs, with others present in the home of the dying person in the days or hours preceding the death, and a few close ones beside the person when she or he expires. People die as they live from the moment of their birth: among others.

One reason for the strong intersubjective cast to many Hyolmo deaths is that members of a community customarily visit relatives or friends if they fall seriously ill in order to help and give support to the sick person and his family, and to keep company with them. The formal term for such a visit is *nhe kor*. While *nhe* means "illness," "disease," "malady," *kor* in this context means "visit" or "gathering" (in other contexts it can mean "circle" or "that which surrounds a certain point or place"). A grave illness prompts a gathering. Within that circle of care there can be a sense of wholeness, completion, and of communal support. "In a lot of ways, it's to make it so that the family doesn't feel alone," Karma noted. A social air usually pervades such accompaniments, with food and tea served and people clustered together, in subdued, drifting conversations.

"Once people know that someone is going to die, then people go there, just to comfort the family."

That was the situation that led people to frequent the home of Sange's father in his final days. "In his case, he knew later on, after he fell sick, that he was going to die. It was cancer. Everyone knew."

Pemba Dolma spoke of those visits: "His room would fill with people who had come to meet him. And we would prepare lots of butter lamps. As we were often preparing a lot of things, he would ask us why we were doing all these things. We would tell him, 'It's for the guests who are coming to visit you.'"

Such visits meant respect for the ailing person and his family in general. Along with this runs the idea that the more respected a person, the greater the number of visitors who step inside the house. Since respect is often earned through engaging in good deeds in life, a bevy of good deeds in life can result in a house full of people at the time of one's death—as so happened to be the case, Pemba Dolma made clear, when her father-in-law was dying. A house rich with people in the days before a death signals respect, compassion, and concern. A house with few well-wishers in times of trouble or during the stage of death, in contrast, can indicate a paucity of good deeds enacted in life by the person who is dying.

"Body lying flat on a last bed," run some words of a poem authored by the Seventh Dalai Lama,

> Voices whispering a few last words,
> Mind watching a final memory glide past:
> When will that drama come for you?[27]

Dying entails a similar kind of drama in Hyolmo households. Scenes of dying are not overly dramatic or melodramatic in any way, but certain roles do take form: the dying person, the grieving spouse, bereaved family members, and visiting relatives play their parts. A subtle but potent semiotics of dying shapes how people act and relate to others. For the dying, the death indicates what kind of person she or he was—and might be in the future. For mourners, the ways they respond to the death attest to their moral character. Dying means a lot.

Yet it would be a mistake to say that relatives show up at the home of a dying person in order simply to heed social conventions on the matter. People are sincerely concerned with the welfare of friends and relatives. They approach death with an ethics of care. That sense of care is an extension of the consideration that Hyolmo people frequently pay to others throughout their lives, be it helping others when they are sick, in need, or building a house. It is especially pronounced when another is in a condition of dying. People visit the home of a dying person, attend to her needs, satisfy desires, comfort her. Friends and family are usually present when another is dying and they try to make that person's passing less painful or solitary. Dying well requires the help of others; a person can't go it alone.

She always used to say to us, "Don't leave me alone. I need your help."

The philosopher Emmanuel Levinas has posited that one of the ethical obligations of human beings is to not "leave the other alone in the face of death."[28] Levinas contends that the sociality of people, based on the presence of the inescapable "face of the other," implies the obligation not to remain indifferent to the death of another, "even if responsibility then amounts only to responding, in this impotent confrontation to the death of the other, 'here I am.'"[29] We can all identify, if we're honest about it, with the occasional urge to get away from the sick and the dying, to walk away from the misery of others, if only because attending to that misery and all the crap that comes with it can be an unpleasant and thankless task. But something usually brings us back or keeps us there among those in need, responsive to their needs, before and after they die. We answer, usually, if we can, when we are called.

Hyolmo communities know well this ethical responsibility and the moral breach implied when it is not heeded. "Here we are, beside you, now and later," families and neighbors appear to be saying through their actions. "We cannot prevent your death. But we can make it a less painful and less lonely one."

Some narratives of dying give a sense of the tender, unassuming assistance given to another in his or her last hours.

I have some memory of the death of Kami's father and mother. The father died some four years before the mother. The father remained sick for a long time, and just before he died, I was there with him. He was laying on the floor and asked me to help turn his body to the other side. Time and again he was saying that perhaps now he's going to die. Hearing this, I advised him to recite mani prayers and to pray to the deity. Soon after I helped him to turn on the other side he died, and he died while reciting prayers. [Temba's grandfather]

: : :

Last year, my cousin's father, Mheme T., died here in Kathmandu. He died in my lap. He wasn't sick. He was too old. He was a drinking man, for quite some time. I went there, and he said, "Nogapu, can I drink a little bit of liquor?"

I said, "Don't drink, Mheme, because you are very old, and you are a little bit ill. Do you want to have a little bit of soup? We can make thukpa for you." He said, "No, no. I'm not hungry." He asked that new clothes be put on his body. And I said to him, "Yes, I've just put some new clothes on you." He then asked for an umbrella. "Why do you want an umbrella?" "I'm leaving," he said. "Where are you going?" "I'm going back to the village." And just before dying, he said, "Okay, I've arrived here, I've arrived in Melamchi. I'm very, very tired. Oh, I'm so tired. I came back very quickly. Now I'm very tired. Can I drink some raksī?" We gave him a little bit of raksī, one cup of raksī. He did a blessing to the deities three times, then he took a sip. But he didn't swallow, it just stayed inside his mouth. Then he died. So I said, "Mheme, Mheme, Mheme." He made a puckered face, and then he was gone. [Nogapu Prakash Sherpa]

Nogapu, the narrator of the above moments, I count as a friend. His words speak to his gentle care toward those others in his world.

Certain forms of contact recur. Techniques of care arise spontaneously: support a dying body from behind, rest a hand lightly on another's body, speak kind and soothing words, place food or drink in another's mouth, respond to their calls for assistance. Being with a dying other can be a caring, compassionate act. Hyolmo people draw on a number of "ethicofigural" acts and gestures in relating to people in life and when caring for those who are dying.[30] They visit the dying person, support and comfort his body, offer him food and drink, speak soothing words, hear his last will, and instruct him as to what he can expect to encounter in death. Through these tangible bodily efforts in care and connection people often die in ways less anxious than they might otherwise.

And less alone. Staying alongside a person in his last moments can make the passing a less solitary enterprise. Unaccompanied dying is a harsh, unwanted way to end a life, much as unaccompanied living is not really living. Through a "gesture of accompaniment," to use words of Paul Ricoeur, family and friends relate in compassionate ways to a vulnerable loved one.[31]

"Compassion, you say?" Ricoeur writes in his posthumously published work, *Living Up to Death*.

> Yes, but once again it is necessary to understand the suffering-with that the word signifies. It is not a moaning-with, as pity, commiseration, figures of regret, can be; it is a struggling-with, an accompanying. . . . Accompanying is perhaps the most adequate word to designate the favorable attitude thanks to which the gaze directed toward a dying person turns toward him, who is struggling for life until death, and not toward a dying person who will soon be dead.

A similar principle of accompaniment motivates the care for the dying in Hyolmo communities, as it does in the care of the living. A person might well be "alone in dying, but he does not die alone."[32]

The stories that people tell of their neighbors' passings are narratives of tender accompaniment. They speak to a modest, abiding co-presence in the hours of dying. The narrators are not so much heroic or prideful in their compassionate assistance as they are quietly accepting of their understated responsibilities. If the fact that people die, often after suffering from anguishing pain hardship, is a grim and unsettling one to accept, then perhaps there is partial consolation in the realization that they do not go it entirely alone.

This, at least, is one way to make sense of the thread of companionship. When I conveyed these assessments to Karma one afternoon in his home in Sunnyside, he said they made sense to him. He also offered a different take on the matter. "It's more the sharing of the last moments," he said. "It's more the sharing of whatever moments they have, together." Gathering in a dying person's home is not primarily to keep that person from feeling lonely or alone in dying. It's to participate together in the significant, communal experience of parting and loss—even if the experiences of the dying person and those who are witnessing that demise are different.

The near related ones are for the times of joys and sorrows, goes one Hyolmo expression. "Joys and sorrows" here is *kyi-dhuk*, a portmanteau word that combines the words *kyipu*, "joy, happiness," and *dhukpu*, "sorrow, hardship." Close family members, "one's own," share in both the good and bad moments in life, from personal and familial successes to devastating losses. "We all gather to share in these moments," Karma explained. It's more a matter of being with than of being for.

"It's out of respect, as well, even if we're not so closely related," Karma added. "It's respecting the fact that now this person will no longer be with us."

There is the memory of a man leaving Nepal on a significant journey. Family members and friends accompanied him to the airport en masse, with the aid of several automobiles and motorcycles, to say goodbye and share in the parting. Gathered together, each person offered a *katha*, a ceremonial scarf, to the departing. That person stepped through the departure gate draped in a cascade of gold and white silk scarves.

Death can be a departure onto new territories in life.

Oral Wills Are Harder than Stone

Speak, before dying, to family and loved ones. Give an oral will, noting debts and finances. Explain to family members how the funeral rites should be carried out. Advise them on the how to live a good life. Respect the morally binding nature of any words left behind.

Pasang's father spoke before dying to family and loved ones. He made clear his financial affairs and he advised his sons on how to live a good life. If speech is an intensive means of relating to others, then speech can also aid in bringing those relations to a close. Words are left, put down. They stand as residual traces of a person's life, his breath. Words can promote connection and continuity, the transmission of values through time.

Pemba Dolma:

When his son came from India he got a little better and he felt happy to see all of his family members together for three days. But again he returned to his previous condition. When everyone came—his sons, his daughters—he left an oral will. Earlier, he and his son had decided to support the construction of a temple in the village, so while he was dying he asked his son to fulfill his wish by giving fifty thousand Indian rupees as his contribution to the temple. And he asked all of his sons to live peacefully and together.

When a person senses he is to die soon, he often calls family members to his bedside and voices an oral will. This is called *kha jhem,* a kind of "mouth oath." *Kha,* which literally means "mouth," is found in compound words that signify speech, oaths, or oral actions of some kind. *Jhem* relates to the Tibetan word *chem,* which can connote "roaring noises," "thunderous sounds," "exhortations." Combined, the words denote a "farewell exhortation" or "last will or testament." *Kha jhem zjhage* is the usual verb phrase for this act, with the verb *zjhagen* meaning "putting, placing, depositing." The last words are placed away from the dying self and left for others. This is language as connection, transfer, and continuity. Words reach out to others.

An oral will designates a finite ending. Its substance involves a person's "last breath." These last words fuse a final engagement between family members, one last transfer from parent to child. After this, once the person is dead, she can no longer speak directly to the living; she is no longer audible. An oral will marks a border, a limit of communication. It signals that the death is soon to occur. Hyolmo people do not consider such wills to be something a person needs to do or is compelled to do before one's death. They belong rather to a genre of speech that a person can draw on if she wishes to. Nor is it the case that, if a person gives an oral will, he needs to do it in a certain way or talk about certain matters in particular. When a person concludes he is to die soon, he asks for family members and relatives, friends, and neighbors to gather around him and says what he wants to. Some die just after giving oral wills, while some leave words months before they die.

A person might address a number of matters when giving his last words. He might talk about financial matters, particularly what money he owes to others, and what money is owed to him. He might detail how his property is to be divided up among their sons and daughters, or how much money should be donated to a temple or given away in charity. "This is kha jhem," Dawa Jyaba Hyolmo once said, "when a person says, 'I have to take this much money from him, and I have to give this to him. When I die, do this for me, and I have got this much property.' He also tells them where he has kept all the money, he tells all these things before dying."

When asked if his father left any last words before he died, Dawa replied:

> Yes, he left kha jhem in the presence of my uncle's son and his wife. My father told them everything, whether he had to take money from someone, or give it to someone. He explained everything. I also did what he wanted me to do. I wanted to do more than that, but before dying he had told my

brother to ask me not to do more than what he had asked me to do. Before dying my father gave eighty thousand rupees to my mother, money he had saved throughout his life. He asked my mother to offer the money to the lamas in the temple. He even added that, if after offering the money to the lamas, if there was still some left, then we should distribute it equally between the two of us, my mother and me. We did each and every thing he asked us to do.

The dying might talk about a number of matters. "He might even tell them about the sins he has done," Kesang observed. Bombos and lamas who have students often refrain from teaching their students certain special, coveted practices until they are close to dying; they then whisper their secrets into the ear of the apprentice. Often the dying will ask as well that certain funeral rites be done on their behalf after they die. They might also instruct their children to act in morally good ways in their lives. "Don't fight. Don't become too greedy. Be a good person. I am leaving now," Nogapu said in English in paraphrasing the gist of the moral exhortations he has heard. He gave a specific example:

> There was a man who died in Melamchi about five years ago. He was always fighting, causing problems. He was a very angry man. When he was dying he was by himself. We were doing some kind of ritual in the temple then in Melamchi. So he sent a message there, asking the boys gathered to come to his place. "Now, listen boys," he said. "I am dying. So listen. Don't get angry. Never fight with anyone. That's very bad. Be friendly with everyone. Don't get angry. I've been an angry man, I was a man who fought—now I'm dying. I did very bad." Then he died.

Death offers an occasion for moral correction. The voicing of any last words can prompt a moral testament that chronicles aspects of a dying person's life and how people should act in life.

Mourners take these unwritten documents seriously. The survivors of a death should heed what a person requested with the last words. "It's the last lecture of the person who is dying," Lhatul noted. "It might include some orders which others, be it his family members or his relatives, have to follow. They have to fulfill his wishes." If they do not, people will speak harshly about the family. The deceased's consciousness might not find the way to a good rebirth.

Kha jhem is an authoritative discourse. The moral contract implied by it cannot be broken. *"Kha jhem dhole sage"* goes one proverb-like phrase voiced by Hyolmo people: "Oral wills are harder than stones." The integrity of willed words is more resilient than stones.

"Hyolmo people believe in kha jhem a lot," Dawa Jyaba Hyolmo told me. "They say 'oral wills are harder than stone.' For example, if I die and I leave kha jhem with my son, then he has to do all the things asked with the kha jhem. If it's not possible, then he has to make it possible, and do it. This is necessary in our Hyolmo society."

As Dawa knew it, the dead person's consciousness looks on from above, hovering in the intermediate bardo realm (between one life and the next), waiting for the acts he requested to be carried out. If they are not, the unfulfilled desires can result in attachments that keep the consciousness from moving on to a new life.

Oral wills are durable, unbreakable.

Still, one never knows for sure what will happen, or what is in another's heart, or how people will act. And so to increase the chances that any and all instructions will be heeded a dying person often utters his will in a public context, such that many people hear his words. He does this by calling relatives and neighbors and asking them to be present while he gives the oral will. The main idea in this is to create an audience which, if need be, can later attest to what the dying person said. When those responsible for organizing funeral rites and the dead person's finances know that others can report on what was said, the reasoning goes, then they are more likely to follow through on the person's requests.

Last words can help a dying person to realize or extinguish his affection for the world, and so further dissolve his worldly self. "Some people die in a difficult way," Dawa Jyaba Hyolmo told us.

In many cases, the person who is dying gives kha jhem, but he is not able to convey his message properly, and due to this his relatives don't understand what he wants to tell them. This makes the death more complicated. But after a few days, he is a little normal, and then he conveys and tells his relatives what he wanted them to do for him when he dies. After saying his last words, the person dies peacefully. He stays alive for two, three days, just to disclose his secrets to his family members, including whether he has to take from or give any loans to anyone. If he is not able to say all these things to his relatives, then it becomes difficult for him.

The ability or inability to give oral wills points to the occasional linguistics of good and bad deaths. With a good death a person can communicate well. He can speak clearly and fully. There are moments of contact, exchange, and reception. Traces are heard, left behind, transferred to a later generation.

A bad death entails obstructions to speaking well. Utterances signal pain more than anything else. Mouths are deformed, blocked, made mute. Continuities, hindered. A person cannot be understood or is unable to talk altogether. Family members cannot receive what is intended for them—how they should handle finances or perform the cremation or funerary rites. No solid linguistic contact or exchange occurs, no transfer of secrets or values. Something remains lacking, incomplete. There is an absence of finality, of completion; a lack of fullness or emptiness. From this, attachment can emerge. Speech and silence figure so often in the circuitries of longing and desire.

All this can point to the karmic worth of a dying self. Bad deeds echo in a difficult death. Reality comes out in the moment of death. So does a sense of history, of changing times. People I have spoken with on the subject told me that kha jhem is not done as much as it was decades before.

"Kha jhem is not so popular these days," Goser Lama noted. "Few people desire to leave kha jhem. But some still leave it."

"I have seen many people die, but I haven't heard kha jhem very much," said Nogapu.

Several factors gird the growing infrequency of the practice. In recent years, financial matters have become less secretive and more "transparent." Families talk more openly about loans and debts. People store money and valuable possessions in banks and keep written records of these deposits. A parent's wealth and belongings are usually distributed equally among children. "So nothing has to be conveyed at the last stage of life, since everything is transparent to all." Many are also living longer than their parents and grandparents did. When parents do die, their children are often adults themselves, and have already come to understand well their parents' finances. At the same time, the need for parents to exhort their children to live morally good lives is less urgent, since the latter, now mature and with families of their own, have already learned how to do so.

Seeing the Face

Regard the face and personal presence of the dying person, before he expires. Help him to meet with loved ones. Be visually and verbally co-present with him. Establish a lasting mental image. Satisfy longings among the dying and the grief-stricken.

In the late 1990s I spent a lot of time with a man called Ghang Lama, "Hill Lama." I visited him in his home in Kathmandu to record his *jāvan kathā*, his "life history." I also liked spending time with him and his family. During our conversations he sometimes expressed concern that two of his sons lived in the Hyolmo region, a long day's walk from the Kathmandu Valley, and thus might not be able to be present when he died. When our talks came to a close in the summer of 1997, I asked if there were anything else he would like to say. "What to say, now?" he replied.

> When I die, will everyone [in the family] be together, or not? I worry about that. If my sons had stayed in one place, then it wouldn't be a problem. But now that they've all dispersed to different places, they're all bound to worry, "If he dies, I won't be able to see him." Isn't that something to worry about? Now, my sons have gone, my daughter has gone, one's own have gone. When a man dies he is cremated. If his children cannot see his face before he's burned, they ask, "Where has he gone?! Where has he gone?!"

When this good man died in 2004, in his home in the village of Thodong, on lands he inhabited and farmed much of his adult life, his daughter and three sons saw his face before his body was cremated. In the summer of 2011 I traveled to Thodong and visited the site where Ghang Lama was cremated. Set within a canopy of breezy young pines close to the house where he lived for much of his adult life, the site, now covered with leafy grasses, looked onto level ground facing the valley to the east. Ghang Lama's grandson and I stood there one rainy morning and took in this scene of silent remembrance.

Vision, like speech, can imply a keen fuse of connection between people, much as it is a means of desire and attachment to the world. A sense of final contact and intimacy can accordingly take place through visual as much as verbal means. Different sensory engagements figure, in shifting ways, in the means and ends of a life.

Hyolmo people talk of the desire to "see the face" of a dying loved one before, or after, she or he expires.[33] The phrase *dhongba tage*, "seeing the face," suggests the act of viewing or being present with the dying person one last time. When people speak of such events they tend to talk about whether or not someone was able to "see" or "meet with" the face of a dying loved one:

Figure 5. Prayer flags. Thodong, 2011.

dhongba thong manyong, "I was unable to see his face." The looks go both ways;
the dying person as well as those surviving him can find value in these acts of
intimate proximity and mutual "engazement."[34]

For a dying person, the act of seeing and being seen by family members
can be a way to say goodbye to them and to enjoy their living presence one
last time. It can also work to diminish his attachment to them. If a few family
members or close friends are absent, if, say, they are living some distance away
and have not been able to travel to the place where the person is dying, then
the dying person can long for them or have a certain "curiosity" or "interest" in
them. One longs for what is absent. If they are present, however, and the dying
person can look at and talk to them in the hours before his death, then that
interest will be abated and he will not be as attached to them. In part because
it's understood that an absence of attachment of any sort can help them to die
well, in their last hours the dying do often ask that certain persons be called
to visit them. If a person's children are absent when he is dying, there can
be undue attachment, because that person longs for the missing, wished-for
loved ones. If they are present, however, there is no need for any ghostbound
attachments to occur, because there is no one absent whose presence is desired. This is the general understanding of the value of seeing the face of loved

ones in a time of dying. There are occasions, however, when interactions do not proceed as smoothly as this: the dying person can long for those around him, and visiting family members can become emotionally upset in the presence of a dying loved one.

For the living, being present while another is dying can help that person to reduce her attachment to the world. Family and friends can help to make the dying process a supported, less lonely one. Seeing the face of a dying person enables a person to behold the loved one visually one last time and sustain a lasting visual memory of that person. Even if they do not utter any words, family members can communicate their love by exchanging glances or by holding the other within their gazes for a time.

This is a poiesis of memory: by looking at the person, her face especially, a lasting visual memory can be fashioned. That look guarantees a future memory. Anthropologist Veena Das notes that "memory is not at the level of representation, but at the level of a particular gesture with which you inhabit the world."[35] Family members cultivate and hold onto memories of loved ones in a gesture of continued relation.

The face is prominent in these actions because it is the most important surface feature of a person's body. People look most at the face of another when conversing with her. A face "shows" a lot about a person's ongoing thoughts, while its features convey a moral character. In looking upon the face of a dying person, a family member can work to retain valued understandings and memories of that person. Vision itself is often a medium of contact, connection, and mutual fusion and co-presence.[36]

The video recording made to document the final days of Sange's father worked along these lines, for it enabled Sange to see his father's "face" one last time. Sange was living in New York City then, but he phoned home often to talk with his family, especially in the weeks preceding the death, to talk with his family. When it became clear that his father was to die soon, Sange considered flying from the States to Nepal to see and talk with him before he died.

"The father knew that he was going to die," Karma told me. "And he himself said to Sange, 'Don't come. Don't come. Once you come back, you'll have a hard time getting back to America. You've tried so hard to get there, just to have the chance to be there. And we'll talk over the phone.' He said that."

Sange agreed to this. But he asked his family to prepare a video of his father's passing and the cremation and funeral rites that followed. That way, he could behold his father one last time and participate, from afar, in his death. He wanted to retain his father's visage before it was no longer possible to do so.

I once asked Sange's wife, Pemba Dolma, why the video was made.

"Sange wanted us to make the video, as he was not here when his father died," she said. "He wanted to see the video and gain satisfaction. It's like seeing the face of a person when he is dying."

Heard in Pemba Dolma's words are efforts to attend to a death in active, generative ways. Families do not respond to a death in ways utterly passive or despairing. They envelop a loss in a craft of words, looks, and gestures.

Liberation upon Hearing

Read sacred texts to the dying person. Provide an expansive spiritual framework for the suffering and transitions at hand. Comfort the dying person through good and soothing words, at once sensate and mythic in scope.

Words, read or heard, can soothe and comfort. Images release a person to other possibilities of life.

Lamas respected for their knowledge of religious practices are called in particular to the homes of the dying in the days or hours before a death. Since it is thought that they know well what happens while a person is dying and after the death itself, they are invited to inform the dying person about such matters and to help her prepare well for the death. This takes place in Tibetan societies more generally. "When a person is approaching death," one commentary observes, "it is customary for the relatives of close friends to seek the assistance of a fully qualified lama. . . . Very often the mere presence of an accomplished lama can create a solid sense of calm and purposefulness, which inspires both the dying person and family."[37]

As Karma once put it, people who are dying are looking for someone to "guide" them, to "have a teacher who gives the good words." These words can be good in several senses. Integral to Buddhist thought and teachings, they are morally and spiritually virtuous, and can fill the mind with dharma. As sets of instructions and explanations, they explain in clear and beneficial ways what a person's consciousness can expect to encounter in death. And as easing, caring intonations, they are received favorably by fraught and vulnerable listeners. The words themselves can soothe.

"Sonam is very good with this," Karma said of his younger brother, an artist accomplished in Tibetan Buddhist thought and practice. Some twelve years of Sonam's youth were spent learning at the side of Mheme Amji, the Tibetan lama who set up a residence above Tharkpa Kharka. Since then, he has continued to advance his understanding of Buddhist principles and his skills as an artist. Sonam has spent much of his time from 1994 on in the United States, where he has been employed to construct and paint the interiors of Buddhist monasteries in Texas, Oregon, and other places. He returns to Nepal every few years to visit with family and to construct Buddhist temples and statues in the Hyolmo region. When he is in Nepal he is often asked to visit the home of a dying person.

"Sonam is calm," Karma noted. "It could be because of his high practices, the lama work and the meditation he has done. When he's in Nepal, he explains things well. He explains things not only to the dying person, but to everyone who is there—something about death. He's very calm. He handles these situations well. And he stays with the person until he dies."

Karma spoke of one such sojourn.

A man from Ningali died two, three years ago. But these days the young people are not there, and so he was worried that, when he was dying, there wouldn't be good lamas around. And then, just before his death, he was well prepared. Sonam had just come from America, and people have good respect for him as a lama. I think the man died in the morning. But before he died, his wife had told him that Sonam had arrived. Just before his death he said, "Okay, I have no worries now."

The dying man took comfort in the fact that Sonam, a "good," knowledgeable lama several decades younger than he, had arrived in the village and would soon come to his home, to attend to his passing. He could submit to Sonam's words and ritual expertise, much as a student yields his welfare to a knowledgeable teacher. A person gives his self over to the immediate presence of another, reliable other. He is cared for, held within another's guiding knowledge and words. That relinquishment of selfhood, which in some ways parallels the release into the encompassing cosmos that transpires after dying, can aid in an easeful death.

One act that Sonam and other lamas often undertake while visiting the home of a dying person is to read the *Bardo Thedol,* or *Liberation upon Hearing in the Between.* Written as *bardo thos grol* in Tibetan, and famously and somewhat inappropriately known in the West as "The Tibetan Book of the Dead," this is a set of mortuary texts which detail what people can expect to encounter during the phantasmagoric journey through the bardo, "between," that follows a death. Usually pronounced as *Bardo Thedol* in Hyolmo, thought to be authored by the great master Padma Sambhava in the eighth or ninth century, used primarily by adherents of the Nyingma sect of Tibetan Buddhism, and more accurately translated as "liberation in the between through hearing/ understanding," the texts explain in great detail what a person can expect to occur in the hours and days after dying. If a reader or listener understands the texts' teachings well, it is held, he or she can achieve liberation from the samsaric world of *khorwa*—hence the use of the Tibetan words *thos grol*, which might be best translated as "liberation through hearing/understanding." As Robert Thurman couches it, "The words *thos grol* mean that this book's teaching 'liberates' just by being 'learned' or 'understood,' giving the person facing the between an understanding so naturally clear and deep that it does not require prolonged reflection or contemplation."[38]

Many Hyolmo people familiar with the *Liberation upon Hearing* are aware of its potential to enlighten, either through its very words or through the understandings it generates on the liberating realities that can be perceived during the bardo states. But most know the text to serve as a guidebook to the liminal, dreamlike "betweens" that a recently deceased person can expect to encounter after dying. In many respects, the text reads as such, for it vividly details, in a day-by-day, perception-by-perception way, what a deceased person undergoes during each phase of death, from a person's last vague moments in life to the consciousness's entry into a new life form. In offering such a guide the text depicts the different psychophenomenal states through which the deceased's consciousness passes, including the diffuse and varied range of perceptions and the sets of peaceful and wrathful deities encountered during the bardo period. One passage helps the bewildered, itinerant consciousness brace for the dreamlike world encountered:

> O, Child of Buddha Nature, the largest of the buddha-bodies of the Peaceful and Wrathful Deities will be as vast as the sky; the medium ones will be the size of Mount Sumeru; and even the smallest will be the size of eighteen of our bodies, standing one above the other. Do not be afraid! All phenomenal existence is now arising as luminosities and buddha-bodies. By recognizing all the present visionary appearances to be the natural luminosity of your own intrinsic awareness, manifesting as lights and buddha-bodies, you will dissolve inseparably within the lights and buddha-bodies, and buddhahood will be attained.[39]

"Emptiness cannot harm emptiness," the text advises. "Signlessness cannot harm signlessness."[40]

Instructions like these help to explain why the book is also read to the dying, for it is understood that if a person becomes more familiar with these states and perceptions before dying, and so gains a better understanding of their apparitional, "signless" nature, he or she will not be so frightened by or attracted to them when they are encountered in death.

The texts' contents also help the deceased to identify and continue along "routes" that can enable them to attain good rebirths. They also instruct the listener to avoid inopportune paths. "Don't be enticed by that soft smoky light of hell!" the narrator in one version warns: "Hey! That is the path of destruction from the sins you have accumulated by your strong hatred! If you cling to it, you will fall into the hells; you will be stuck in the mire of unbearable ordeals of suffering, without any escape."[41]

The texts sound prayers, mete out instructions, and describe the look of deities. They urge their readers to act in certain ways, contemplate certain visions, and avoid some options in death while attending to those that will lead to either liberation or a good rebirth in a human body. How different this territory is when compared to the zones of indistinction found in hospitals in North America and elsewhere. Finding great value in these narrations, Hyolmo lamas read the book during several of the funeral rites for a deceased person, with the understanding that the deceased can still hear their words and so continue to be guided by them. Since the text is penned in a Tibetan script rich with esoteric Buddhist terms, family members of the deceased and other lay persons attending a funeral usually understand but a few of its words. But they too understand that the collective, oral reading of the book serves as a guide to the deceased.

The text circuits as a guide to the living and dying more generally, for it offers a rich canvas of what can be expected in the first hours and days of death. One efficacy of the *Bardo Thedol* is that it teaches people how to die. It gives people an exemplary model of death, much as works of literature sometimes do, as French philosopher Paul Ricoeur has observed. "As for death," Ricoeur writes, "do not narratives provided by literature serve to soften the sting of anguish in the face of the unknown, of nothingness, by giving it in imagination the shape of this or that death, exemplary in one way or another? Thus fiction has a role to play in the apprenticeship of dying."[42]

The *Liberation upon Hearing in the Between* gives an imaginal shape to death and contributes to any rehearsals of dying. The text is one of the great

Figure 6. Thodong, 2011.

human efforts to perceive, in methodic, intensely detailed ways, what happens in death. Through an imaginative inhabiting of the bardo betweens, the text opens up the imagination, releases it, even.

Hyolmo lamas read the book to people who are dying in order to prepare them for what they will encounter in the days and weeks after their consciousnesses pass from their bodies. Sitting close to a bedridden person, the lamas will often read for a while and then pause to explain in everyday words the significance of the terms recited. As Temba explained it,

> When someone gets quite seriously ill, the first thing we do is try to cure them, we try to get the person better. If they cannot heal the person, in some cases the *Liberation upon Hearing* is read to the sick person, so that he hears it. The people believe that, if the sick persons hear all those words, they can understand what happens when they die and keep all those things in mind. When they die, they face all those things they have to face, and they die in a calm, peaceful way.

This was the text that Sange's father asked Sonam to read. "Before dying," Pemba Dolma explained, "he told me that he wanted to hear the *Liberation upon*

Hearing. My brother Sonam was here in Kathmandu at that time, so my father-in-law asked if Sonam could read the *Liberation upon Hearing* for him. So we asked Sonam if he could come here and do that. He agreed to this, and he came and read the text through an entire day. My father-in-law listened carefully."

"He did not die in a bad way," Karma said of Sange's father. "He wanted to be here and to listen to whatever he could learn about dying."

After Sonam left Kathmandu, the family called Goser Lama to read the text to Sange's father, a few days before he died. As Goser told it, that reading fulfilled the father's last desire in life. Temba and I asked Goser his thoughts on the death during one of our conversations with him.

"Recently we watched the video that shows the death of Sange's father," we said to him. "It appeared that he died in quite a peaceful way, without much pain, and in the presence of his children and other family members. Would you agree? Do you think that he died in a good way?"

Goser nodded his head and replied:

Just a few days before he died, his daughter-in-law Pemba Dolma came to my house and asked me to recite the *Liberation upon Hearing* to her father-in-law. She said that he wanted to hear the *Liberation upon Hearing* in the Between before he died. In line with this request, I went to his house and read that to him. Before he died, he told me that if he could hear well all of the *Liberation upon Hearing*, then all of his desires as a human being would be fulfilled. In the course of our conversation he said he was well satisfied with his life, because he had accomplished everything. He got everything he desired, everything he wanted. He also was able to make donations to the places he wished to. . . . So he died well. He died in a good way.

The dharma holds people, and reduces fear.[43] A dying person can entrust herself to the rich emptiness it offers. More than semiotic meanings are involved in the "work of the text" here, however. Reading is an active doing. When heard, the texts can inform, clarify, and reduce attachment, even if little if any of their actual significance is gleaned by those listening to them. "It's a kind of hearing therapy, for the person who is sick," Temba told me. "When he hears the *Bardo Thedol* he might not understand everything, but he will have a kind of consciousness, a kind of understanding: 'Oh, I am hearing the good words.' So, even if the words aren't understood at the moment, they will have a good impact."

That good impact is multichambered. For one, the words spoken and heard can help to streamline a consciousness. "It's like receiving guidance right to the end," Karma told me. "Right to that point the person is receiving the very relevant guidance, and then he is not worrying about something else. His mind is not diverted to anything else. Because he knows they are good words. It keeps his thoughts from wandering. It's giving a direction to those thoughts. Any confused or unsettled thoughts—it works against that. You're channeling thoughts."

You are fashioning a consciousness.

They can keep all those things in mind. The texts are lined with ornate intensities, much as Tibetan *thang ka* paintings hold an abundance of images, colors, and significations. The texts make clear other dimensions of a person's existence, beyond the pain and futility of dying itself. A body's suffering is painted, by implication, as signless, as empty of inherent meaning and substance— and signlessness, after all, cannot harm signlessness. The coarseness of dying is steered into something sacred and transformative. When heard, the texts emit a semantic, syllabic, and emotional fullness which stands in contrast to the sparse banality of dying. They couch the singular intensity, the lonely thusness, of the person's cessation within an expansive spatial and temporal landscape. A kind of "temporal stretching" occurs in which the suffering and death itself are placed within an encompassing cosmic totality which extends beyond the confines of the present moment, such that any suffering or transitions are rendered more meaningful and transcendent.[44] This rich expansiveness is promoted both by the subject of the texts—namely, what transpires during the successive intermediate periods to be encountered after death and the rich significance of these "betweens"—and the temporal quality of the recitations, with sentences following sentences, for hours at a stretch. Dying itself is impermanent; it won't last for long. More life is to come, more time is to occur. The texts, anticipating all of that, make anticipators out of its listeners: *this will happen, keep this in mind, you can expect this to appear.* The fading listener comes to think of more than her immediate, anxious, finite plight. Situated within the space of dying, and beyond it, the dying person is led to imagine what is to come in the near and distant future, past her current life. She is taken outside and beyond, beyond herself, beyond her dying, in a line of flight, a magical flight, into the intermediate states. If shamanic spirit-calling rites work to invoke a sense of presence or "hereness" among persons bereft of vital life forces, then recitations of the *Liberation upon Hearing* can be said to invoke a sense of elsewhereness.[45] They also link a here, the known felt world, to an elsewhere, as do many religious efforts.

The sensory grains of the recitation can themselves be soothing. "The voice of the lama who calls out to the dying person should be very melodious," notes one commentary, "so that merely upon hearing the sound of the instructions the person feels soothed, elevated, and attracted."[46] The words touch a suffering self. Along with informing the dying person of what to expect in death, and so appeasing a number of fears and concerns, the vocalization of the text, read in sonorous, evocative ways, in synch with the cadences of the human breath, can be calming, extensive. "It has some flow to it. It's soothing," Karma said of the text when it was read out loud. The sounds are reassuring.[47] Shared syllables and breathing recur. Arrhythmia turns rhythmic. The voices are embracing, guiding ones. The words, at once familiar and mysterious, can comfort a person as much as a supporting hand or a sip of water. They can help a fading self dissolve inseparably into a vast and incessant murmuring, with the "name" and identity of the person flowing into a larger, more anonymous stream of language and a more fluid, dreamlike sense of time.

Rhythm can hold people ("Know what rhythm holds men"—Archilochus).[48] It can also help them to let go. Emmanuel Levinas once wrote critically of rhythm and of art in general by suggesting that "in rhythm there is no longer a oneself, but rather a passage of oneself to anonymity."[49] Yet such a perspective neglects the fact that there can be great value at times in passing into anonymity, to the point where a more expansive ambit of consciousness, integrated within a larger whole (or not), removed from the scaffoldings of ego, attachment, and suffering, can arise.

The texts, when heard or imagined, provide guidance and a theory of signlessness. They introduce a sense of fullness, expansiveness, elsewhereness. They promote the easeful dissolution of a self through a linguistic and sensorial canvas of unmaking. They teach people how to die.

Liberation upon hearing, indeed.

The Pulse of Life

Encounter the extreme limits to the human comprehension of death. Come to appreciate the ways in which the pulse of life takes on new vital possibilities, even in the wake of a loss.

"And it's the only thing a lama can do before a person dies," said Goser Lama of the efforts of Buddhist priests to read the *Liberation upon Hearing* to a dying person and to explain any procedures of death more generally.

Figure 7. Reading Buddhist texts. Gulphubanjang, 2011.

What Goser meant by this, I think, was that, outside of being present in a respectful way, comforting a person, encouraging him to think in certain ways, little else can be done by a lama or anyone else. Since the death itself cannot be prevented, a waiting game ensues. Rituals help little here. What is most at stake is the destination of a dying person's consciousness. A person's climate of mind and body at the time of death, and the ease with which she dies, influences where her consciousness travels to in death. People try to create a situation that can contribute to a good rebirth while alleviating undue suffering. But this assisted cessation is all they can do. The rituals come later.

The pulse of dying is sometimes sharp and sudden, as when a radio is turned off. The pulse is slow and gradual at other times, with people taking measure of that ending and changes in the social positioning of the dying one, getting used to the death, anticipating it. Either way, death interrupts the flow of life. It tears at the social fabric. A knife slice in time, death severs relations.

Hyolmo people know well the truth in Georges Bataille's observation that "death is in one sense the common inevitable, but in another sense, profound, inaccessible."[50] Death is a pure white blankness. Terribly present, it is seemingly within reach yet ungraspable and unperceivable. Thoughts and stories only faintly reflect its actuality.

Yet it's also true that people sustain relations with the dead after those loved ones enter into silence. When I began this research more than a decade ago I saw in death endings only, a terminus of life and relation. It's now clear that new connections take form, in vast swirls of continuity. Similar to the ways in which new plants repopulate a burned-out tract of land, or the neurogenesis that can occur after a stroke, there is a kind of vitagenesis at work in people's lives in the wake of death: new strands of life take form, in forms actual and virtual.[51] Rupture comes with creation. The pulse of life finds new channels.

PART II

Passing from the Body

Death, Impermanence Has Arisen

Observe the moment of death. Mind what it says about the fleeting, impermanent nature of all life. Make something of death beyond its sheer brutality.

I never met Karma's father. I wish I had. He was by all accounts an exceptional person. His second son showed me a photograph once, enclosed in the sheets of a photo album. A composed mustached man stood among others in a sunwashed village. He looked straight at the camera, intelligence quick in his eyes.

Tenzin Choephel Lama was an artist, political figure, community leader, and a knowledgeable Buddhist lama. One of six sons in a Sarma Lama family rooted in Takpakharka, and known from an early age to be uncommonly bright, he learned in his youth how to craft Buddhist paintings and statues. He painted Buddhist deities and images in a number of temples. He traveled to Darjeeling and other regions of India and partook of arrangements of life other than those cobbled in Kathmandu and the Hyolmo region. That exposure led him to decide on ways to refashion the conditions of life in his home region. He served in the Nepali government for a stint, representing his home district in the national Panchayat system. A leader in his community, he toiled to improve the political and economic status of his family's village of Takpakharka and that of neighboring villages.

"He was a special figure," Karma told me. "He had visions. He was in fact the one who started planting apple trees in the region. He was also one of the first to start up a carpet-weaving factory there. He would say from time to time, 'If I wanted to earn money, I could have earned a lot of money. But I'm doing all this for the villages.'"

Karma's father also invited a knowledgeable Tibetan lama, known as Mheme Amji, to the area and provided a modest retreat of a home for him on the mountain ridge above Takpakharka. Anyone who lived in the area could then seek out Buddhist teachings from this lama.

"He was very well respected," said Karma. That social regard has carried over, long after his death, to the reputations of his brothers and children. He had high standards for his family and others. He was strict. When he came upon boys gambling with coins he would snatch the coins from them. Later, he would laugh and say to them, "See, I am not doing this for myself. I'm doing it for you. You're like pencils, and I'm trying to sharpen you."

He left marks. Karma's father was an exemplar of human poiesis, of someone actively fashioning the world. He tailored the landscape itself, "writing" on it as though he might paint a canvas. Yet it's often the case that the world emits turnings of life at odds with the creative strivings of those within it.

He died in the early 1980s, in his home in Takpakharka, after suffering for several days from a severe headache. He was fifty-four. The specific cause of the death remains uncertain. Karma was living in Kathmandu at the time, studying for important college exams. He was twenty-one.

In the spring of 1998, while I was living in Boudhanath, six years after the sudden death of my own father, Karma and I often met in the flat where I was staying, a one-room haven next to an apartment inhabited by his elder sister and her children. While snacking on tea and Tibetan dumplings, we engaged in hours-long conversations about Hyolmo culture and social relations and, in those days, understandings of life and death. Toward the end of one conversation I asked Karma if we might discuss people's involvements in grief the next time we talked. He said we could do this; he knew the importance of fathoming the subject better. He returned a few days later and told of how he learned of his father's passing. He spoke in a calm and clear voice as the tape recorder coiled on and I listened quietly. The audio measured the pauses when still-sharp grief overtook him.

Near in age and temperament, Karma and I share similar vantages on life. Despite the different cultural worlds we inhabit, we've been traveling similar paths since we first met in our mid-twenties. It pained me to stir grief in this virtual brother of mine for the sake of supposed research. It troubled us to give birth to these words, but we both knew this had to be done, or could be. I relay his words in respect to those involved, in sorrow for the loss, in appreciation of his willingness, while aware of the wounds and the uncertain value of repeating traces of them here. The words tell me not to study them too much. They prefer to be left as they are. Yet making something of a death is perhaps what we all need to do.

In relating the events of those days Karma's narration made clear that his relatives, who knew his father had died, hesitated to tell him and his sister of the death too soon, lest the shock of it hinder their progress to the village. They said he was seriously ill and implored Karma and others to hasten their way. Karma:

I was here at that time in Kathmandu, preparing for a very important examination. And then two people from the village came, cousins of mine. On that day I was at my sister's place, my oldest sister. She was living in Mahankal, with her husband Binod. Our cousins came there and told us that our father was really sick. But then, when people come like that, it's definitely very serious.

They said he was sick, so my mother wanted us to come. I really thought he was just sick, but he had already passed away by then. They didn't tell me that. They didn't tell us.

I immediately thought of giving up the exam, and my sister—who else was there?—there were other relatives who also wanted to go, because they had respect for my father.

We in fact wanted to leave that same day. But then we couldn't get cars or anything like that, so we said we would leave the next day. But apparently it seems they didn't tell my sister and me, but everyone knew that . . . that he died. So they weren't really in a hurry. We waited till next morning.

We left early in the morning. We rented a jeep. We left, but a cousin and I decided to go early on, before my sister and everyone else. Because I had the thought that, if he was really sick, then we should even bring him down [to a hospital in Kathmandu]. That was my idea. But then except for my sister and me everyone knew that he passed away. But anyway, they let us leave early.

When we reached the village it was quite early, I think it was two o'clock. Of course, we can see our village before reaching it. My cousin was still saying that my father was still really seriously ill. So if he had died, we would hear the lamas playing the horns. I was really trying to hear everything, but I didn't hear anything like that. So I still had hope.

When I reached home quite a few people were outside, and then I went inside and I saw a lot of people in there. The lamas were at break, it seems, which I didn't know. As soon as I got there my mother started to cry. Even at that point I couldn't believe that he had died. It didn't cross my mind that he had died. I thought people were there to visit. My younger brother was there and I asked him how father was.

He also cried. "Now we're the unfortunate ones," he said. That's what he said. I then understood that he had passed away. And my brother was crying, and everyone was crying there.

For me, that was really the unhappiest moment.

When I arrived people started crying. My mother, and my younger sister; she was there too. Everyone was crying. And then I was quite angry with them also—at my cousins, for not letting us know earlier. But they explained that everything happened in a very short time. They said for just two days he had a severe headache and he passed away like that. So they couldn't do much.

And then I think that, at that time my younger brother was also not in the village, but he was working in another village. He was doing work in a temple, constructing statues. He said he had really bad dreams. What was it? I think he said he saw our house on fire. Just in seeing that, he came back. He found that my father was really sick. He couldn't talk.

He couldn't talk then. At that stage, maybe he didn't want to talk to others because he was doing his phowa [transference of his consciousness]. He was doing it, and maybe he didn't want to say anything to anyone. And since he had really practiced this—because he knew about the intermediate state, the bardo—I think he was really concentrating on that. That's what people said.

Then later in the evening my sister and everyone else arrived. She had the same shock. And everyone started crying again.

After my father passed away, I think we sent a message to our brother also, in India. I don't think he got the letter, though. Someone told him that father was no more. He also came. I was already in Kathmandu then. He was very upset too. Yeah, at that stage, whenever we met a new relative, there was a really emotional situation.

. . . And yes, there were dreams as well. The day when I received this news from the village, when these two people came, right from the morning I was feeling so restless. I was supposed to be studying hard, but I couldn't do that. I was feeling so restless. I don't know how many times I went to my sister's place, going back and forth. Because I did say, "I don't feel like studying today." My sister had even said, "What are you doing today? You've been here, I don't know, three or four times already." From the morning on I was feeling restless. And I told her, "My heart is not really feeling well." It was beating fast. I told her it was getting like that. And my brother had seen this dream which was really very significant: our house being on fire.

Karma's restlessness that day and his brother's fiery dreams of a household in flames marked the intense interrelationality between father and sons. The elder's suffering touched the latter's moods and imaginings, though they were miles apart.[1]

Back in Nepal two years later, I was immersed in another round of field research. Karma arranged it so that we could meet with a relative of his, Goser Lama, to elicit his thoughts on the ways in which people had died in the Hyolmo region. After relating to us several incidents Goser spoke of the end of Karma's father. As we listened, it became clear that Goser was speaking most to Karma, as though he were passing on to Karma an accurate ledger of what happened, what was done and said in those hours.

At the time Goser Lama was undertaking a meditative retreat with his teacher, Mheme Amji. His sister took a message to him informing him that Karma's father was gravely ill.

As for your father, my meditation was in its ninth day, and the night before he called for me. So the next morning my sister came with the message and Mheme Amji relayed the news to me that your father was very sick. When I arrived at his home he was not in the prayer room. He was in the room where your mother used to sleep.

I spoke to him, calling, "Uncle, Uncle," and he asked, "Are you Goser?" I answered him and asked why he had called for me. "Ah . . . it was nothing."

He asked me if any rituals were going to be done on his behalf. I told him that Mheme Amji had told me to do so, to recite some texts, so we were arranging everything in the dharma room. I said this. Then I asked him to move to the dharma room, as so many people were coming there. I carried him to the dharma room and from then on he slept there. He never woke up. He didn't say anything to Sonam or to me—or to your mother either. Even if we lifted his head up, he would round his mustache but he did not open his eyes. Outside of this, nothing was said.

When he was about to die he straightened his legs by himself. We all knew he was dying then. Your mother cried out, saying he was dying. She

told us to ask your father if he had anything to say. We scolded her for having
uttered these bad words [bad because, when spoken, they could bring about
the situation spoken of]. Sonam also knew what was happening. He placed
a text on your father's head and asked him to meditate on *chhiwa mitakpa*,
death and impermanence. Outside of this, nothing else was said or done.

Before, his legs were quite bent. At the time of dying, he straightened
them on his own, making some cracking sounds. He stayed in that position.

Sonam placed a sacred text on his forehead. The phrase *chhiwa mitakpa*,
"death, impermanence," carries several threads of sense. One is more philosophical in spirit. By contemplating the ways in which death and impermanence characterize life, a person can better orient himself to the nature of
existence. Keeping such a perspective in mind in the moments of dying can
help a person to die easily, without attachment, to dissolve inseparably into
emptiness, and possibly enable him to achieve enlightenment during the transitional moments between one life and the next. For many the understanding
of *chhiwa mitakpa* can be largely conceptual in nature; people can know about
death and impermanence without tasting of it directly. When someone dies,
the fact of impermanence hits home. It makes its presence known in the most
direct way possible.

People often say *chhiwa mitakpa sharche bhekyo* when speaking of scenes
in which a person is on the verge of death: "Death, impermanence has arisen."
These forces have come into fruition. "It's a way of saying that death has come."

It's a way of giving death a name in the very moments when the force of it
is most anguishing. People work on death. They turn it. They make something
of it beyond its sheer and unstoppable brutality.

Transference of Consciousness

Transfer the consciousness from the body. Send it to Dewa Chen, the
buddha field of Amitābha. Care for the dead person in those hours when
he or she is ceasing to be a living person.

Without the aid of others, a dead person is likely to remain a ghost, a shyindi
or "death-demon" caught between one life and the next—unless he is learned
or enlightened enough to command his own passing. Survivors do a lot to
promote a good rebirth. They host family and friends who pay their respects.
They prepare the corpse for cremation, incinerate the body in a sacred ritual

of sacrifice, and sponsor a set of funeral rites in the weeks following the death. They also complete a memorial rite a year later while attending to swells of grief that never fully dissolve.

"It's really something that you *need* to do," Karma said of such matters while at his home in Queens, New York, in 2009. "It's your responsibility, in fact. That's what people feel. This is for the deceased. And if you don't do it, you're not completing things for the deceased person. In other words, it's important to complete everything, in the sense that, after a person dies, you can't just leave it like that."

The living can't just leave the body there, vitality stuck between lives. Survivors have to step up, shake off the devastation, and respond to the needs of the passed-on one. They have to follow through on that person's dharmic journey. This responsibility to act on behalf of the other is at once moral and practical. The mortuary rites are the Hyolmo version of technological interventions in the face of death. In contrast to contemporary medical procedures in hospital settings, where the main aim is to keep the body from dying, the rituals aid in the post-life continuation of consciousness.

Lamas undertake many of these tasks. "We need bombos when we are alive, and lamas when we die," runs one expression. People need bombos to heal them when they fall ill, for these shamanic healers are skilled in recovering lost life forces and restoring them within an ailing body. Lamas help to bring a person into the world, and they help to transfer a person's consciousness from the body toward a new rebirth. They work to fashion a good death and rebirth.

Dying is not dying. It is shifting. Death entails a transfer from one life form to another. A common euphemism for death is that it is a "passing from the body." What leaves the body are a person's consciousness and life forces; as the body begins to decay and then is cremated, these spiritual forces become disembodied, making for a handless, touchless existence. Death occurs when the "external breath" of the person detaches from the body. Since the *nam-she* or "consciousness," a person's "inner breath," still resides in the body, it needs to be extracted from the body. To achieve this, family members usually summon a knowledgeable lama to perform a rite known as *phowa*, "transference." They also refrain from touching the body until the lama arrives in the home, for fear of disturbing the consciousness or contaminating the body.

Phowa is a Tibetan and Hyolmo word that means "to transfer, to change place, to move from one place to another." The rite that goes by that name serves to transfer the deceased's consciousness out of the now-defunct body and to send it, ideally, to Dewa Chen, the blissful buddha field of Amitābha.[2] This is crucial. The inner breath resides in the veins and muscles of a body. To extract it, the lama performing the act of transference engages in a ritual process that combines deep meditative visualizations, the reading of a Buddhist text, and tantric acts. He sits in a meditative position close to the body, about a foot and a half away from it and a foot and a half higher than it. He puts himself into a meditative state of mind and contemplates with deep mental concentration Amitābha, the Buddha responsible for sending a person's consciousness to the Pure Land, and he visualizes Amitābha's form. The meditation and concentration should be sharp and deep, such that the person gains all the features of Amitābha and in effect assumes the spiritual powers of Amitābha within his own form. After this meditation is done, a religious prayer known as *soldev* is recited. This prayer works as an "appeal" or "invocation" to deities to assist in the act of transference.[3]

The lama "pulls" the inner breath, the consciousness, from within the body's veins and muscles, by focusing his mental-spiritual powers on this act, and by saying "ek," a hiccup-like utterance that accomplishes the extraction. While the consciousness can leave the body from several different openings— the eyes, ears, mouth, nostrils, navel, and so forth—the most beneficial passageway for it to depart the body from is the *chyir-chsug*, the fontanel area at the top of the cranium. The chyir-chsug is the purest and most sacred opening in the body; if the consciousness leaves the body through it, it has a greater chance of reaching the Pure Land. The lama tries to draw the consciousness out of the body through the chyir-chsug. He does this by "closing" all the other holes present in the body by engaging in a set of meditative acts and by reciting mantras, and then "extracting" the consciousness from the chyir-chsug. He then converts it into the Tibetan letter "a" and sends it to the Pure Land by uttering "phet" three times while visualizing and meditating deeply on this process.

Ideally, the dead person's consciousness reaches the Pure Land through this process. Lamas and others know well, however, that this is only an ideal possibility. Since so much depends on the karmic status of the deceased person, both where the consciousness leaves the body and where it "transfers" to upon its departure is largely a result of the deceased's karma. Getting the consciousness to the Pure Land is determined more by a person's deeds than by the lama's efforts.

If the transference is not done, or if it's not completed in an effective way and the consciousness still resides in the body, the body can turn into a zombie-like creature known as *ro lang*. The word *"ro lang"* can be translated as "corpse-recovered/arisen." With the body bereft of the external breath and so not properly alive but still invested with the mute and errant vitality of the consciousness, the corpse can "awaken" and linger as an ambulatory remainder that contains an unnatural combination of post-life body and aimless, predeath consciousness. A nonliving vessel, a dumb, amoral subject with little sense of self or others, a zombie attacks any living persons it happens upon. If it touches any living person, that person will also become a zombie. Zombies are easily killed, however, since they move stiffly and slowly and they cannot bend over; "You have to chop it apart and then burn it. Then it won't come back again," Nogapu explained to me. While Hyolmo people still speak of rolang, they also note that such zombies are only a rare occurrence in modern times, at best. "Not long ago there were a lot of rolang," Nogapu continued, "but all that has stopped. I don't know why." Mostly there are stories of zombies of times past: "A few days after that person's death," went one account, related by Nogapu, "some people were bringing his corpse to be cremated. While being brought to the cremation site, it began to break through its cloths. So they had to kill it."

Since transferring the consciousness is one of the most important rites conducted on behalf of the deceased, and since there is a lot at stake in performing it properly, lamas need to become skilled in doing it. Lamas usually learn to perform the transference by undergoing trainings with knowledgeable teachers who instruct them as to what they need to do—which deities need to be visualized, for instance, and which mantras and texts need to be recited. In these sessions, students of the process practice on themselves. A student tries to extract his own consciousness to the point where it's close to departing the body through the chyir-chsug. To determine whether their students have performed the transference effectively, the instructors take strands of a broomstick and place it on top of the fontanel of each student. If the strand sinks in a bit and the fontanel appears soft and yielding and slightly indented, this is an indication that the student has "pulled" his consciousness toward the top of the skull in an effective way, and they have become qualified in performing the consciousness transference. The practice is difficult and dangerous. If practitioners do not perform the transference well or extract the consciousness beyond the surface of their own fontanel, they can harm themselves and endanger their lives.

Once students learn to do the transference well, they begin to practice on their own. They do so in order to become expert enough in the process to successfully perform it on others when they die. Yet since so much of the practice is undertaken on their own forms, the adepts also become able to conduct the transference themselves when they are dying. Given this, it's often thought to be unnecessary to perform the consciousness transference on lamas who have practiced the act a lot and understand well the processes of dying and death, for it's understood that such men will be able to perform the transference themselves in the moments before dying. A strong indication that a person has been successful in this endeavor is the presence, just after he dies, of white and red blood-like substances just below the nostrils: the white substance comes out of the right nostril, and the red from the left. These substances, known as *jang-sem kar-mar*—literally, "pure-mind white-red"—are an indication both that the consciousness has departed the body and that the deceased person has a spiritually pure heartmind.

Those who witnessed the death of Karma's father concluded that he successfully transferred his own consciousness. Several people were in the room where he lay dying. He appeared to have some awareness of their presence, but he did not engage with them. Karma:

> At that stage, maybe he didn't want to talk to others. Because a lot of people were saying that perhaps he was transferring his consciousness. And he was really practicing, because he knew about the intermediate state, the bardo—I think he was concentrating on that. That's what people said.
>
> My cousins were there. They said later on that, when he was close to dying, he was doing his consciousness transference, it seems. They said they heard a long sound just before he died, which happens when someone is trying to do the consciousness transference. Suddenly a noise came— Crack!—and that was it. At that time he was not really struggling with pain. He died quietly, in a comfortable position, with his hands under his head. He was aware that he was dying. Our lama said he died in *singhi ngyalthap*— "the position of the sleeping lion," which is the way the Buddha died as well. The lama said he was fully aware of his death. He was really prepared.

Karma and his brother and cousins traveled to Kathmandu soon after their father's body was cremated. While there, they asked several Tibetan adepts residing in monasteries, monks who knew and respected Karma's father, to perform funeral rites on his behalf. When they informed these lamas about the manner of his death, the priests told them that, given the way in which he died, there was probably no need to perform the transference on his behalf.

But Karma's family asked them to do so anyway and several monks completed the transference in the father's name.

As in the case with Karma's father, consciousness transference can be performed on many occasions. Performing it more than once doesn't hurt the deceased's chances of reaching a buddha field after death, or of obtaining a good rebirth. Repeated performances can in fact help with this. The transference is taken to be most effective when it is enacted soon after a person dies, which is to say soon after the external breath has departed the body. But since the act works not only to extract the consciousness from the body but to promote its journey to the Pure Land, multiple transferences can help the consciousness reach that destination. "It's to help the consciousness on its way, wherever it is," said one man. Each successive performance further promotes the consciousness's chances of reaching the Pure Land. Ritual repetitions work to good effect.

Consciousness transference can be performed in the absence of a body. It can take place after a corpse is cremated, and it can be enacted when a person is presumed dead, even though the body has not been recovered. On some occasions, residents of Hyolmo have performed the transference (and other funeral rites) on behalf of a person thought to be dead, only to have that person show up quite alive in the Hyolmo region later on. "There have been times when someone would go to India and he wouldn't be heard of again," Karma related. "People would then do the transference for those people. Sometimes, they would later appear from India. I heard that when one man, who we thought had died, came back to the village, people told him that they had performed the transference for him on a particular day.

"The man said, 'Yeah, I felt really miserable that day.' It had an effect."

We care for the dead in ways known and shown to us. "Any death raises the question of the obligations of the living toward the dead," writes anthropologist Veena Das.[4] Hyolmo people aid in a passing from the body. That kind of care aids the living as much as it does the dead. It enables mourners to act responsively on behalf of the deceased. The fact that others have to care for a person's body after death shows how interdependent all of us really are.

Between

Read the *Liberation upon Hearing* to the deceased as he finds himself in the liminal, phantasmagoric realm between one life and any next life, uncertain of his plight.

Figure 8. Gulphubanjang, 2011.

What lies between two lives? What is involved in the passage between one life and any next life? Once the consciousness skirts the body, it wanders about a liminal, phantasmagoric realm between one life and the next. In death, a person is deprived of his or her body, a "heap" of matter that decays soon after its soulful inhabitants vacate it. Everything else also has to be parted with, including his family and possessions, his "name" and worldly identity. He increasingly becomes a subjectivity without a subject.[5] Although the recently deceased can see, hear, and voice words to family members, those loved ones cannot perceive the invisible, inaudible shade of a consciousness. They must go about their mourning without being able to converse with or see the face of the imperceptible figure of the deceased, hovering beyond the threshold of perception. Mutual visual and verbal co-presence cannot be maintained.

A body of sorts does emerge for the traveler in the betweens after death, but it is an illusory, subtle one, similar to a subject's body sensed while dreaming. One version of the *Liberation upon Hearing in the Between* refers to this form as "the mental body of apparitional experience in the intermediate state."[6] His awareness now separated from its physical support, the deceased becomes an apparitional consciousness, and a dreamy, karma-driven one at that, in realms riddled with apparitions.

Bardo is the word used to depict the liminal "between" one life and the next. The term draws from the word *bar*, which means "between" in either a temporal or spatial sense. The word "bardo," in turn, literally means "between two." It can designate any intermediate period between two actions or two stretches of time. The moments between sleep and waking can be said to be a bardo, as can a pause between utterances, or a years-long stretch of migrant labor in a foreign land. Many of those who have migrated to New York City, to work and provide for their families, find that they are a "bardo generation," squarely between the past of their parents' lives and the futures of their children; "Queens Bardo." As the lamas tell it, any intermediate moment in life is a bardo. An interval of sleep between states of waking consciousness is a bardo, as is a dream between stretches of sleep. In the stretches of their own lives, however, Hyolmo lamas and laypersons most commonly invoke the word when speaking of the transitional, intermediate period that is known to occur between life and rebirth. During this stretch of betweenness, thought to last up to forty-nine days, a recently deceased person travels about in a disembodied, dreamlike state until she or he achieves liberation from the cycle of rebirths or obtains another rebirth.

The bardo is a liminal phase of passage, akin to transitional experiences known to peoples throughout the world. As Claes Corlin notes in a discussion of Tibetan understandings of death, "The succession of bardo states after death thus bears the mark of a true passage rite: a dramatic separation from the world of the living, a liminal phase which is subdivided into successive stages but apart from the time and space of everyday reality, and eventual reintegration into society by rebirth. The difference from a common passage rite is that there are 'special exits' in the form of possibilities of liberation from the cycle of rebirths."[7]

Flux, unfixed changes, and dreamy uncertainties are the mean in the bardo realms. The deceased's consciousness is thrown into a betwixt and between life and death. Both the deceased's condition and the environment he traverses are without solid grounding, "unstable and fluid." The consciousness wanders about the countryside in a dreamlike fugue. Without a stable body to anchor it, its kinesthetic grounds are altered. The consciousness moves about quickly, unsteadily. "The consciousness wanders to many places, sometimes here, sometimes there." The dreamlike qualities of the death between entail confusion and opacity and an inability to think or see clearly or converse well with others. A deceased person travels alone, without the help of friends and family or the agentive abilities that a human body usually affords. He or she is guided only by previously acquired knowledge and the oral instructions of lamas, who read from lamaic texts as funeral rites are performed. Despite such instructions, opacity and confusion are the mean. The perceptions of the wayward consciousness lack the sober, single-minded abilities that usually coincide with daytime realities. Visual and acoustic images appear and then disappear, or morph into other chimeras.

The consciousness encounters a frightening array of apparitions, including the visitations of peaceful and wrathful deities. As Buddhist teachings tell it, all of the images and deities perceived are projections that emanate from the deceased's mind. Many Tibetan peoples understand that a person's consciousness and body in the death betweens are "structured by the imagery" that result from that person's karmic heritage, which is to say that the shadowy images that a deceased person encounters in the death betweens are manifestations of his or her psychic and karmic disposition.[8] They are the fanciful product of the generative poiesis of a person's karma and of dharmic forces more generally. More the substance of "dream" than "reality," such images "appear" more than they exist on their own. All is subjectively rendered; nothing has a stable, secure existence outside of self-consciousness. While humans are in fact the karmic authors of the images they perceive, they are far from being in command of their senses or of any phenomena perceived after dying. A person's perceptions in the days after death are dreamlike, altered, radically subjective, obscured, unsteady, and ungrounded. They are immaterial and "signless." One passage of the *Liberation upon Hearing* encourages any recipients of the text's instructions to develop and affirm an understanding that all sights and sounds perceived during the "death-between" are one's "own":

> May I recognize all sound as my own sounds.
> May I recognize all lights as my own lights.
> May I recognize all rays as my own rays.
> May I spontaneously recognize [the characteristics of] the
>   intermediate states.[9]

Elsewhere the text advises its readers to recognize that all visions encountered in the death between are "but empty images," the product of one's "own creations," with one's body itself "born by apparition."[10] The recently deceased find themselves in situations where they are being overwhelmed by a dizzying array of images of which they are, ultimately, the karmic sponsors, for karma is the shaping of the self by the self. It is like someone writing out a set of intense, dreamlike scenarios, many of them long forgotten, which return and spook their author.

All this helps to explain why it is that, the more one knows what to expect during the death betweens, the better off one will be when actually in their midst: if a recently deceased person can keep in mind such understandings when mired in the bardo states, then he or she has a better chance of identifying and grasping the subjective nature of fearful emanations. This is the critical moment to realize one's nature and achieve liberation. Correct decisions and perceptions must be made, on the spot. "Now, if you continue to be distracted," runs one caution, "the lifeline of compassion, suspended to you, will be cut off and you will move on to a place where there is no [immediate] prospect of liberation. So be careful."[11]

Be careful.

For these and other reasons lamas often read the *Liberation upon Hearing* text, with the deceased's reception of it in mind, in the days and weeks after a death, usually in that person's former home or during the performance of various funeral rites. Lamas voice lines of the text in the hope or expectation that the deceased is listening.

O, Child of Buddha Nature, at this time, you will try to find shelter [from the hurricane of past actions] below bridges, in mansions, in temples or grass-huts or beside stupas and so forth, but this [shelter] will be momentary, it will not last. Your awareness, now separated from your body, will not rest and you will feel reckless, angry and afraid. Your consciousness will be faltering, superficial and nebulous. Again you will realize: "Alas! I am dead, what should I do now?" Reflecting on this, your consciousness will grow sad, your heart will be chilled and you will feel intense and boundless misery. Your mind is being compelled to move on, without settling in one place. Do not indulge in all kinds of memories! Let your awareness rest in an undistracted state![12]

It's not just the apparitions of the bardo realms that are illusory and ephemeral. All of life is as well, or so these teachings suggest. The *Liberation upon Hearing* texts encourage readers and listeners to recognize that all phenomena of waking life as being illusion-like and impermanent. One passage asks the deceased person to meditate on the fact that "all substantial things are unreal and false, like a mirage." Another segment details a line of thought on which a bardoic traveler should meditate:

Now, I must realize that all these phenomena are completely devoid of substantial existence, even for a single instant. In reality, they are like a dream, like an illusion, like an echo, like a celestial city, like a mirage, like a reflection, like an optical illusion, like the moon reflected in water. It is absolutely certain that these are not truly real, but that they are false. Through this singular resolve, I will blow apart my apprehension of their true existence.[13]

Anyone listening to these words is encouraged to consider the ways in which the swampy elements of our lives are devoid of substantial existence. They are like a dream, an unworldly city, the apprehension of which should be demolished, making way for more enlightened perceptions. People often get a general sense of this conception in their lives, in one way or another, through Buddhist teachings or hard-traveled roads. Death drives home the point. Death becomes the means to realize that life is built of emptiness, an interdependence of nondualistic forms.

Knowledge of one's death comes fitfully. The deceased person is at first unaware of his demise. Only gradually does he realize that he no longer has a flesh-and-blood body.

"When someone is dead, he's confused," Ghang Lama told me. "He doesn't know what's happening to him."

A common narrative image in Hyolmo villages is of a deceased person roaming the countryside in the days after his death, unaware that he has died. Each day at dusk he returns to his home to eat and be with family members. But since the dead lack corporeal form, he goes unseen and unnoticed by loved ones. "He talks to us. But we don't hear him." Horrified by such negligence, the dead person leaves in despair and slowly learns that he no longer remains with the living. "At that particular time he realizes, 'I am a dead person.'" The deceased also often comes to know that he is dead by noticing that he is not leaving footprints on the ground, or that his feet do not leave wet imprints on boulders after stepping through a stream or river. Or he might fathom that his image no longer casts a shadow on the earth, or a reflection in any mirrors, water, or windows.

The subjective condition of death is one of marklessness. A person cannot leave graphic traces and tracks, nor engage with others. He has no effect in or on the world. The deceased becomes passive, reactive, and no longer capable of full-bodied worldly action. These nonqualities suggest that having a body grounds and stabilizes us. A human body enables us to act in the world, engage with others in a direct way, and to leave footprints: it enables us to be able, to think clearly about the circumstances of our lives and engage with them. From a Buddhist perspective, such an existence offers a highly favorable situation, as it provides the opportunity for karmic action and the practice of dharma.

Death brings the end of such reflective agency. The recently deceased finds himself in a glut of non-poiesis; he cannot act in creative, generative ways. This is a notable image for many Hyolmo people, adult men in particular, who invest a lot in the idea that their lives can be bio-graphic, that they can leave marks in the world, have an impact. Dying marks the ends of action. A dead person can feel, sense, yearn, and remember, but he can no longer "write" in any directly legible ways.[14]

Field of Apparitions

Words reach out to him as he roams about, alone, intangible, free-floating, without grounding, unable, unnoticed, driven by past actions, signed and signless.

Death entails a stretch of time at once disconcerting and transformative. It offers the possibility of rebirth or escape from the samsaric world. The death between is an obscure, phantasmic realm, in which humans, adrift and alone, rely on sensory and cognitive abilities unlike what they are accustomed to while alive. The bardo implies a dangerous passage, one that holds the potential for insight and creative transformation.

While there is a cultural precision to the qualities of the bardo, cued as they are to Tibetan circles, these qualities speak to something rooted in liminal situations familiar to peoples more generally. We all know of intermediate moments in our own lives, be it moving to a new place or taking on a new identity, losing a job, starting over, traveling in unfamiliar lands, falling ill, ending or beginning a relationship, drowning in the madness of love, where we find ourselves alone, tumbling through turbulence, frantic with uncertainty, feeling powerless, feverish with images and perceptions, time and space thrown off kilter, unsure of who we are or how we might best get along in the world, what is real and what is imagined. In passing through these dangerous straits and facing the redeaths and rebirths they entail, we can become keen to who we are and how life proceeds for us and others. The betweens speak to moments sensed on the margins of everyday life, from dreams and other liminal states to times of slippage, rupture, swirls of intoxication.

Grief is a struggle in liminality. It's no coincidence that the singular

changes that deceased persons undergo in death parallel the unsettling devi-
ations from life that come with mourning, in Nepal and elsewhere. Thrown
in the hollows of a loss, we find ourselves removed from familiar certainties.
Any reliance on stable truths is undermined. The line between truth and fiction grows blurred, if it does not collapse altogether. A film of irreality coats all
we see and touch. We lose a sense of who we are, while grasping what makes
us who we are. Vacant, intangible, we inhabit an apparitional field swirled by
specters of the past.[15] We try to navigate our way through dangerous regions.
We go it alone. No one else can carry the burden of our loss. But we can be
helped and guided by others. Powerless at times, we are caught in sways of
force beyond our control. A sense of self can dissolve, fall apart. From those
remnants another kind of life can emerge, one that bears the marks of a previous existence. Still, the betweenness of mourners never ends.

The qualities of the bardo speak to the ends of selfhood found with threshold moments known to us. Incisive is the *Liberation upon Hearing*'s elemental,
bare-soul depiction of the afterlife, with its subjects hobbling through phantasms
of their own making. The minimal subjectivity within a vast cosmic order; the
disappearance of a stable, reliable body; the sway of past events; the aloneness
linked to the care of distant others; the emergence of new "apparitional fields";
the creative dissolution and re-emergence—all of this recurs in situations of
passage, illness, aging, loss, and transcendence. A strong measure of truth and
beauty runs through Tibetan depictions of the death betweens. This exact fantasy holds insights on extremes which rival those more familiar to Western audiences, such as Shakespeare's *King Lear* or Beckett's *Texts for Nothing*.[16]

As the days of a death sear on in Hyolmo communities, mourners go about
what they need to do while their lost relatives encounter hardships of their
own. The longing and anguish is much the same on both sides, but there's a
gap in what they can convey to each other. Unclear to the living is the precise
nature of the consciousness of the deceased, whether it is close or far away
from loved ones, whether it is attending to the lives of the living at any given
time or in time and space more generally. Uncertain are the kinds of changes
the consciousness is undergoing as it makes its way through the between. How
or when the consciousness fades into emptiness or when precisely it transfers
into another life and body goes unknown. What kind of consciousness lingers
in the days and weeks after a death? When does the deceased stop listening? It's
like trying to communicate with a person as he steps silently into a dense fog,
while not knowing when that person's form has fully dissolved into that vapor.

The structure of the situation implies that the consciousness becomes other than what it was while the person was alive. That continuum of self-hood becomes more spectral, more diffuse and anonymous, removed from the affairs and circumstances of the living, drawn more to other realms. Ultimately there is no longer a "you" or "I" invested in that increasingly obscure domain of consciousness, until perhaps consciousness is not the most apt term for what that airy field of apparitions implies.

Shifting, Not Dying

When the last breath leaves the body,
do not think I am dead
it's not that I will be dead,
I will have transferred somewhere

The material life might have changed,
but the spiritual life will be the same
Family relationships might be altered,
but spirituality and emotional relations will continue

You might not know,
to where I have shifted
And you might think,
I've left with my last breath

I may get out of this net of material desires,
but I won't be free from the totality
Although the existence of the physical body might be erased,
the internal knowledge will not be emptied

When the memories drag me back to you,
do not ignore me, thinking I am nonexistent
Even if I cannot appear physically,
I will come in the form of memories of the past

I have arrived as a guest for one life,
not for hundreds of lives
A guest has to leave,
to stay is impossible

Today I am here,
but where will I be tomorrow?
Our migration is temporary
so say farewell to me with smiles, instead of tears
     —Temba D. Hyolmo (translated from the original, in Nepali)

"Yes, It's Death"

See or hold the lifeless body to comprehend that death has truly occurred. Make a visual record of the death, such that those far away can also participate in the parting of a life.

Dawa Jyaba Hyolmo, a compact man articulate in speech, owns a thriving dharma shop set along the main road that roars through the ever-growing bulk of Boudhanath. Prayer flags are his specialty. It was there, in the cool of the storage room, with the drone of buses and truck horns faint along the roads outside, that he spoke of his father's passing. Temba and I had come that morning to hear him tell what he knew of ways of dying in the Hyolmo region.

The death took place when Dawa was thirty-six and his father eighty-five. He was living in Kathmandu at the time, while his father and mother were living in Sermathang, a village on the eastern ridge of the Hyolmo Valley.

"Is it true," I asked, "that some people return from far away to see the face of a family member when he dies?"

"Earlier on, families used to stay together," said Dawa. "But now some live away from their parents, due to work and the like."

When my father died I was here in Kathmandu, building my house. Someone came to me at around four in the afternoon and gave the message, "La, your father has passed away. You need to go up to the village." At that time I didn't have a telephone hook-up in my home. Somebody else gave me this message and asked me to go immediately to the village. I was shocked. I thought, "I won't be able to see his face now."

He had typhoid, I later concluded. In the village he was given unnecessary medicines, and in this way he died. He was suffering from this typhoid for a month but neither my mother nor anyone from the village informed me. They only told me after his death at four in the afternoon. It wasn't possible for me to go at night, so I decided to go early in the morning. But at eleven that night a man came to my home and told me that my father was still alive, that he had not yet died. I was shocked. "What has happened? First they said he was dead, and then they said he was alive. I've never heard of such a thing before."

So we started for the village early the next morning. When we reached Melamchi Pul [at the southern base of the Hyolmo valley] we met two relatives who were coming from the village. One of them told me that my father was fine, that there was nothing to worry about; he had gotten better. When I asked what had happened yesterday, he told me that my father had suddenly become unconscious for several hours. He also told me that if we brought him down to Kathmandu for treatment he might get better. After that we again started our journey.

There were a lot of us—my older sister, many relatives. I was walking ahead of them. I was waiting for them in a small teashop when I saw two people coming from the village. They were people who worked in the field. The two men said they had gone to Sermathang. The woman shopkeeper told them, "You could have gotten something to eat in Sermathang. It's a big village." The two men replied that they had been working in a field in the village, but as an old man had died in the village, everyone went to see him, so they couldn't find anything to eat. As I was sitting outside the teashop I heard the two men saying all these things to the owner, and I rushed in to ask them in whose home a person had died. They said they didn't know who had died.

I hurried toward the village and again we met two old women there. "Who died?" I asked. "Hawaldār Māmā [Uncle Sargent] died," they said. When the two women told me of his death I became sure that it was none other than my own father who had died. Before then, I could talk with him about everything, he still had his breath. But now I couldn't.

I again asked them, "Are you sure he has died?" Both women said, "Yes, it's true. We went there and had a bit to eat, and now we are returning back from being inside the home there. Many lamas are reading texts and reciting mantras." Just then my brother came along the road and told us not to stay there, but to come directly home. We again started for the village.

I wasn't able to talk with my father before he died. Not having been able to talk with him, I went to see him. In seeing him I got a little satisfied. "Yes [he's dead]."

Because without having seen him I was wondering, "Is he dead or not?" I didn't quite believe he had died. In seeing this with my own eyes I knew he was really dead. As I was unable to talk with him at all, I went close to his body and embraced him tightly. It was so cold, a dead body feels very cold. I had never touched a dead body with my own hands like this before. I embraced him and touched my cheek to my father's cheek. I knew then he was already dead, and I felt satisfied.

Dawa's fretful trek from Kathmandu to his family's home in Sermathang involved a passage from distance to proximity, obscurity to sad certitude. Mixed messages and teashop chatter alerted him to his father's demise but left him confused. Only when he encountered his father's corpse did he know for sure that his father had died.

Family members should share in the event of a death, and confirm its reality. Seeing the face lends itself to this. Family members will try to view the countenance of a dying loved one both before and after she or he expires. If they cannot be present before the person dies, often because they've had to travel from some distance away, when they do arrive at the house where the dead body lies they often ask to see the body, the face especially, of a loved one before the corpse is cremated. This is most often the case when sons and daughters arrive at the home of a dead parent. In situations where the corpse has already been wrapped in white cloths in preparation for the cremation it will be revealed enough to enable recently arrived mourners to view the face.

Efforts to see the corpse can involve a desire to behold the person visually one last time. People are aware it's the last glimpse, to last forever, and they try to make it so. It's like retaining a photographic image, but in the realm of mind and memory only.

"They can't look at the body after it's cremated," said Nogapu when asked about this. "That's why they want to look. So they have to open up the cloth and the people look, and cry." Lhatul Lama put it differently: "As the body is burned after the death we won't be able to see the face again in the future. So, for the sake of remembrance only, the face is shown to the rest of the family, even if it's just for a moment. If only to satisfy themselves, they see the face of the dead person before performing the cremation rites."

Hyolmo people often talk about efforts to see the corpse as consisting of attempts to become "satisfied" (*sem lo dhesin*; to have a settled mind) with the fact of the death. Mourners can satisfy their longing to visually caress the face one last time, and thus not feel that there is a strong gap or disconnect in their recollection of that person. Viewing a face before it becomes impossible to do so helps to instantiate lasting relations and memories. This helps to increase the chances that the deceased does not appear after death in more ghostly, apparitional forms.

Encountering the dead body introduces people to death and impermanence. They come to know of finality, of how a life ceases to be.

The embraces also help them to realize that the person is no longer alive. They can reach a certain assurance as to the reality of the death, one that can help them to begin in full their grief. "This is just to satisfy oneself whether the person is dead or not," said Kesang Lama when speaking of the act. "Just by seeing the face, they get satisfied and realize that the person is truly dead."

A sophisticated, psycho-sensorial reasoning is at work here. Without viewing the corpse, the idea that someone has died can be too ungrounded a possibility. A person comes to know of the death through sensate means, body touching body. The presence of a corpse verifies the absence of a person.

People throughout the world have found that the tangible presence of a corpse helps the grief-stricken to come to terms with a death. Families of individuals "disappeared" in Argentina's Dirty Wars, for instance, have had difficulty accepting in full the loss of loved ones without a body to mourn. As anthropologist Marcelo Suárez-Orozco observes, "The disappearances subverted the mourning process and added fuel to the tendency to deny: without a corpse to ritually mourn, there is always the fantasy that the person is not really dead, the atrocities not real."[17] An American friend of mine speaks of the presence of her late grandfather, whose dead body, which she never saw, is still quite "tangible" in her life. Hyolmo people, perhaps knowing of similar situations of interrupted mourning in their own lives, grasp the value of seeing and holding the lifeless form of the person that was.

Technologically mediated visual images can help in this endeavor. "In a few cases," Temba related, "if, say, a mother dies, but not everyone was able to attend the funeral, people will take photos or videos to confirm to people who were absent that the mother has died and to show how all the processions were done." As is the case when people see the face of a dead person outright, the images recorded help people to view the person—and his or her "face"—one last time.[18] This can help them to realize that the person is dead. The images can also register to an extent the way in which the funeral rites were undertaken, as well as demonstrate that the rites were carried out with appropriate care and respect.

This was the kind of video made to document the passing of Sange's father. The video recording served as a substitute body of the deceased. An effigy of sorts, it provided Sange with a body to touch and to perceive, however virtual that body and his contact with it might have been. We are left to wonder if, by engaging virtually in the events of the dying and ritual care, Sange was better able to attend to the loss of his father and the grief it spawned.

Corpses, Fashioned

Cleanse the corpse, keep it uncontaminated. Wrap the inert, mute body in white cloth. Treat the body respectfully and imbue it with sacred value.

The survivors have a person's remainder to work with in aiding in his progress toward a good rebirth. Fashioning the body, rendering it sacred and beautiful, mourners act on behalf of the one who can no longer act. This is a labor of body and soul, as a Hyolmo "pain song" conveys it:

> This body of flesh and bone
> Will be stuck in the cremation grounds
> This consciousness like air
> Will be left in the land of bardo

A corpse is an incongruous presence, uncommon and extraordinary to most people. Not a matter of everyday life, it is perceived by the living, and yet not of their world. It is at once sensible and insensible. "What we call mortal remains escapes common categories," observed Maurice Blanchot. "Something is there before us which is not really the living person, nor is it any reality at all. It is neither the same as the person who was alive, nor is it another person, nor is it anything else. What is there, with the absolute calm of something that has found its place, does not, however, succeed in being convincingly here."[19] A corpse is at once here and not here. Bound to be soon gone, it spots a marker between life and death. A corpse is the locus for a person who is no longer here but not fully somewhere else.

A corpse is mute. It is flat, unresponsive. It carries a quality of thingness, of inert matter, like other material objects in Hyolmo lives, and like matter more generally—"existence without being," to use a term of Blanchot's.[20] This quality is obvious to adults who encounter a corpse: bodies do not move on their own, they become stiff and silent and cold to the touch. But this quality is also significant, for it speaks to the painful absence of the vitality of a person who a few hours before animated that body. The absence of life, of a quickness of limb, stresses that very thing. A corpse, a *phungbo*—a "heap," literally, an "aggregate," in accord with Buddhist parsings of the self—is a material remnant of something once alive, easily dismembered, a vacant echo. Yet it's through engagements with that emptiness that people grasp that a person has died.

Women and children usually do not touch dead bodies; only adult men contribute to the preparation of a corpse, for they are thought to be of a stronger nature. Men carry out these preparations with care and purposefulness. Although in death a "person" no longer inhabits the body that has died, the body is still an important vehicle and bearer of selfhood, worthy of respect. "Of course, the physical body is dead there," Karma once put it. "It has no meaning at all. It's just a physical remnant. It's only the consciousness that is important. But because the body is so much linked to it, this is a means to reach out to the consciousness."

The body and its consciousness are "linked" to one another, due to their close affinity and mutual influence. Although the person does not exist, its former body continues to serve as a ground of being. The corpse stands as a powerful image of personhood, one that can be worked on even in death. A corpse is like an effigy. As is the case with the mimetic simulations evident in the rituals of bombos and lamas, by acting on the physical model people act on the force or agent represented. *Reach out to the consciousness.*

"The image does not, at first glance, resemble the corpse," Blanchot contends, "but the cadaver's strangeness is perhaps also that of the image."[21] Corpses are like images, and images are like corpses. Both stand for something else, something separate that is not fully present. By acting upon them, mourners can act upon what they entail. In a stretch of sympathetic magic, mourners and lamas act on the body in positive, generative ways, with the idea that the deceased will benefit from these actions. These efforts correlate with the fact, common to many societies in the world, that "death is not simple demise, a privation of life; it is a transformation of which the corpse is both the instrument and the object, a transmutation of the subject that functions in and through the body."[22] Mourners turn the body into a vehicle of transmutation, into a corpus which carries qualities that aid the deceased. The living work to change the condition of the body and thus the existential and karmic status of the subject who once inhabited it. The temporality of this work is prospective and anticipatory, nodding toward the conditions of a future life.

A lama places coins or pieces of gold or silver in the mouth of the corpse soon after the death. One explanation for this placement is that the coins pre-

vent the consciousness from departing the body through the mouth and increase the likelihood that it will exit the body through the chyir-chsug at the
top of the skull. Another reckoning is that coins help alleviate any attachment
the dead person has to his or her wealth or belongings. Having pieces of wealth
enclosed so integrally in the body, resting on the crest of the tongue, the dying
or dead person will not long for the possessions or wealth it possessed and
valued in life. Knowing this, a dying person might instruct family members
to place gold or silver ornaments in his mouth after he dies. Some say a single
coin can stand for all the monies and wealth earned by a person in her lifetime,
and setting a coin within her mouth insures that the wealth will transfer over
into the next life.

Goser Lama offered another explanation. "It's said that, when a person
dies, the body becomes empty, as there is no breath, no consciousness, and
no other element of life," he told Temba and me. "In our Hyolmo tradition
anything empty is not good. And so it's not good to cremate the body in such
a condition of emptiness. So, to give value to the body and to make it worthy,
at least one coin is put in the mouth."

Anything empty is not good. A gift of a jewelry box should be presented
with something in it. Trash receptacles shouldn't go empty. A body void of life
should not remain vacant.

Family members bathe the corpse by hand, with water, soap, and cloths.
They do so in a separate room, or hang blankets around the body, so that
others cannot look on. Washing removes any dirt, soiled materials, or surface
impurities.

Sacred inscriptions, known as *tag dol,* are written on pieces of paper, which
are then pasted on different parts of the body: the forehead, mouth, chest,
stomach, and genitals. The images usually consist of five inscriptions, in Tibetan script, printed on five sheets of paper:

> *sku*
> *gsung*
> *thugs*
> *yon tan*
> *phrin las*

These mantra-letters refer to the five aspects of Buddhahood: body,
speech, mind, qualities, and activities.[23] The inscriptions invest the person with the qualities denoted by them. The term *tag dol* translates as "lib-

eration upon wearing." When these mantra-letters are "worn" on the body, the wisdom intensive to them can provoke a spiritual liberation from cyclic existence—much as a profound "liberation upon hearing" can be achieved by hearing the *Liberation upon Hearing in the Between*.

One commentary on the usage of *tag dol* in Tibetan settings deems it: "At the time of death [this mantra circle] should not be removed from the body, and when cremation takes place it should not be removed from the corpse. As a consequence, liberation may occur through seeing, hearing, recollection or contact."[24]

An indirect consequence of applying the tag dol to the body is that the corpse takes on the qualities of a text: sacred words imbue it with value. The body is a font of writing, of inscription and imprinting, in life and in death. Yet the present words are not to be read or decoded so much as they emanate intensive value and sacred effect. As with comparable imageries worn by Tibetan Buddhists at the time of death, "these mantra-letters are the resonance of the pure awareness of the deities expressed in the form of letter shapes and sounds."[25] The living write on the textual equivalent of the deceased, who can no longer tread in marks himself.

The body is laid straight and wrapped in white cloths, such that no part of the body is exposed. The ubiquity of this practice has led the covering to signify an icon of death: if a person dreams of lying with a white cloth draped over his body, the image foretells a death to come. "If we don't have fun in life," lilts a Hyolmo folksong, "then all we get after we die is a piece of cloth." A body covered by a white cloth is a lonely, meager image. Still, the covering keeps the body uncontaminated: white signs as purity for Hyolmo people; covering the body protects it from immediate visual or tactile contact with the world external to it. The fewer the number of people who touch or look at the body, the better it is for the deceased's measure of purity.

Few people touch the bodies of spiritually advanced persons when they die because "ordinary people" can contaminate their corpses and diminish their spiritual purity and power.

Before his death, Karma's father instructed several relatives to prevent people from touching his body after he died, out of concern that they would render it less spiritually pure and sacred, hindering the passage of his consciousness in death. Goser Lama spoke of this:

> While we were painting the temple in Thalo, quite a long time before he
> died, your father told us what should be done and what should not be done

in the event of his death. He said those words in front of all of us. He told us
that, after his death, we should prevent people who smoked, and people who
could not keep their promises, from touching his body. "Although Khendo's
father uses snuff and tobacco, let him touch my body, because he is a good
friend. But as for others, don't let them touch it."

Washed and wrapped, the body is set up in a room and elevated—"put
above" others. The corpse is usually laid flat on a table that stands above the
place where people would typically sit. The corpse is dressed in clothes and
ornaments worn by the person while alive, and then tied up with its arms
and legs bound together and set within the structure of a large pot such that
it "stands" upright, with arms crossed at the wrists, and legs at the ankles.
The face remains covered only by the white cloths wrapped around the head.
A crown, known as *rig nga*, is positioned on the head of the corpse. The crown
contains five sides; each side designates one of the five Buddha families (the
Buddha, Vajra, Jewel, Lotus, and Action families), with each family associated with one of the five directions: east, south, west, north, and the center.[26]
These five Buddha families make possible the transfer of a deceased person's
consciousness to *dewa chen*, the Pure Land. With the placement of the images
of these buddhas at the top of the person's corpse, it becomes more likely that
he will reach this heavenly realm. The crown "empowers" the deceased by activating and demonstrating his inherent buddha nature.

The corpse is kept uncontaminated, given value, empowered, and envel-
oped in care. The living protect the body from visual and tactile contact with
the world external to it. They straighten it, set it above others, and inscribe it
with intensive, transformative words and images. They render it a semi-sacred
presence. Something is made out of the body, beyond its inert, post-life matter.

Karma noted this direct and generative fashioning himself when we were
discussing the role of poeisis in Hyolmo lives. "For instance, after people die,"
he said, "the way they treat the corpse even this is really guided by poiesis.
Here, you are not doing it just for the sake of doing it, in itself. It's done with
the graceful unmaking of the present life, and the making of the afterlife, in
mind. It's done to make the journey to the next life more meaningful, more
beautiful, and more fashioned."

The transformation occurs in direct but inverse proportion to the decay
of the cadaver. As the body darkens and decomposes, mourners render it
brighter, fuller, purer, more sacred. Creation countermands decay.

Implicit in this striving for increase, for something *more* than what might occur otherwise, is the development of a temporal flow that halted in the dead time of death. In moving matters forward, the living situate the deceased's inert body within a broad reach of karmic time and a series of rebirths and redeaths. Mourners do not shape the form of the corpse simply to help establish a good death. They do so to set up the terms of the next life, within a principle of generative fashioning. What is done with the body can bear fruit in the person's next life. These actions form one sequence of a larger sequence of actions that contributes to the dharmic career of the deceased, who will soon, it is hoped, move on to another human life or achieve enlightenment altogether. There is work to be done, a next life to augment and anticipate.

"Where does that drive to do that with the corpse come from?" I asked Karma.

"It's the respect to life. The life is impermanent, but death is not the end of it. It continues. So your respect for life doesn't end there either. It's a continuation of your respect for the person's life — and life more generally."

"And you're doing it an artful way," Karma continued. "That's my point. We probably wouldn't need to do it that way. But then, even if the corpse is changing more and more, people are making it more and more artful. It's not artful just for the deceased, but for the people to see and observe it in a more artful way. These things aren't really necessary. But they are creating it. . . . It is their poiesis. It's not really a conscious action, but what's being done is an expression of love and respect for life and for the body's graceful passage to its next form."

A steadfast generativity is in force here which goes beyond any instrumental logic of treating the corpse in certain ways. Fashion the body, goes the imperative, because the life that it once held continues on. Make more of it than what it is in the pall of death. In these modest efforts we find elements of lifemaking more fundamentally. We strive to compose something notable, artful or sacred even, if for fleeting moments, out of the scant bones of our lives.

Bodies That Wound

Be wary of the dangerous impurity of corpses and of death more generally. Heed the startling vivid starkness of a dead body.

"A relative had an accident," Karma Gyaltsen Lama told me. The day after the death that young man's body was taken to a hospital for the postmortem and placed in the morgue. Karma and others came there to retrieve the body

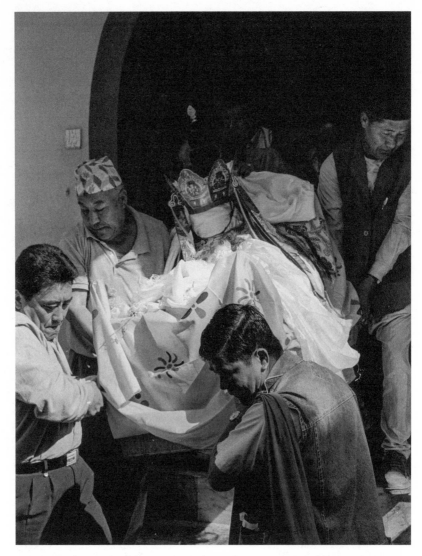

Figure 9. Transferring a corpse to a cremation ground. Kathmandu, 2001.

and take it back home. The corpse was in a room, alongside other cadavers. It wasn't kept well.

I was one of those who touched the man. He was naked, with just a small cloth covering him. And I felt some kind of chill. It was the first time I touched a dead body. Suddenly I got very dizzy. I had to go outside immediately. It was as though I was fainting. I don't know why that happened—because I was perfectly healthy. I wasn't sick at the time. I never felt that way before. Since then, I've tried not to touch dead bodies. I was prone to *shyi dhip*.

The effects go both ways: people can soil a corpse, and a corpse's aura can disturb people.

Corpses are polluting. Entailing a marker between life and death, they are transitional, transitioning matters. As with other liminal matters, a potentially dangerous impurity is associated with cadavers. When a child is born, the act of transferring a new life into the world brings with it certain impurities. These "birth impurities" (*kye dhip*) linger amidst the bodies of child and mother and within the household where the birth took place. Within a day or two, and before outsiders can visit the household, a lama must be summoned in order to wash away the impurities through a set of ritual practices. It is at that time that he bestows a name on the newly arrived person. While some find that the birth impurities result from the blood and other bodily substances present, there is also something in the transfer of a new life into the world that is, in itself, defiling.

The passage from life to death carries similar impurities. That leaving is also associated with dangerous, contaminating borders, outflows, and seepages. A miasmic force, known as *shyi dhip*, "death impurity," emanates from the corpse and "spreads" in the air about it. Hyolmo people associate *dhip* of any kind with obscurities, hindrances, darkness, vagueness, defilement. Dhip brings the inverse of purity, clarity, preciseness, sharpness, and good and proper forms. A person affected by death impurity becomes imbued with its qualities; he can become sickly, slow-witted, sluggish, lightheaded; she can feel dull and lazy and find herself unable to act, think, or remember well. If people come in contact with a corpse, or if they have stepped within a household where a corpse lies, they will try to prevent any death impurity from afflicting them by drinking pure water or by sprinkling such water on their bodies. Death comes, dangerously, from the outside.

Hospitals are rife with death impurity, as so many people die on beds and in hospital wards. The cadavers effect death pollutants which linger even after the bodies have been removed, for hours or days even.

Few men and women see or touch corpses early in their lives. "When I was very little other kids and I were very curious to see a corpse if someone had died," Karma recalled. "But usually our parents wouldn't let us into the houses, so we would try to peek into the homes. We would see the bodies only after they had been wrapped up and prepared for the cremation. . . . I do remember seeing parts of the body being burned."

"Did this bother you?"

"No. Not really. I wasn't bothered by it, or frightened, or made worried by it. But I was struck by the smell. The smell of human flesh is unlike any other smell."

Parents and older relatives often try to keep children from viewing corpses for fear that the visual image of the dead person, particularly the face, will linger in a child's mind.

Temba told me that he never saw any dead bodies when he was young. "Because people used to tell me, 'If you see the dead body, it will frighten you.' So with that kind of fear in our minds, we never dared to see dead bodies."

"How old were you when you first saw a dead body?"

"I was eighteen, I think. At that time one of my friends died in an accident and I saw his dead body then."

"What did you think about this?"

"Before I had seen a dead body people used to say, 'The dead body is like this, it's like that, and if you see a dead body, then you will often come to remember that face. It will be imprinted in the mind and it will come time and again into your memory and it will frighten you.' I used to think the same thing, and I never dared to see any dead bodies. But at that time a friend of mine got into an accident, just before he was to begin school in Kathmandu. We were the same age. He was on a bicycle and a big lorry came from behind and hit him and he died on the spot. I saw the dead body at that time, and still sometimes the memory comes into my mind. I come to remember the body."

Temba's recollections spoke to the serious power of images of the deceased. His friend's body was not deformed in death and did not trouble him in the way his elders cautioned. But the look of it shadows his mind.

"I still see him in my dreams," said Dawa Jyaba Hyolmo of his father. "I still remember the way he died, the way he was taken to the cremation ground. In our culture, we tie the dead body and remove the clothes, and after we wash the dead body with incense and camphor, it's put into a bag. I still remember all this, the way he was tied."

A sharp vividness lingers in people's recollections of a corpse. The event of a corpse leaves a mark, an etching or "imprint" on a person's mind, recursive in time and memory. *"Mi tsola yit yit tonge"* is a Hyolmo sentence sometimes voiced in such situations: "What I've seen keeps flashing in my eyes."

The dumb inert matter of corpses can hit people hard. A dead body's un-responsiveness can be unnerving and unforgettable. A corpse can provoke a sense of what French psychoanalyst Jacques Lacan called "the real"—a state of nature that is unresponsive and indifferent to human concerns or strivings in life. A cadaver is a "thing in its dumb reality."[27] That vague, uncommon inertness can leave a mark.

Most people do not come into contact with the dead on a regular basis. The main exceptions are men engaged in "lama work," who labor in close proximity with corpses when performing death rites. They wash and dress corpses, sit by them, sleep in the same room with them when necessary, and eat food close to their sides. In so doing, they can become more comfortable with the reality of death. Years ago, one lama was known to brew tea at cremations by setting a pot of water atop embers in the cremation fire.

Hyolmo biographies are marked by the fact of whether and when people have seen or touched a corpse, and the effects such contact has had on them. Corpses can wound, through the dangerous miasmata they generate or their haunting presence. The appearance of a corpse is an event, and events leave marks.

Grief likewise dulls a person. The fog of grief can stun and overwhelm. It makes one dumbstruck, inarticulate. It disables us and clouds our abilities to think and perceive well.

The Five Sensual Pleasures

Dedicate sensual pleasures to a deity and transfer the karmic merit gained from that act to the deceased. Satisfy the dead person's sensate appetite for the world. Satiate the sensory grounds of his existence.

The living must take the dead seriously. The recently deceased are plaintive, needy, desirous, even if there's no clear way to know the force of such cravings. The recently dead, like those they have left behind, are grieving, confused. They pine for what is lost to them, absent life and connections.

Attachment often sticks around after a person dies, for the person's consciousness can continue to be hooked on the elements of its world. The dead person might suffer from thirst or hunger or continue to "remember" and long for certain loved ones or yearn for cherished possessions. In death, attachment is an unwelcome, inappropriate remainder of an expired life. While grasping is understandable among the living, to be attached while dead is "unnatural."

Clinging to life is incompatible with that post-life condition, much as some-one who stalks a former lover after the relation has ended goes against what should be.

If the living survivors deem that this is happening, measures are taken to extinguish the attachment. If they determine that a dead person's attachment is affixed to certain objects, such as valuable clothes that the person liked a lot while alive, then those objects are given away, or sold, with the money earned from the sale donated away in charity. If a mourner sees the visual image of a dead person in his dreams—generally an unwelcome sight—then it's thought that the latter is pining for the person who saw the image in the dream or he is hungry and desires some food. If the images continue to appear in the mourner's dreams and nothing is done to arrest the attachment causing them, the mourner can fall ill. "In the dreams, the dead person sometimes tries to take us with him, or he says to follow or accompany him." The dead person's desperate attachments can drag a loved one into death. Unlike what many in Western settings so often think, among Hyolmo people these days it's not so much the living but the recently dead who have a tough time coming to terms with the reality of death and who, sometimes unable to let go, linger within harmful states of attachment.

One way people try to satisfy a dead person's longings is by preparing an offering called *sur*. Sur derives from a mixture of sweet foods, such as sugar, butter, milk, barley, fruits, and flour, which is formed into a paste, then put on lightly burning coals, held within a clay pot, placed either in the household or just outside the door of it, and offered in the name of the person in question. As the mixture slowly burns, a light, syrupy smoke rises from it.

Hyolmo lamas trained in Buddhist studies understand that the sur is of-fered to protector deities and to all sentient beings of the six realms, including hungry ghosts. The merit from dedicating this offering goes to the deceased person, to increase his karmic merit and to aid him in the path to liberation. For many others, the aromatic smoke, which the dead find to be beautiful in scent, also serves to satiate the desires of the dead person, who is not able to eat owing to his bodiless state. Once satisfied in this way, the deceased's at-tachment to the world goes away—"it drifts away with the smoke"—and the dead person no longer pines for the distant loved one. As Goser Lama put it,

> When the dead person is dreamed of, it's thought that he has either remem-bered the person who dreamt of him longingly, or is hungry and wants to have some food. So when sur is offered, it satisfies the dead person and he

will no longer harm the living. It is said that, if sur is not offered in such cases, then the person longed for will fall ill. . . . Sur is the best food for a dead person. Because when the mixture of flour is burned, the smoke comes and the deceased's consciousness can have the smoke and satisfy itself.

Sur is used often to appease a gamut of deities and hungry ghosts as well as the recently dead. I have come upon sur in my visits to families in Boudhanath; the aromatic smoke lifting from burning embers, placed close to the door, mingled with odors, sights, and the sounds of car horns and rooster crows thick in the urban air. In cases where a person has died, the mix is prepared daily in the household where the person lived, through the first seven weeks after the death—until, that is, it can safely be said that the deceased's consciousness has reached the Pure Land or taken a new rebirth. Sur serves as food for the deceased and, more generally, as a way to satisfy any lingering cravings. "Be satisfied now," Karma said in characterizing the intent of the offering. "Don't be attached now. We're giving you everything you're attached to."

Much the same message carries through other means. People offer foods to the dead person's consciousness. Mourners and lamas advise it to cease staying around the living. Lamas sometimes warn the consciousness that, if it sticks around the world of the living, they will force it to quit the world.

Lamas also perform an important rite that takes place while the deceased's body is still at the house, sometime during the days before the cremation, while people are visiting the house and consoling the mourners and lamas are reciting words from sacred texts. The rite, known as *doyen ngogen*, usually takes place after people visiting the house are served a meal, but before they begin to eat.[28] Lamas visualize the deceased person as a deity and then dedicate "the five sensual pleasures." They do so by invoking five offerings to the deity while reciting accompanying texts. Each of the offerings is associated with one of the five senses: sight, hearing, smell, taste, and touch.

For an offering of *zuk*, a word which literally means "figure, form, body" but which also denotes visual forms more generally, a mirror is held up to the corpse, such that it reflects the deity's image.

For an offering of *dha*, the sense of hearing, the lama's bell (*dilbu*) is sounded.

For an offering of *dhi*, the sense of smell, incense is lit and its aroma is offered.

For an offering of *rho*, the sense of taste, varieties of foods are set before the deceased in the understanding that the deity will consume them through their vapors.

For an offering of *rhecha*, the sense of touch or sentience, the deity is presented with a *katha* ceremonial scarf or some clothes.

Dedicating these sensual pleasures to the deity accrues significant karmic merit. The merit transits to the deceased person, thus "empowered" with great karmic merit.

The rite delivers desirable objects to the deceased to satiate his craving for worldly things. In offering the pleasures, the living aim to satisfy desires that occur through the medium of sight, sound, smell, taste, or touch. This helps to diminish, and perhaps extinguish altogether, that person's attachment to the world. It is important to do this, since it's possible that the deceased is still grasping for features of its prior existence, from tasty meals to a child's laughter. Also, since the living eat food directly in front of the deceased, it makes sense to sate any possible hunger of the deceased, so as not add to any cravings for the provisions of the world.

"It's to fulfill the sensual desires of the deceased," Karma said of these actions. "So that no more desires should remain. Everything transforms into emptiness. No scope of sensual pleasures should remain, and no senses should remain. Then, 'There's nothing remaining now. Every kind of longing should be fulfilled. Now you are fulfilled. We have offered you everything. Nothing exists now.'"

A sense of completion and fulfillment characterizes the rite. There's also an air of reduction, nullification. The offerings quench the deceased's consciousness out of existence. There is no longer a personal, flesh-and-mind assemblage that engages with the world. There is no longer a reason to seek an existence on earth, to cling to the living. An absence of desire equals an absence of existence. To be a person is to desire, to want, to seek out others. When a consciousness no longer desires anything, it ceases to exist.

"Everything transforms into one, becomes universal emptiness," Karma added to the above words. "At least this is the motivation."

Consoling Mourners

Visit the home of the deceased. Console the mourners, and be with them in their distress and grief. Create an ambiance of social support, comfort, and presence.

Word of the death pulsed through the villages. A good man from the hamlet of Ghyang had died. He had a quiet way about him, with a trim mustache and Clarke Gable eyes. Close to his fifties, he was feverish for a week, delirious at the end. His body soaked in sweat. Rabies, it could have been. A fierce dog had bit him a few weeks back. *Nyingjua,* "compassioned one," people said. He was worthy of the sentiment. This was in 1998.

The morning after the news I joined with families in visiting the home. It felt right to be included. I knew the man and his wife and had shared words with their two sons. I was with others in that moral fold of care and connection.

We set out after breakfast. The women carried woven bags holding uncooked rice and liquor in glass bottles, corked with strands of plastic bags. Two men brought dharma books with them. A younger man cupped a set of cymbals in his hands. We sloshed through a sandy wash and hiked up a narrow footpath that angled through a bluff of hills, pausing on level ground by a watery mill and a quarry of stones. Wet, reedy grasses greened the laces on my sneakers. We climbed to the house, caught our breaths. We came to an open door and I sensed the mood. We discarded shoes and sandals and stepped inside.

The glow from votive candles, newly oiled in the main room, softened the dark wood. Fresh water stood in receptacles on the altar. Juniper incense fused the air. People we knew sat on the floor, cups of tea on small stands before them. Somber greetings, familiar looks. Unsure what to do, I squatted by the door, waiting for a guiding word or gesture.

A lama from the village huddled close to the corpse by the lone window, on the wood bed frame where the man used to sleep, keeping company. The lama, the widow's father, was reading from the *Bardo Thedol,* his voice gusty in assertions. He flipped a page and delivered words cast on the second side. Raspy, ornate syllables filled the room.

A body sat upright, seated in form, decked in fine attire. Stiff arms, elbows bound inward, flesh bundled with cloth, the dead man looked tousled by a long sleep, muffled in death.

Each arrived family placed a bottle of *shalgar* (a ritual offering of liquor) on tables close to him, dabs of butter touched to the rims. We offered ceremonial scarves. Someone handed me a khata ceremonial scarf and showed me where and how to place it. I unfolded the white silk and draped it round the man's neck, atop the pure fine fabrics there.

I had seldom been so close to a dead body.

We took our place in the room, quiet conversations, glances toward the body. A dark gravity weighed on our thoughts.

The man appeared to be resting, his face white and mute.

Women in an adjacent structure prepared food—potatoes, rice, smoked meat, brewed tea, *tsampa* (roasted barley flour). Two men labored with axes in a clearing outside to produce more firewood. Wood chips spliced to the ground. Chickens clucked about the level ground outside.

The man's wife looked to the floor, shoulders heavy, her eyes worn. Her sons sat with their backs tight against a wall. The men from our village moved to the window, close to the older lama. They took out the texts and unwrapped their silk coverings. They found their place in the reading and joined in the recitations. The youngest called to me and told me to sit by him, down the line. The boy to his left shimmied over to clear a space.

A young woman walked to the men. She held an open thermos.

"Please drink, uncle," she said to one. The man reached into his vest and produced a low round cup and placed it on the table.

The readings continued. The corpse kept still. They weren't going to shunt it away any time soon. A girl in a faded blue dress, slight tear at the waist, pranced into the room, humming the lyrics of a Bollywood song. Her mother reached for an arm and brought the child to her lap. She fed her some tea and tsampa.

My neighbors that morning were showing me how to feel, how to console a family. Those who visited stepped into a mood of mourning. The tones were of somber sadness, of respects paid, with clipped expressions of sorrow or casual conversations. Some cried out. There was little clear joy.

Immediate family members take on a number of "mourning restrictions" (*dhu zemge*) in the wake of a death. The self-imposed restrictions usually last until the final funeral rites some weeks later, when the end of social mourning is ritually noted. Mourners do not sing or dance, nor do they participate in games or forms of play and entertainment, or wear good clothes. Some persons decide to bear the restrictions for a year's time or more, depending on their "heart." "As our hearts do not want to dance or sing, so we don't dance."

The practice of mourning restrictions allows people a culturally authorized span of time in which one can live distinct from others, within the pace of one's sadness, apart from the pleasures of play or entertainment, for there's no mirth to that. The restrictions provide a standard for grieving, a method for a certain kind of consciousness. For many, there is a visceral force to adhering to the sanctions. Doing otherwise does not feel appropriate, despite urgings from others. There is a pacing to grief, if discordant and dolorous.

> The year our father passed away,
> we had to sing songs of pain

Or so recalls a Hyolmo pain-song.

"When my father died, I did not dance for one year and four months," Dawa Jyaba Hyolmo told us.

> I usually dance a lot, and at wedding ceremonies people tried to force me to dance, because they all know that I dance well and I am fond of dancing. But I would tell them that I was a little upset, so I'll dance some other day. But they pressured me to join them, and told me that the person who has to die has died, but let's not spoil our mood, and enjoy life. During a social gathering of Hyolmo people one woman organized a cultural program and she asked me to take part in that program. But I refused to dance. She then said to me, "It won't make any difference if you dance." I got angry and upset when she said this to me. In reply I said to her, "You will come to know how one feels when someone who is very near to you dies, when you have to go through the same state that I am going through." After that she didn't compel me to dance.

Grief is singular, bound to those who suffer from it. Grief itself cannot be shared, much as a wound cannot be shared. That cut is a person's burden alone. "When people come to the house, we try to comfort people, and say, 'If it was some other work, we could share it,'" Karma said of this. "'But it's something we can't do. So still you have to bear it.'" On your own. "We're saying this, but it's not easy to. 'If it was some kind of load that we could help to carry, then we could share it, to make it less for you. But still you should comfort yourself.'"

This take on the matter addresses the truth of the situation in an honest, nonsuperficial way, while allowing for a sympathetic, compassionate relation to the sorrow of others. People keep company with those racked by a loss.

"How is the sorrow of death made less?" I once asked Nogapu, using language that he might not have used himself. "How do people make the heartache less?"

"If somebody dies in a family," Nogapu answered, "and if, say, there is a wife whose husband has died and maybe is very upset, all the relatives, all the people go there, and help with the works, talk with that person, sit with her, then I think—"

"That makes a person feel better?"

"Yes. If nobody goes there, if everybody is just watching, without interest, then they get very upset."

"What kinds of things do they say?"

"They say things like, 'Everybody will die. Don't worry, we all have to die.' That kind of thing. 'Once we have to burn. Once we have to die.'"

"If people are very sad," Nogapu added, "then others help them. They say, 'We all have to die someday. It's not only your wife who has died. Everyone has to die someday. Don't be sad. You have to take care of yourself, because you have children your house, you have to look after these things. . . . You are not too old. You have to marry someone else.'"

We all have to burn once.

It's not easy to say or do anything useful at all. Any such statements might be heard as platitudes, reassuring discernments on the nature of life, or something in between. We know the sense of helplessness in such situations.

And yet it is terrifically important to give heartfelt condolences to bereaved family members. *Semso bheke*, "doing or performing semso," is the name for this act. The phrase builds on the words *sem*, "heartmind," and *so*, a term which relates closely to the Tibetan *solba*. Solba is a verb which carries connotations such as to feed, nourish; to bring up, nurse up, rear, train; to cure; to put an end to (such as fatigue); to mend, repair; to restore, rebuild, re-establish what has been destroyed; to refresh, recreate.[29]

These acts are relational. Someone comes, compassionately, to the aid of another. The phrase *semso bheke* might be translated as "to console, to comfort, or to appease the heart of another." Along with that is a tonality of nourishing and mending, of efforts to repair what has been destroyed, the poise and integrity of spirit of persons devastated by grief. People console immediate mourners and try to alter the pain a shade. They create an ambiance of social support and comfort. They pay respect to the deceased and his family. They share in the loss.

A portion of this consolation occurs through visitors simply being there in the household, with and alongside the grief-stricken in a situation of co-presence. Talking with them, sitting with them, through a stretch of time, it's what people do, should do. This kind of communal accompaniment, an *active withness* which is an ethical act in its own right, might help to keep some mourners out of the deepest of funks. There are other people right there, next to you, and they are not going to leave any time soon. But there's more to it than companionship alone, as the physical and conversational presences suggest rhythms distinct from those solely of grief.

These alternate rhythms can keep a person out of a pure and singular aloneness of despair. The rhythms indicate that life continues on, possibly enabling mourners to go further on in life themselves. It's similar to situations where, say, someone who is distressed is comforted by talking with a friend, with that solace coming from the patterns of the talk. The exchanges offer strands of awareness that bring a person back into the world. They give perspective on the distress. They remind the person of who she or he is, of what life is, and they create distractions which take a person away. "We're there for you," the sentiment goes, "but we're there for you in ways, significantly, that are distinct from your own ways of being there."

Quiet withness. An elderly woman reads entries from the day's newspaper in a clear and conversational voice to an even older man as they ride on a Metro North train into Manhattan one December afternoon. A man sits at a table in a faculty dining room on a college campus in New York one morning, keeping company with another man, who learned the day before that his son had died. A man goes for a walk with a friend in a wildlife reserve in Massachusetts in an autumn season when the friend was plagued by hallucinatory memories from his past. The friend says he finds the companionship helpful. A son stays with his mother in her home the weekend after his father dies so that neither mother nor son have to face alone the terrifying suddenness of the loss. A woman talks by phone with a friend soon after she arrives in a city in southern California unknown to her. The conversation brings her back to thoughts and relations familiar to her.

An ethics of care is found as much with supporting mourners as it is in helping a person to die well. Families clearly value the support of others. The compassionate presence of others, offering sympathetic words, is comforting. If people aren't there, or if they are "just watching, without interest," then family members can get upset, as they are left to go it on their own. A lack of engaged care or "interest" implies a contemptuous lack of moral responsiveness. An absence of consolers also signals the social unworthiness of the deceased.

A scarcity of mourners besets some accounts of death. Temba's grandfather related to us a stark scene of asocial mourning, which took place decades ago.

In those days there wasn't the tradition of going to the cremation ceremonies, as there is nowadays. In those days just a few people gathered and then took the dead body to the cremation ground and cremated the body. Also during the funeral ceremonies only close relatives were invited, and very few people used to gather and perform the rites. There was a scarcity of money and food. If all the villagers were invited, lots of foods were required, so in order to minimize the cost they invited just a few people and performed the rites.

The grandfather spoke of a death in a family that had recently settled in the region, without kin ties to count on.

I still visualize the scene of the death of a woman in Sermathang. I was going to Lhashisa, carrying my luggage, and on the way I saw the scene. Just then a few people were trying to prepare the dead body [for the cremation ceremonies]. There wasn't even a *surku* [traditional dress women wear, made of pure silk] to put on the body. The body was so big, and it was put into a thin transparent sack of cotton cloth. At that time, I didn't even have the thought of helping them. I saw it while I was going to my work. It was such an unsocialized scene then. Only the very close relatives gathered and undertook the cremation. Other people, even from the same village, didn't care about these events.

A bareness to life and death marks such dire situations. These days, people have the thought of helping other families, in part because they now can afford to do so.

The spirit of consolation continues to evolve. In recent years, particularly among families who have set up lives in the New York area, news of a death impels people to bring ritual offerings, chiefly in the form of food, to the home of the mourners. This often leads to a bounty of nourishment, however, with some going to waste. Some families have taken to passing along money along with their gestures of semso, of consoling, to help the family cover the expenses of cremation and funeral rites. In speaking of this, Temba tells me of how he and his friends joke that, given the increasing busyness of people's lives, there could soon be a day when the money is transferred with the speed of a phone call, to the touch tune of 1-800-SEMSO.

Alternate Rhythms

Read sacred texts to increase the karmic merit of the deceased and of all sentient beings. Perform prayers that accompany these readings. Establish rhythms of life counter to the harsh despondency of grief.

Mend and repair, or at least try to do so. Restore and rebuild what has been destroyed. Comfort, console. Sit and talk with those in grief. Provide alternate rhythms, because that's what should be done.

It's important not to cry or lament the death too overtly, as any crying or tears can disturb the deceased's passage to a new life. A man named Kesang Lama spoke of the genealogy and implications of this sensibility. "It's natural that when any member of a family dies, then his family members will definitely feel bad, and sad," he told Temba and me.

In older days, people were very uneducated and they didn't have knowledge of anything. So in this case, it's natural to get or feel sad. But as compared to older days, now people are educated, due to which they don't feel sad. It's because they might have read in some text that we should not cry when anyone dies, or they might have learned from lamas that one shouldn't weep when their dear one dies. What I think is important is to go to any of the gompas, and to light butter lamps or to give some donations to needy people. Earlier in Hyolmo society, many people would cry when someone died. It's because they were uneducated. But now I have seen very few young people who weep when someone dies, because they have read and learned from the lamas that it is not good to cry when someone dies—and it's not useful for the dead person.

This man related a tale known to many Buddhist peoples, for centuries now, in one form or another—the story of the mustard seed oil.

Once there was a king, and his only son died. Then the king took his son to Gautama Buddha, and begged the Buddha to make his son alive, and said to the Buddha that, if you do this, I will give you anything you want, my property, everything. After listening to him, Gautama Buddha said to him, I will definitely make your son alive if you bring some mustard oil from a house where no one has died. The king went door to door to get some oil and asked whether anybody has died in their family. But the king got disappointed because in each and every family someone had died. So after that the king went to the Buddha again, and the Buddha said to the king that anyone who takes birth on this earth has to die. And even lamas tell us that we should not cry or weep when someone is dying, because it only gives the dying person pain, and he won't be able to die peacefully.

People have to accept the fact that death touches all households. The presence of others at the home of the deceased serves as an implicit reminder of this fact, as they too have faced such losses.

Many help to participate in the work that needs to be done after a death. If the house is large enough, different activities take place in different rooms or areas. Women, especially close relatives of the deceased, work in the kitchen to prepare tea and food. Young men often assist in the preparation of materials needed for the funeral rites. Lamas read several sacred texts. Another lama or two lead a group of women and men in chanting and singing prayers known as *mani* on behalf of the deceased.[30]

The word "mani" works as an abbreviation of the sacred Buddhist mantra, "om mani peme hung," which invokes the powerful benevolent attention and blessings of Chenrezig, the embodiment of compassion. In a more general sense, the word stands for the sacred prayers performed during the funeral rites. These prayers can augment the karmic merit of the deceased, as well as other sentient beings, and so increase the chance of liberation of those receiving the merit. Most of the chants consist of prayers recited by a lama, followed by melodic refrains sung by lay women and men. Sometimes more than a hundred people participate in the performance of mani, which can go on for several hours. The refrains involve words that work as a coda for the prayer as a whole. The structure of the mani is a dialogical one, and a gendered one at that, with a lama reciting prayers and a group consisting primarily of women chorusing a refrain. A readerly male voice proceeds in counterpoint to the collective orality of women, text and voice woven together. The refrains, which many women know by heart, are sung in beautifully lyrical, heart-reaching terms. Voices generate a long white banner of a prayer that soars toward higher, purer realms.[31]

A mani refrain usually begins with a line, sung slowly, that includes the mantra "*om mani pe me hung.*" The prayer then advances words that appeal to a deity for guidance or assistance. One refrain, recorded at a funeral rite and later recited by Goser Lama, sounds as

Om ... ma ... ni ... pe ... me ... hung ... rhi
yidam thu-zjhi chhenpo rang khyeno.

Yidam is an adjective that means "tutelar." *Thu-zjhi chhenpo* is a name for the deity Phagpa Chenrezig. *Rang khyeno* can translate as "you yourself may know." Goser Lama glossed the meaning of the second line: "Yidam thu-zjhi chhenpo, you know all these things, and whatever deeds we have done, we have done, and now we are dependent on you. It is up to you where to guide us." Another refrain reads as

A ... la ... om ... ma ... ni ... pe ... me ... hung ... rhi
chhi ma denbe lama yidam thu-zjhi chhenpo
chhi ma bardo gi dhang le denbe chyakyu deno.

A loose translation of the second two lines reads as "You, tutelary lama The Great Compassion, the guru guide for our next life, like a hook that can snatch us from the bardo of the next life, guide us."

Any karmic merit generated through performing mani prayers is due to the fact that the prayers are enacted on behalf of all sentient beings. Since that act is a meritorious deed, the deceased receives the merit generated by it. "With the merits of this mani, may the person be liberated," goes one sentence of the prayer. By voicing powerful prayers, lamas, grieving family members, and supporting friends and relatives help the deceased in his aspirations for liberation or a good rebirth. Such is the intensive force of words.

Mourners perform the mani prayers in the first days after a death, during the tearful procession to the cremation site, and during the conclusion of the funeral rites several weeks later, when lamas ritually demolish the last tangible embodiment of the deceased. Any performance of the prayers invokes a larger sequence of transformation in sorrow. The sounds link to critical moments of transfer and farewell, of the deceased leaving the world and the living saddened by that passing. As each death brings a cycle of these prayers, any new voicing can recall previous deaths.[32]

"It's a kind of praying, but it looks like singing," said Karma when I was talking with him and Temba about mani prayers. "People are dying, and they are singing! But see exactly how much of poeisis is involved in that. And that's one thing that's specific to Hyolmo. Nowhere else is this found."

The two went on to tell me that other ethnic groups in Nepal, such as Sherpa and Tamang, find something "fascinating" in the mani prayers voiced at Hyolmo processions to cremation sites, so much so that they have come to imitate that practice in their own processions. They have also taken to hiring Hyolmo singers to hymn the prayers at cremation and funeral rites. "This has started here, in New York, as well—inviting Hyolmo people to do that."

"It's beautiful," I ventured.

"Yes, it's so beautiful," Temba said. "And it's so meaningful." "It's not just the lamas chanting mani," Karma added. "It's *singing* mani. But of course it's not singing to make merry."

"It's to generate good karma."

"Yes."

"But in a beautiful way, too."

"Yes."

Why is there such beauty here, in a space of death and mourning? Does the sonic force of this art form promote sentiments among mourners that they might not otherwise have in the days after a death? There's much to be heard in the mani prayers, even if there's no secure way of knowing whether such interpretations are correct or in play in any given situation. For one, we can hear the refrains as working within a broader service of *consolation*. The refrains are potentially restorative, recreative; they have the capacity to mend. They counter the despair and seeming pointlessness of a death. They provide an expansive terrain for the death. As the prayers are recited, the death continues to take form within a rich cosmography, a vast stretch of dharmic time and space stretching from the most compassionate of bodhisattvas to the neediest of sentient beings. A fragile, beseeching eloquence of a voice sounds out in the cosmos. In such eloquence there is defiance in the face of death, if defiance is the right word for statements counter to the banality of the death. Someone has died, but life perseveres. That life can entail a difficult, delicate joy, where there is at least the possibility of happiness.

Rhythm is needed. That's what's called for, a counterpoint to the heartbreak of grief. We seek patterns in time and space when life throws us off our stride, when we're struggling to maintain some sense of vitality. In the days after my father died, my mother, stunned by grief, took comfort in a rocking chair set by her kitchen table; she found the repetitive motion soothing. This cadence in a smooth, rhythmic space reminds me of the ways in which residents of a homeless shelter in Boston resorted to routines of pacing or reading in order to "zone out" for a while and keep their suffering and the distractions of life at bay.[33] I have found solace in listening to the alto flights of Charlie

Parker (tragic in his own death), or to Miles Davis's pensive clarity of mood, or to Bach's fugues, or by talking with friends or in reading or writing. Like others I step into forms of consistency not unlike what others call prayer. Notable within the institution of mani prayers is that friends and family provide a sustained, sustaining rhythm to those most in need of it. The solace comes by nourishing what has been destroyed.

The prayers are a matter of compassionate accompaniment, of assisting the deceased in his passage through the betweens, of staying close to the grief-stricken. Alternate rhythms pulse alongside the dark tones of death. How different this is from a world where mourners are left to go their grief alone, without the aid of institutions of consolation beyond those found in the first days after a death.

The mani prayers harmonize patterns of dying and grief. The melodic rhythms of the words stand in contrast to the disjointed speech and arrhythmia found with many acts of dying.

The tones bid a counterpoint to the despair of grief. "No worst, there is none. Pitched past pitch of grief," writes a poet.[34]Grief is destructive, singular, interior, isolating. It's unbearable, fracturing, obscure, and lowly. The mani refrains are generative, collective, inclusive, uplifting, lucid, and artful. They take people to a different place; they take the self away from itself. In showing forms of consciousness otherwise than grief, they articulate a different mood which, if never fully felt by the bereaved, at least lingers within the horizons of their thoughts. A person can lose himself in this kind of sonority. He might come to know death in a different light, or at least know that other rhythms can be voiced in death, some of them beautiful and heartening, alongside the hollow gasps of grief.

"Death is a void," Karma wrote on an earlier version of these paragraphs. "Music and rhythm reverberate in this void. The void works as the means to reflect on passed life and to connect to the next life. It gives positive perspective on the negative, for the dead and the living alike." There is more perspective in a stark space.

The music gives mourners a different kind of death than that which might stand otherwise, not one of dying happily but of attending to the loss in ways that suggest the continuation of life and sustained generation. This might help mourners to find a world again, and rejoin it.

The prayers create a calming sense of order within the chaos of death. They demarcate a space juxtaposed to the despair of death. They offer rhythms counter to the discordances of dying and grief. These different potentialities within the refrains are, plausibly, ever-shifting, taking form in variable ways with diverse intensities in effect at different times.

If we end up in between, kindly hook us. Art hooks us, transports us elsewhere. Music snares and turns us, consoles and shelters. It draws us outside of ourselves and leads to new perceptions in and about the world. "Music has a thirst for destruction, every kind of destruction, extinction, breakage, dislocation," suggest Deleuze and Guattari.[35] The mani refrains disrupt the stark aloneness of grief. The music moves people along. It turns them, leads them into different realms of consciousness. The prayers show the way (*lam den*), down along a path a bit, to a domain of feeling beyond the anguish of grief. The refrains offer mourners a way to feel and think otherwise about a loss that can be so devastating for them. While those wrecked by grief might not want or be able to heed that way of proceeding otherwise in the hours that the refrains are sounded, they might take on their sonorities down the road, in the weeks and months that follow, when something other than pain is possible.

Creative textuality, of a merit-making, sense-making, becoming-different sort, recurs in the days after a death. The prayers are a generative practice, a way of fostering marks, echoes, and karmic merit. They constitute a graph of writing on the karmic form of the deceased, whose consciousness and mental body, now somewhere adrift in the bardo betweens, lack the ability to act or to signify.

I first encountered the mani prayers as they were sung at a funeral. This was in 1988, in the initial months of my first stint of fieldwork in the Hyolmo region. I was living in Gulphubanjang. A woman had died in the neighboring village of Thodong several weeks before, and now the final funeral rites were being performed on her behalf, at her family's household, a homestead of a place set along a sloping hilltop ridge. Several lamas were established in a temporary temple set up behind the house, conducting the rites necessary to transfer her consciousness to the Land of Bliss or to a good rebirth. The woman's husband and sons sat there, looking blankly.

Just as these rites were coming to a dramatic close, toward the end of the third day of the funeral, another set of mourners gathered in a clearing alongside the foot road that branched through the village, in counterpoint to what was taking place on the other side of the house. I happened upon these efforts by chance, after watching the main funeral rites for several hours. The prayers started slowly as the women and men gathered discussed how they wanted to proceed. Dawa Lama, Ghang Lama's youngest son, took the lead in voicing mani prayers and using a set of cymbals to mark a rhythm.

Figure 10. Singing and dancing at the close of a funeral rite. Ghyang, 1989.

Women joined in on a few prayers at first and then participated in greater numbers as the pace gained in energy and coherence, the lama touching the cymbals together in time to the women's refrains. *So graceful,* I thought. Responding to the lama's statements with prayers of their own, the women formed a circle to which they walked, circumambulating an intangible center. Other women joined in, one by one or in groups, their footwork intricate, stepping along with the gait of others timed to the music. The force of their efforts and voices, the sounds of the lama's voice and the majestic clash of the cymbals took on an uncommon beauty as dusk set in. Soaring, becoming lighter, becoming rhythmic, moving on, life and death, life in death. Transfixed by the scene before me I stood to the side, watching, listening, waves of beauty surging through me, the sounds and gestures taking me outside of myself, turning me. The funeral rites now completed, the end of the mourning period formally marked, the rotating circle took more and more participants, women and men alike. The prayers turned, in the darkness that followed, into folk songs, songs of pain and heartache, flirting songs, drinking songs, with the men exchanging clever lyrics with the women gathered, back and forth, in counterpoint with each other, arms clasped in arms, intricate footwork, a sense of pleasure, excitement, verbal flirtation, being alive through the night among others.

Figure 11. Mani prayers performed at a funeral rite. Thodong, 1988.

Wearied by fatigue after midnight, flush with all I had taken in that day, I walked with neighbors back to Gulphubanjang, our flashlights in hand, voices and fires from the house behind us growing fainter as we scampered down the road, past boulders and soil. Back in my cabin of a home, snug in a sleeping bag and a sooty blanket, I could still hear some voices, carried by occasional winds. I fell to sleep, stunned still within the artful beauty of the sounds voiced around sunset, on that jagged hilltop. I wasn't expecting this kind of beauty at a funeral.

Years later, I came across these words:

> I reach from pain
> to music great enough
> to bring me back.[36]

PART III

Dissolution

Trouble

Prepare the body for the cremation rites. Decide on an auspicious time for the elimination of the corpse. Call on neighbors and relatives to help with these often stressful efforts.

This much I knew: that a woman had died the day before, and her body needed to be cremated. The ceremony was being delayed for some reason and I did not know why. When I asked when the rites would take place, several people told me they weren't sure. I found this odd, as usually an astrologically auspicious time for the cremation is quickly determined. News of the death soon was sowed throughout households in the area, and there was talk as to how to proceed, with raised voices. My grasp of Nepali and Hyolmo wasn't good enough to keep up with all the assertions and no one was inclined to explain to me what was happening. From what I gathered, lamas capable of performing the rites were reluctant to do so. They held off despite urgings of some. This ruptured the flow of ritual time. The body lay back at the woman's house in a remote area near Thodong.

I sat among others in the open area in Gulphubanjang, the village just north of Thodong. A meeting had been convened and men had just stepped into the home of Lhatul Lama, a respected and influential resident of Gulphubanjang. Krishna Bahadur Gurung (K.B.), a generous man who had introduced me to the region, was mediating the situation, drawing on skills from his trade as a social worker and diplomatic peace maker. There was a congenial air to his round face and kind eyes.

"Can I go inside as well?" I asked K.B.

"No," he said. "It's better that you stay outside, for now. You don't need to hear all this."

His response threw me. This was the first time I was excluded from a gathering.

K.B. joined others inside the house. I sat outside, on a painted wooden bench not far from women and children going about their days. Two boys drew diamonds and mandalas in the sand with small sticks. I heard the voices of the men, rushed and impassioned in the main room of the house. I thought of my first summer in Nepal, when I strolled through the streets of Kathmandu on dusky evenings and passed by homes with interiors warmly lit, families eating *dāl bhāt* and speaking languages I did not understand. That arrangement of interiors and exteriors came to mind while I sat on the bench.

K.B. came outside the house and sat beside me.

"What's all the talk about?" I asked. "Is it concerned with the delay in burning the body?"

"It's nothing too much," he said with a smile. "There is a dispute about animals grazing on another family's land. They're trying to sort it out now."

I took it that K.B. and others did not want me to know too much about the conflicts. They were perhaps concerned that I would write about them and characterize the region as vexed by disputes. "When you write about our village and our lives here, and the beauty of this place, the fresh air and water, people in your country will want to come visit, and that will be good for us," K.B. had told me that same season.

K.B. went back into the house. Twenty minutes later the men present at the meeting spilled out of the house onto the open path that runs through the center of Gulphubanjang. Some returned to their homes. Others loitered about. The mood had changed; ritual time cranked again. People's bodies relaxed, expanded toward the world. K.B. and others told me the cremation would be performed early the next day. I asked if I could attend the event.

"That would be fine," they said.

I did not learn more details of the dispute during that stay in Nepal. To press the issue would have been pushing against what people in the region wanted. I did not ask about it again. I took this as a strategy meant to gain the confidence of people whom I had come to know and trust in the villages.

I would not slice into any soreness. The tacit social contract was that my research should be attentive to some topics and not others.

Only in 2001, when I was living and conducting research among Hyolmo peoples in Kathmandu, did I learn more about what had taken place that October of 1988. I visited the home of a man who had been present at the meeting in Gulphubanjang and spoke with him about some deaths that occurred in the region. An audio recorder looped between us, preserving our words.

"A woman once died in a place near Thodong," I ventured between sips of tea. "The lamas did not do the cremation at first, because they had an argument with the family. I never understood what the cause or reason for that was. And, after having a big discussion, the lamas agreed to it. What happened then?"

The man's wife, seated in the room with us, took in my words. She looked at her husband and said a name.

The man nodded his head. He placed his tea on a small table.

"We thought that she was beaten by her husband and due to that she died," he said. "So the lamas refused to do the funeral ceremony. They thought that if they did the cremation then the blame might come to them, and they might have to go to the police. But later, after settling the dispute, they agreed to do the cremation. The husband was a drunkard."

"Why did they agree to do the funeral ceremony later?" I asked.

"Everyone later agreed that she did not die due to the beating," the man said. "It was all due to her *kal* [destined time to die]—and her husband's ignorance. As everyone became one in their words, the lamas agreed to perform the funeral ceremonies."

The man related his take on what happened in tones serious but straightforward. In situations where a person has possibly died at the hands of others, the police are supposed to be summoned to determine the cause of death. A few men did not want to cremate the corpse without clarifying the cause of the death, for fear that they too would be accused of wrongdoing. No one delighted in getting the police involved. The patrols, stationed a few miles away and fueled by the Nepali kingdom, could threaten or beat and liked to "eat" money.

The man appeared comfortable telling me what had happened, perhaps because the events were some years in the past, or because the dispute had been resolved in an unstaining way. Or he trusted me more now. Perhaps the tidiness of his explanation included only some of what happened. It's likely there was ongoing strife among families that piled onto the strains of those mournful days.

A group of men decided the fate of a woman's body.

The woman had lived with her husband and their children. This family struck me as different from the other Hyolmo families who lived in the region. They lived as if apart from others, the two parents, their four sons, and two daughters-in-law newly married on a homestead. They farmed terraced tracts of corn and potatoes sloping into a western valley and they gathered cut logs in neat piles by the side of the house. The mother, the woman who died, had two sisters who lived in the region with families of their own. I did not know her well. I passed by her home one afternoon on my way elsewhere. She sat in sunlight on a low-lying porch outside the house. Her hands were repairing the weave of a wicker basket. I voiced a polite "Namaste." She answered the same. I kept walking. This moment returns like a two-second clip of a home movie. I never came to know the woman's name. She had a calm formality and a quiet smile, as though the world amused her slightly.

They cremated her body the morning after the meeting. Residents of neighboring homes and villages came to the family's home early in the day to prepare for the procession to the cremation site. We sat in a somber room with little direct sunlight. The morning's dew chilled the room. We kept our coats on. The family placed cups of tea and bowls of *chang* before us on the mud-polished floor. "Please drink the tea," the sons said graciously. The tea's vapors wafted upward. The widower was slumped over, eyes to the ground. He shook his head and mumbled into his drink.

When all was set, a group of men and women began to sing mani prayers. The husband, wrecked with grief, was crying. He spoke to his wife, mumbled words toward the ground. We set off for the cremation grounds.

Seven weeks later, on a clear, crisp night in October, the family held the final funeral rites.

Eliminating the Corpse

Cremate the corpse. Perform a ritualized farewell as the body is brought to the cremation grounds. Dissolve the body into the elements of wind, earth, fire, and water.

A corpse poses a problem. An inert body is both of this world and of another. "He who dies cannot tarry," writes Blanchot. "The deceased, it is said, is no longer of this world; he has left it behind. But behind there is, precisely, this cadaver, which is not of the world either, even though it is here. Rather, it is behind this world."[1] For this and other reasons a corpse must be rendered into something more or less than what it is in that strange, hovering moment of lifeless life. "It's like a house," said Ghang Lama as we talked one morning in 1998. "If there's no one living in the house, then what happens to it? It decays." Anticipating the erosion, mourners eradicate the lifeless heap in a respectful, generative way.

Cremation is the most common method for disposing of a corpse. *Phungbo jhyanghe* is the Hyolmo wording for the cremation or "elimination" of a dead body. *Phungbo* can be translated as "corpse" "heap," or "aggregate"—the same Buddhist term used when speaking of the five "aggregates" or components that come together to make a person. We are reduced to fundamental forms in death. The verb *jhyanghe*, meanwhile, carries connotations of freeing, wiping out, taking away, subtracting, dissolving, extinguishing, clearing away.[2] A corollary aim of a cremation is to "wash away" all of the sins and impurities carried by the deceased. The body of the deceased is disaggregated in ways that clear away its existence as a built form in the world. This act is accomplished by burning the body, dissolving into the four basic elements that make up composite forms: wind, earth, fire, water.

"The body transforms into the four basic elements," Karma noted. "Everything turns into ashes, and then there's nothing there."

After a person dies, lamas conduct a set of astrological "calculations" (*tsi*) to determine a favorable day to cremate the body, as well as the best hour in the chosen day to transfer the body out of the household, and sometimes from what direction it should first be taken away from the house.[3] Most of the cremation grounds in the Hyolmo region lie on elevated lands, above and apart from where people step during their everyday traffic; these "pure lands," *sa tsangma*, are good places to extinguish bodies. In recent years Hyolmo people in Kathmandu, elders in particular, have preferred to return to the Hyolmo region when on the verge of dying in order to expire in the villages they take as home. Sometimes these elders walk on their own. Sometimes they are carried. Rarely, those from wealthy families are trafficked by helicopters hired for that purpose. If such a journey proves impossible, many want their corpses to be carried to the Hyolmo region in order to be cremated there, in part because the riverside cremation grounds in Kathmandu are thought by some to be spiritually polluted by the "burnings" of "outsiders," non-Buddhists. "I've seen five, six bodies brought up to Hyolmo in the past ten years," Nogapu told

Figure 12. A cremation site near Boudhanath, Nepal, 2001.

me in 2001. "Because they don't want to do the funeral here, they want to do it in the village." Bereaved family members can be seen transporting deceased parents and children wrapped in white clothes up into the foothills north of Kathmandu, by taxi or bus until the road runs out and then bodily along winding footpaths. Many Hyolmo families now residing in Kathmandu have held cremations at one of several sites in the Kathmandu Valley. Along with a place known as Jambu Ghang, a cremation pyre which rests on a sloping hill on the outskirts of Boudhanath, close to a neighborhood of intersecting roads called Jorpati, people often use a cremation site close to Swayambhunath, a sacred complex of temples that has stood for millennia now atop a lofty hilltop in southwest Kathmandu.

This is where Sange's father was cremated. "At that time," Pemba Dolma related, "there was no cremation place at Jorpati, as it had recently been made. His wish was to be cremated in Swayambhunath. Before his death he always asked us to take him to Swayambhunath when he died. He used to say, 'It would have been better if I died in Hyolmo, and was cremated in my own village. But as this is not possible now, take me to Swayambhunath.'"

Dhiti Rhama Dho, Teku Doban in Nepali, is another sacred site that rests at the confluence of the Bagmati and Vishnumati rivers in southern Kath-

mandu, close to Patan. I attended a cremation there in September 2001, held
for a wealthy lama from Tarke Ghang, three days after his death. I did not
know the family. Temba alerted me of the cremation the day before and said
that I could attend.

The home that morning was filled with mourners when we arrived. Each
family affiliated with the deceased had sent at least one representative to
home. They came to show their respect, to accompany the body, and to help
the family with the rites. Many mourners brought rice, fruit, and shalgar to the
household. These served as *tsho*, accumulated foods that are offered to deities.
Family members accepted these offerings and placed them close to the corpse,
close to the *shukpa*, a sacred, purifying incense from juniper trees.

Mourners arrived at the house in groups. They approached the corpse,
draped ceremonial scarves around its neck, and found seats on the crowded
floor. The family served food.

Temba and I waited with others on a narrow street beside the house. The
sun crested the rooftops of an unbroken line of houses and warmed the air,
cool from the night's chill. I had a camera with me. I asked Temba if it would
be agreeable to the family that I took photographs. He located a son of the
deceased. "He said it would be okay," Temba told me. "He has a nephew who
will be filming the cremation with a video camera, so you won't be the only
one taking pictures."

The appearance of the corpse at the doorframe brought a heightened intensity in the crowd. The body was held, upright, in a wooden box. This carriage was supported by two long poles, which the men rested on their shoulders. The body bore the clothes, ornaments, and the *rig nga* crown. The face
was covered over with a white cloth; to show the face itself would have been
too graphic a display. It would be too much, to have to look at the face itself,
too much to see, to remember. The covering over the face also detailed the loss
of the man's singular living identity.

Adult men only carried the corpse. They were sons- and brothers-in-law
of the deceased, Temba told me. Men of this social category often assist the
families into which they have married, during social occasions or ritual events.

The corpse faced its former home as the men carried it out of the house,
and the women sang mani prayers. They placed the carriage on the ground.
Several lamas performed the rites of farewell. Family members enacted gestures of farewell and good wishes to the deceased. The lamas blessed the body
with mantras and then touched butter to the forehead as a further blessing
(*yarka*).

Several men unraveled a lengthy white banner, some forty meters long. This banner, known as *lam-den* ("way-showing") or *lam-nga* ("way-leading"), showed the path to a good rebirth. The men held it in their hands and began to walk slowly with it, heading northwest along the road. The men lifted up the carriage, the end of the banner tied tightly to it. Some men blew conch shells and trumpets in a gust of percussive accompaniment. The group transitioned as a whole, their pace deliberate, in time with the lamas' music and the women's mani prayers, the white banner leading the way. Some shed tears.

"In our culture," Goser Lama later told Temba and me, "when a dead body is taken to the cremation site, all the members of the community join in as mourners and accompany the family in taking the corpse to the cremation site. It is a farewell, and a final departure from the human world. It's a support for and assistance to the dead person."

We threaded through the neighborhood streets. A young man on a motorcycle wanted to pass the group. Straddling his idling machine, he walked through the rows of mourners, horn quiet. They made way for him without missing a step of movement and music. A minor traffic jam formed around a man in an automobile who wanted to get past. In this bottleneck of the mundane and the ceremonial a ritual form was making its steady, patient way along urban streets on a weekday morning.

We came out onto the main street of Boudhanath. The procession recomposed itself along a busy thoroughfare and progressed toward the great chhorten (stupa) in the center of Boudhanath. We walked along the side of the road, passing electronics shops and markets, skirting food stands and restaurants. Cars and trucks jostled by; children watched us pass. The deceased's nephew wielded his video camera. I walked with the mourners and took photographs.

We cut through a jagged side street lined with clothes shops and arrived at the chhorten. The group walked clockwise around the chhorten. A man from Germany, a traveler unknown to us, recorded the spectacle with a compact video camera, light in his hands. The mourners circumambulated the chhorten three times, supporting the corpse and the white banner draped before it. They walked to the main street outside the area of the chhorten. Buses waited to transport them to the cremation site, along with the corpse.

Some mourners filled the buses and others climbed onto the backs of open-bed trucks. I moved too slowly to snag a seat on one of the buses. I spotted Nogapu starting up his motorcycle, on the side of the road. "Could I ride

Figure 13. Procession to a cremation site. Boudhanath, 2001.

with you?" I asked. Nogapu looked at me, glanced at the bike, and put his helmet on. "That would be okay," he said. "But the seat is kind of small."

I leapt on, slid off the back of the seat, and hopped on again. The buses started out. Temba hitched a ride with a friend on that man's motorcycle. We joined the procession as it sped around the Ring Road that circles the bulk of Kathmandu. I sat snug behind Nogapu, half off the seat, my hands clutching the back of his nylon jacket. Several young men traveled to the site with motorbikes of their own. They led the procession along the highways and side roads of Kathmandu while carrying five colored prayer flags.

Nogapu and I trailed behind. The flags, held upright, fluttered in the wind. "They look like a motorcycle gang," Nogapu quipped. The contingent of buses, cars, and motorcycles sped along the western curve of the Ring Road through a satellite of neighborhoods which had not existed twenty years ago. I tried to recognize locations I had visited by bicycle years before. We cruised past slower cars and taxis, a tractor driven by a man smoking a cigarette, a bus with no passengers in it, a large commercial truck from India painted in yellow and reds, a boy riding a bicycle, two dogs sniffing through trash, a three-wheeled taxi burning cooking gas. A group of schoolgirls dressed in light blue shirts and dark blue pants walked alongside the road toward a stand selling fresh mangoes. A man pulled a cart. A young woman wearing a white sanitary mask ambled alongside an older woman. We curved past Swayambhunath, its noble temples on a hilltop to our right. We threaded through a sudden cluster of buildings and stopped at a makeshift dirt parking area.

Mourners descended from the cars and buses and walked in groups to the cremation site. Many gathered in the shade along the steps of a magnificent temple, known as Japanatha Dagah, built in 1792, just south of the cremation site there.[4] The family had permission to construct a pyre to be used solely for this cremation, and they had built one of bricks several yards removed from the usual pyre. A lama purified the cremation grounds by chanting powerful mantras and sprinkling ambrosia water on the soil and cremation pyre.

Men retrieved the corpse and its carriage from one of the buses and set it on the ground. They lifted it up, circumambulated three times around the cremation pyre [pur-khang], and placed it on the ground. Mourners approached the body. They performed prostrations on behalf of the deceased.

The men took the body from the carriage. They relieved it of clothes and ornaments and placed it on the wood arranged on the cremation pyre. They encircled the body and wood with the white banner and laid incense branches on top of the body, now covered. The other mourners sat far from the pyre, near the temple, and collectively recited mani prayers. The family dished out potatoes and flattened rice, sweet tea, and salt butter tea.

Two men fixed the five flags in the ground, one flag for each of the five directions—east, south, west, north, and center—and their respective deities.[5] The funeral pyre and the corpse were associated with the "center" direction, the cremation site manifesting as the world more generally, a microcosm of the macrocosm. "The main thing," Karma later explained, "is to change the environment of the cremation site into the world at large. It's not the world of the living. It's the world beyond life, beyond the living."

The cremation site held the area where bodies are cremated as well as an open-sided structure set some fifteen meters from the cremation pyre, where the lamas could sit comfortably while performing the rite. The structure was architecturally synonymous with the temple adjacent to it, though graffiti clashed against the delicate woodwork on one of its walls. Someone had scratched out letters of the Roman alphabet, a few letters facing backward.

Built of brick, the pyre lay alongside a stack of bulky logs cut from trees. Two hundred meters away, the Bagmati River flowed within its banks. Between

Figure 14. Preparing a body for cremation. Kathmandu, 2001.

the area of the cremation site and the river, a strand of empty turf was drying in the September heat. Susceptible to flooding in the monsoon season, in this dry month a level patch of ground showed signs of recent soccer games, white chalk markings, a goal and sidelines.

The lamas prepared for the cremation rites. Once all of the texts, thangku scrolls, offerings, and ritual instruments were arranged and the corpse was appropriately positioned, they invoked the deities associated with their lineage.

Figure 15. Cremation ceremony. Kathmandu, 2001.

They performed a puja to Mhe Lha, the deity of fire, who represented certain other deities, and they transferred to that deity the responsibility to consume the corpse.

The head lama walked to the pyre and circumambulated it. An assistant handed him a lit stick and he set the woods and cloths on fire.

Burnt Offerings

Offer the corpse, along with other burnt offerings, to the Deity of Fire.
Wash away the misdeeds and impurities of the deceased.

When cremating a corpse, survivors are not burning any inert thing, like a log or chunk of stone. A body needs to be cremated in a calm, peaceful, and respectful way. The body is not so much burnt as it is dedicated to deities, as a sacrifice, which the lamas keep contemplatively in mind while performing the cremation rites. They should pray to the various deities to help the deceased's consciousness to reach the Pure Land and to refrain from sending it to any of the hell realms. The main text read during a cremation is known as *thu-zhji*

Figure 16. Prostrations performed by mourners. Kathmandu, 2001.

chhenpo, a name for Avalokitśvara. The words hold a series of prayers related to this bodhisattva.

In dissolving the body, eliminating it by fire, mourners offer a gamut of substances known collectively as *jhin-se*, to Mhe Lha. Jhin-se literally means "burnt offering." *Jhin*, *sbyin* in written Tibetan, means gift, present, offering, while *se, sreg* in written Tibetan, entails something consumed or destroyed by or with fire.[6] Families use jhin-se in several situations where a sacrificial offering to deities is appropriate. When a family completes the construction of a house, its members might perform a rite of jhin-se to give proper offerings to certain deities, an act which can bode well for the new household and those living within it. Within the context of a cremation, the substances are offered in a similar way, though here the fire also consumes the body of the deceased. The deceased can benefit from the offerings in any next life of his, in terms consistent with the qualities of each element.

At Dhiti Rhama Dho, the lamas placed the substances in the fire one after another, in a rotating manner, until four sets of offerings were bestowed to the fire. The head lama performing the rite placed small amounts of each substance in a special, long-handled iron ladle held by an assistant. The assistant carried the ladle to the fire and deposited the substance held by it into the fire.

Figure 17. A rite of burnt offerings. Kathmandu, 2001.

Those seated in the lamas' area shouted out the amplifying count of the offering being added to the fire.

"*Chi chog! Nyi chog! Sum chog! Zki chog! Nga chog! Druk chog! Dun chog! Brgyad chog! Dgu chog! Bcu chog Thumba!*"

"Onefold! Twofold! Threefold! Fourfold! Fivefold! Sixfold! Sevenfold! Eightfold! Ninefold! Ten and One hundredfold, complete!"

The assistant walked back to where the lamas were seated, held the ladle out to the head lama to have another substance placed within it, and returned to the fire, joined by another round of shouts.

"Onefold! Twofold! Threefold! . . . Ten and One hundredfold, complete!"

Through this calculus of increase, which lasted over two hours, lamas recited the prayers and mantras that accompanied the rite. Substances offered, other assistants tended to the fire, adding incense and ceremonial scarves dense with oil.

The fire grew in intensity. The corpse seared until it collapsed into the fire. The assistants took pains that all of the body burned within the flames. We watched, quiet.

The first substance offered to the fire was black sesame, known as *til*. This grainy organic substance was used because, when added to the cremation fire, all the sins and impurities embedded in the corpse would be transferred to it and cleared away through its incineration. After the assistant put til on the fire, the lamas offered several household grains, such as wheat, barley, and rice. These grains would be richly available to the deceased in any next life of his, and he would not go hungry. A species of a long, reedy grass known as *tabang tsa* was made into a burnt offering: the man's next life would be longer than his present one. The assistant placed pure branches of a broomstick in the fire. The branches wiped away all the sins and impurities of the dead body, which could help the deceased to reach the Pure Land. The lamas fed plants and woods to the flames. The deceased, if born into any next life, would live in a place abundant with vegetation and other forms of prosperous growth.

The lamas delivered some fourteen different substances in all. When each rotation of substances offered was completed, the men performed a rite called *mhe-chu*, in which oil was heated in a special container and placed on the woods of the cremation pyre. The head lama poured a pinch of liquor on the heated oil while reciting sacred words and engaging in a meditative visualization. The liquor hit the oil and a huge flame blazed fiery and explosive.

The burning of the substances benefited the deceased in two ways: they served as offerings to deities on the deceased's behalf, and they added to the deceased's store of karmic merit. After some time, the qualities associated with them—plenitude, long life, purity—would appear in the deceased's next life. "All of these substances are used," said Goser Lama, "in the understanding that, through their support, whatever kind of hard or bad life the person had in his present life, life after death will be full of joy and plenitude."

Dissolve, augment, transcend, cleanse, merge, sacrifice, burn away, transmute, complete, respectfully so—the rites were polyvectorial. The immolation was an artful, sacred elimination of the dead man's body. It built to the creative subtraction of a now-gone life. The eradication established a second death, one more glorified than the mortal demise that occurred days earlier. This death was regenerative, fruitful in spirit. It was a beautiful end, skilled in its means, transformative to its core, beyond the reach of the living—and point blank in its demolition.

Thirst

Be wary of the potent force of a burning body. Witness the fiery incineration of a once-living form and reflect on the fleeting grounds of human existence.

Figure 18. Mourners at a cremation ceremony. Kathmandu, 2001.

I watched as they prepared the corpse for its immolation. I watched as they set the body on fire. The nephew with the video camera stepped about, filming the events. He knelt on the ground, angling for a better shot. He looked like he was gathering different scenes for a documentary, cinema verité. I followed suit. I asked Temba if he could check with someone in the family, to make sure it was acceptable that I take photographs. He did so. I walked to where the lamas were, caught the eye of a man close to me, held up my camera, and said, "*Photo kichne, tik chha?*" The man nodded his head yes. Two other men, seated to his right, looked up and nodded. I took photographs of family members performing prostrations, of two men arranging the corpse, and of the body settled on the pyre. No one seemed to mind.

I did not know who the immediate mourners were. Nogapu pointed out the widow. She was seated at the base of the temple alongside other women, looking on.

The afternoon sun bore down on us in a cloudless sky. Many of the mourners and their guests were trying to find shade by the temple. Women placed their shawls on the tops of their heads to screen the heat of the sun. I finished the purified water I had in a plastic bottle. I began to feel dehydrated. The tourist's dilemma: no drinkable water. I did not see any place nearby to get some.

I looked toward the river, lax in its movement, trash lining sadly its banks, and spied a set of shops past the bridge that spanned it. It would take a good twenty minutes to reach the shops and walk back from there, and I didn't want to miss out on any of the burning. I considered asking someone to get some bottled water for me, an older boy or two, but I hesitated to impose on anyone.

I went thirsty. My throat clamped tight. I felt a cold coming on. The sun was unrelenting. There was work to do. The body, set on the pyre, sat like a king on a throne.

Most people left once the fire was lit. Women and men climbed into the buses, trucks, and cars and left for Boudhanath on dusty roads. Temba asked me if I wanted to go with them, back to the home of the deceased.

"I'd like to stay, if that's okay," I told him. "I want to see what happens, and then go back when the lamas do."

Temba boarded a bus. Nogapu stayed on. Remaining at the site were the lamas, their assistants, and a few others, like us. Few words were exchanged. We looked on. We grew pensive, watching the flames, the assistants plying their ladles.

Ashes swirled, soaking the air with a cloudy whiteness. The smoke hit us when the winds shifted. I moved places to get away from the funk. Clumps of soot lay in my mouth. I felt thirsty. I watched the pyre. This was the ash of a dead man.

The flames seared the man's clothes and the cloth covering the face. An arrangement of form was coming undone. The cloth melted smooth against the face. His face looked out at us. The head gleamed face-like at times, his human features, eyes, sockets, nose, mouth, jaw, cheekbones. In other moments it was less than a face, a bundle of features. A body's structures were shifting in ways I had never seen or imagined. The face was shorn of its protections, the man's demeanor, his garb and schemas, this man who was a husband and father, a child once.

The rites added on through the afternoon. The sun sloped over the canopy where the lamas sat. The midday heat broke. Children from the neighborhood idled on the margins, watching what we were doing.

The fires ate into the wood beneath the body. They touched the body itself. My photographs marked this passage. The assistants took the katha scarves, soaked in oil, and tossed them on the fire. Flames burst up, a wealth of combustion. Black, grainy death.

Smoke silted the air. Pieces dropped from the fire's bulk. Those tending the flames pushed these embers back into the burning mass. The body shifted from corpse to person, back to corpse. The body was turning into something else, eroding into nothing at all, collapsing into flames. Part of the crown slipped from the head.

The body was not a lifeless corpse, not fully alone. The face looked as though its owner was aware of what was happening. It looked resigned to its fate, bemused. The face was passive, inert, with no glint of sensation. Oil juiced into flame which burnt wood, grains, grass, cloth, and flesh of and beyond the world of the living.

We stood and watched. The body appeared to have consciousness to it, as though the dead man sensed he was being eliminated by fire. I identified with the corpse's plight. I did not want to do that too much, though. There was no awareness in the body to speak of. I wavered between distance and identification. I was conferring consciousness onto something unaware of its surroundings. That's me some day, I thought. That's everyone else here, too. The ends of a life.

I stayed on, throat parched. The lamas had dedicated the offerings to the fire. The body had blistered into embers. The men wrapped their texts in cloth and put them into cloth bags. They packed up the cymbals and conch shells. They walked away from the cremation site and boarded a bus. Someone must have stayed on and tended to the smoldering fire. I went back with Nogapu, hands clasping his shoulders, half off the motorcycle. I strained to balance. We stopped at a small bazaar on Ring Road to get some water. We drank, liquids cooling our throats.

We came to the dead man's house. We washed our faces in the water set out for those returned from the burning. We approached the burning juniper, set in a copper vessel outside the entrance. Nogapu bathed his limbs, torsos, and clothing in its vapors, and I did the same. We stepped inside, climbed a flight of stairs, and came to the main room of the house, an elegant quarter with an altar alongside one wall and thangku paintings draped on others. I spied Temba and stepped to his side. Mourners and guests sat leg-crossed, tea, chang, and liquors before them, spiced potatoes and dried meats served on shiny metal plates. Two lamas led the women and men in the performance of mani prayers. Voices lifted in their ascent. Several men occupied a separate room, preparing for further rites in the funerary process. Temba and I stepped to the threshold. Men were molding aspects of deities out of rice dough and barley flour. The men looked up, exchanged glances with us, and returned to their work.

We walked back to the main room and sat among others. The mood lightened as people ate and conversations hummed. I saw some smiles. Had the fullness of rice, camaraderie, and warm tea replaced the stark vacuity of death? Temba and I sipped from cups of salt butter tea. Liquid salts warmed my stomach. My right hand reached into a plate of rice and lentils and my fingers funneled the cooked grains into my mouth.

My brain and body wanted most to sleep. My eyelids sought to close. The force of an imminent cold, fused within my skull, gripped my throat. Temba told me they were going to perform a *ne par*, the first funeral rite, later that evening. I was welcome to stay and observe it. I wanted to do this. It had been years since I had seen a *ne par* ceremony performed, and never in Kathmandu. I was exhausted. "I'd like to stay," I told Temba. "But I think a bad cold is coming on. Maybe I should just go home and sleep."

Night had fallen. Women and men left after eating the meal. Many of them took with them a share of the food set up earlier in the day on the altar. Representatives from different households, men mostly, stayed on, to decide when to hold subsequent funeral rites.

I decided to leave. I gathered up my bag and bottled water, nearly empty, and stood up. I thanked the hosts and walked down a flight of stairs. I took a few steps from the house, dejected. A stronger, more intrepid researcher would have stayed on, to get that data.

I found the way out to the main street in Boudhanath and hopped on a three-wheeled tuk-tuk that took me a jumpy mile west, to Chabahil. I walked the rest of the way. The evening's car horns and people dashing about, their glances snared within mine, two children playing by the stoop of their house, a taxi driver cruising for passengers, a beggar's beseech, wore on me. I wanted to be free of the particles of life's intrusions. Once home, I told Pemba Dolma and her mother- and sister-in-law what had occurred during the cremation. I answered their questions as best I could, who was there and who was not. I went to bed and fell into a fugue of a sleep. Choppy images flitted through the dark. A man's arms reached toward me, vaguely.

I woke up late coming back to the world. Thick with a cold and a runny nose, I went through bundles of tissues that day. I wasn't sure of a good way to dispose of them. Constant swipes with the back of my hand made the tip of my nose raw. I managed, groggily, to write up notes on the previous day's events on my laptop. I saved all the words on my hard drive and made a back-up file on a diskette. "It's the face I remember most," I typed out, fingers soft against the keypad.

I nursed myself the rest of the day. In the evening I joined the family as

they watched television in the main room of the house. I rifled through the white tissues in my hand. We took in CNN World News. Video replays of tall, tall buildings, collapsing in a foreign city, filled the screen.

"Do people live in those buildings?" asked Ani, Pemba's mother-in-law.

"No, not so much," I said. "But a lot of people worked there. And many of them didn't get out in time."

I labored to blow my nose.

Ani set her eyes upon me.

"You see," she said. "You went to the cremation, and you stayed there. Because of the impurity you're sick now."

I nodded my head. *Ro dhip*. Corpse impurity. The dark, staining contaminants of the burning body had debilitated me, that was her comment. I had no means to argue with her.

It took a week to recover from the cold.

Ashes, Burnt Bones

Avoid the harmful impurities of the burning corpse. Leave the cremation grounds and cleanse bodies and minds of any lingering contaminants. Purify the deceased's cremated remains. Gather the remaining bodies and some ashes. Keep a single piece of bone.

Most of those who are free to quit the cremation site have the good sense to do so once the pyre is lit. The burning of a body is not a public event. Only those who need to stay at the site, lamas performing the rites and men assisting them, some ten or twelve in all, usually do so. There is no reason for others to stay on, close family members included. They can be more helpful by participating in prayers and contributing to activities back at the home.

Another reason people vacate the cremation site is that the burning of a corpse generates a harmful impurity known as *ro dhip*, "corpse impurity." Corpse impurity is a stronger form of *shyi dhip*, "death impurity." The miasma which emanates from a corpse intensifies when that bulk is burned. People say that those who are prone to "catching" this impurity can fall ill, or die even.[7] Many hold that, since women and children have weaker constitutions than men, they can be more greatly disturbed by the corpse impurity. Accordingly, women and children usually do not stay once the pyre is set on fire. It's not good for children to see a corpse being cremated, people say, since that unnerving sight can be "imprinted" in their minds. But any men not needed for the cremation rites leave as well.

When mourners return to the home of the deceased they cleanse themselves of the impurities brought on by the burning corpse by washing their faces with water and cleansing themselves with the smoke of burning juniper. Some also drink pure nectar, *dhichi*. A clean break is made from the grim perils of the cremation site. People move away from forces intense, obscure, and dangerous.

Once the lamas complete the cremation rites they return to the home of the deceased, usually some four to five hours after they commenced with the burnt offerings. The family offers them a kind of "gift," known as *ku-yen*, "body worth," for their religious service. One or two men will often stay on, sometimes through the night, until the corpse is little but ashes and charred remains.

"Gone to ashes," say Hyolmo people of the result of cremations. *Thala ghalsin.* "Ash" is the same word for "dust" in the Hyolmo language: *thalbi.* Like dust, ashes are disintegrated remainders of something once more fully formed. A cremated corpse is reduced to the four elements of the world. "There's nothing there now." There's no longer anything composite, assembled. A person's body is irrevocably transformed. And yet tangible, material traces remain. "I would prefer *ashes* as the better paradigm of what I call the trace — something that erases itself totally, radically, while presenting itself," or so writes Jacques Derrida.[8]

In the days following the cremation, until the smoldering fire is extinguished, lamas visit the cremation site early in the morning and "purify" the remains and "wash away" any bad deeds and sins of the deceased by sprinkling pure water on the remaining ashes and bones while reciting sacred mantras. This process is known as *thi sol* or more simply as *thi*. *Thi* carries connotations of "bath, washing, ablution"; when conjoined with the verb stem *sol,* the phrase implies a purification or ablution of a subject, commonly through the sprinkling of water on that subject's body or representative image.[9] Once again, by working on a dead body or its cremated remains, something is being done to the spiritual and karmic condition of the deceased. The act of washing also purifies the cremation ground in general. "It's to clear everything away, to purify it."

A single piece of bone is often preserved for use in the funeral rites. This bone, known as *rhiba,* serves as a material element of the deceased during the funeral rites.[10] The bone "hooks" and draws the deceased person's wayward consciousness to the location of the funeral rites. Later on, by pouring pure water over the bone through another act of purification, the lamas deem to wash away the deceased's impurities. The bone is the seat of the soul, say centuries of Tibetan lore.

Once the cremation fire is completely out the remaining bones and some of the ashes are gathered together. Some of these remains are deposited in rivers, some are thrown into the air from an elevated place, and some are crushed into powder and mixed with clay and made into small conical figures known as *tsha-tsha,* clay figurines. In this way, the four elements which constitute the body are offered to the four elements: fire, water, wind, and earth.

Along with the religious significance of these practices, a measure of care and respect is evident in the treatment of a person's cremated body. As Goser Lama put it, "The tradition of purifying and collecting the cremated remains and disposing them to the different elements seems quite good. It is a compassionate and worthy tribute to the deceased."

Odd, disrespectful it would be to leave the remains as they are. A fullness of effort comes with this. "A day after the cremation, the ashes and the remains of the cremation are also not left without doing anything," Goser Lama noted. The remains must be attended to, as though everything, including the remnants of the cremated body, calls for something to be done with it, through ritual deeds or respectful care. The situation calls for a repletion of activity. Everything has its ceremonial act. The family honors the body even after it is gone.

Finality

Reflect on the memorable, unnerving sight of a body being cremated. Consider what the elimination of a corpse says about the transient, fleeting nature of life.

Cremations weigh on those who witness them. They can stun and unnerve and reshape a person's take on life. They introduce the fact of death in a direct and tangible way. Those who watch a body collapsing into flames often retain vivid memories of that event. *I still see him in my dreams. I still remember the way he died, the way he was taken to the cremation ground.* What a burning body looks and smells like can leave its mark in the mind's eye.

Dawa Jyaba Hyolmo spoke of a cremation he and a friend helped to facilitate in the summer of 2001, the unsettling graphicness of which disturbed both men's sleep that night.

A few days back a child of a laborer died. There were many people at the cremation but among them no one agreed to go near the dead body. They didn't even know how to set up the logs. I have a friend who asked me to help him to burn the dead body, because the child who had died was the daughter of a laborer who worked for him.

I went with him and did the cremation and stayed there until the dead body was burned properly. Actually the place where the dead body was cremated was on a sloping hillside, and at that place the woods burn well enough, but the dead body wasn't burning easily due to the winds. This made me frightened. At around seven o'clock in the evening the two of us were there when the dead body was about to be burned. At that time an old man came and shouted at the people who were watching the process and told them that they were guests and they should be helping us. "Why aren't you helping them?" They slowly approached the pyre and helped us to finish.

The day after the cremation my friend phoned me. "The whole night I didn't fall asleep," he said. "Why is this so? *Hatērīka!* [Damn!] What we two did together, I could see it exactly. The whole night I couldn't fall asleep." And I told him, "If you're not used to it, this is what happens. This won't happen after a while." I myself felt scared while sleeping. I remembered for a while, but later on it didn't affect me much, and eventually I fell asleep.

The fire was burning the leg but the fire went out and the foot fell on the

ground. And my friend kept seeing that time and again. And after that I put
the foot inside the fire with the help of a long stick. I also remembered that
while sleeping. The foot falling, I could see it exactly. I thought that I myself
put that foot in the fire and it has already been converted into ashes. So it can
do nothing to me. And I fell asleep. But my friend couldn't fall asleep.

"I could see it exactly." Sharp sights linger acutely. One man told me of a
cremation performed sadly for a child who had died: "At that time, the baby
looked like it was sleeping, with her eyes open a bit and the mouth in a normal
condition. So she looked just like she was lying there."

"But my friend couldn't fall asleep." A common theme for those who witness
cremations—men, chiefly—is that, when they are young, the elimination of
a corpse frightens and disturbs. Later on, they are more familiar with this act
and become more comfortable with its terms. *"So it can do nothing to me."*

"And the foot fell on the ground." The limb's incongruent flesh, severed from
the body and charring flames, jibed with the harsh interrupt of the cremation
itself. The burning is an occurrence unusual, disruptive—something out of
joint, seared beyond the fabric of the everyday. People tend to these ghoul-
ish disjecta by giving congruence to them, telling stories, joking about them,
dreaming and fantasizing their presence, or holding true to the funeral rites
due a loved one. We want to put the foot back where it belongs.

The scene and scent of burning flesh entails a "limit situation," as philosophers and anthropologists have used that term in speaking of times in life
where something unconditioned appears—struggle, death, chance—which
brings people face to face with the existential realities of their finite presences
in the world. This can cause a person to face himself and the world in unprecedented ways. Suffering from a severe illness, facing a death, moving to a new
country, stunned by displacement or violence, or challenged in pressing ways
can bring a person to the border of what she knows of the world, with that encounter with uncertainty leading her to reflect on the grounds of her existence.
As Karl Jaspers put it, limit situations "possess finality": "They are like a wall
against which we butt, against which we founder."[11]

Cremations can stir a sense of finality among those who get close to them.
They breach the complacencies of the everyday and throw the mind off balance. They lead many to think about their lives and the nature of life and death
more broadly. Cremations work as a *memento mori*: you too must die. In many
Buddhist societies, adepts undertake a meditative practice wherein they sit in
charnel fields and contemplate the nature of death and impermanence. Get-

ting schooled in cremations drives home similar realizations. Confronted by the terminus of human forms, watching a body dissolve into emptiness, people grasp the futility of most human endeavors.

"When I was a little boy I would go to the cremations and I used to become very scared," Nogapu related. "Now when I go, I don't get frightened. But I get very sad, because we're also in the queue."

Standing at the precipice reminds people that we are all in line for what is slated.

They come to know of death and impermanence in a direct way. As Dawa Jyaba Hyolmo put it, "Those who participate in the cremation process gain at least some knowledge about death and the worth of life. With this knowledge, some people change their behaviors and attitudes toward others, thinking that love, compassion, and good deeds are all that we keep after death. In viewing the dead body being cremated into ash, Hyolmo people, even the young, come to realize that one should not act in ways that hurt others, such as cheating, troubling others, or other sinful deeds."

Nothing lasts for long, except perhaps the legacy a person and family can achieve in life, through good deeds and a good name. Cremations prompt the question of how a person might transcend time and impermanence. The burnings introduce an uncommon lucidity that makes clear the fact of death and the tenuous line between life and death. They force into effect a moral education. A perceptual and moral heightening occurs, making clear what matters most in life. I have faced such heated acuities as well. *It was the body of a dead man.*

"This is it. This is death," said Karma of the impact. "This is how our lives end. This is *chhiwa mitakpa*, death and impermanence." A feeling of frustration comes with that, he said. "But along with that comes the sense that, since we are going to die, we need to do something that helps others and start accumulating merit for the next life."

Witnessing the annihilation of a loved one's body can be especially alarming.

"What do you think is the experiential effect of the corpse being cremated?" I asked Karma. "How does that affect people?"

"The physical body turns into nothing, it turns into ashes," Karma answered. "And then, after that, people shift their attention to the spiritual domain of the person and the importance of cultivating merit. That's very important for the afterlife. That's the only thing you have, for the future. All the bodily things are nothing now. Whatever remains goes into *tsha-tsha*, and that's it. It reminds us that it's a phenomenon, everyone has to die. It is a phenomenon of impermanence."

"And for the near family, it's like a separation," Karma added. "That's the hardest thing to accept. It's difficult to realize."

"Because it's so final?" I asked.

"So final. There's nothing more now. That's the end of your relation to the physical body of that person—to the body that has done so much in life."

"Do you think the fact that this is so explicit helps people to move on. Or is it—"

"For some, it can be too much, really."

"Like a shock?"

"It could be a shock. Just to see the body turning into ashes, the body which has meant so much to you, so much to your life, turning to ashes, just like that. For someone really close, it could be really, really, ah—"

"Traumatic?"

"Traumatic, in that sense."

"And is there a way they can recover from that trauma? Do the funeral rites help with that?"

"Yes, in fact that's what's comforting," Karma said. "The funeral rites convince them that this is what they can do now. This is what you can do for the person whom you miss so much. That is it. There's nothing else you can do. The only thing you can do is dedicate whatever you can in the name of that person, and that's how you can connect yourself to this person."

PART IV

Transmutations

Resting Place

Conduct a series of rites within a spirit of relational care and support. Prepare a "resting place" for the deceased, made of bundled clothes. Consider this temporary haven as the material ground of the deceased's consciousness.

This is what you can do now. There is nothing else to be done for the person missed but to labor ritually on his behalf. Survivors have to step up, shake off the devastation of their grief, and respond to the needs of the passed-on one. Family members can no longer see or touch or talk or share food with the loved one in any reciprocal, tangible way. Yet the rituals mark a way in which they can convert their affections into new kinds of relation, more ethereal and removed from those of everyday life, grounded in ritual practices and the dedication of karmic merit to the deceased. Loved ones sustain allegiance and intimacy. Ritual becomes a medium of familial care and connection—of love.

This abiding sense of care was evident a few years back when an elderly man we shall call Mheme Mingmar died in his home in Thodong. I was residing then in Gulphubanyang, the town just north, but was in Kathmandu in the days of the death. I returned the day after the cremation, making the long, exhausting hike on foot, backpack crammed with muesli and rolls of color film, and a visa extension stamped in my passport. I learned of the death soon after I arrived. Some men were talking about it at a teashop. The sun had fallen behind the houses lining the street, a day's work done. One man held his son in his arms. They spoke in measured pauses. They looked outside the shop, at the glasses of milk tea, at the burn of cigarettes. They ventured a few more words. He had died of old age, after a mild illness. It could have been his destined time, his *kal*. He had spent years farming and "carrying loads." He cultivated a taste for millet beer. His family had long ties to the area, with strong kin connections to other families. He was well liked. He had an understated, gentle way about him.

A woman came to the teashop and stood by the door, listening in. She drew a cigarette out of her husband's pack and held the open end to her husband's lit beedi cigarette and drew in the heat of it. She listened, cupped the cold end of the cigarette in her fist, and walked toward her house.

I imagined the body being incinerated at the remote spot atop the ridge to the south, its ashes still there. I gave thought to hiking up there soon, to take a look.

The next morning I walked with a few women and men along the trail to Thodong. Two of the men, lineage lamas, had invited me to join them. We came to the house where the man had lived. My companions stepped inside. I shucked off my shoes, set them to the side of the stone, and followed them into the cool shade.

We sat on handwoven mats flush against the clay floor. The home was a modest one, a large, rectangular room and a loft of a storage area above the entrance. A hearth was built into the floor the long way from the door. A shiny metal chimney flowed from the back of the fireplace up to and through the roof, itself covered with sheets of aluminum siding. On shelves built along one wall stood well-kept, polished pots, pans, and dish wares, alongside jars filled with colored waters. I could hear chickens cooing in a coop fixed to the wall's outer side.

A young woman newly married into the household placed cups of tea before us and spooned out servings of tsampa. The man's wife sat to the left of the hearth, a ladle in her hand. She looked dimly into the embers of the fire. To her right sat her sister, tending a pot of simmering dal. A black pot dense with white, water-cooked rice idled on a back burner. Ghyang Mheme, a respected lama from Ghyang, a neighboring village set along the craggy hill jutting north, was performing a series of offerings close to an altar, his raspy voice the strongest, most reliable sound heard in those hours. We waited, expectant. The morning's wind picked up. The man's body was no longer there but his

Figure 20. A *malsa*, resting place. Boudhanath, 2002.

presence filled the room. Two dharma books wrapped in bright yellow cloth lay by the window, next to a worn paper notebook and a blue toothbrush.

Just before the altar, close to the hearth, sat a compact of clothes bundled in good form. The light brown fabric of a shirt and pair of pants could be seen, and a dark vest, folded together. These were the same clothes that Mheme Mingmar wore in life. A silk scarf lighted atop them. Food had been set before the bundle, along with *sur.* This burnt offering, a mixture of flour, butter, sugar, and milk, was producing an aromatic smoke, streaming into the air, an offering to sentient beings, consumable by the deceased.

The bundled clothes, together with the foods and burnt offerings, served as the *malsa*, the "resting place" for the dead man. Lonely and adrift is the deceased's consciousness as it wanders about during the liminal bardo, between one life and the next. Mourners treat the consciousness as being, presumably, confused, distraught, or hungry. It should be attended to, fed and kept company. To provide a mooring where the consciousness can repose and find a measure of stability, family members prepare the resting place in the home of the deceased, starting the day after the cremation. Some of the person's clothes are gathered together and arranged in a compact bundle. The family places new food before it each day, and sur is lit several times a day. The area that holds this bundle and the nourishments set before it offers a suitable way station for the itinerant consciousness through the weeks-long course of the funeral proceedings. The consciousness can rest at home, abide in the company of family members, take nourishment.

The clothes set in the resting place compare in a crisply visual way to a person resting in his home or on his bed. In effect, the bundled clothes stand in as a post-life, effigial body for the dead person. Clothes suit this purpose well, as they are closely identified with the person who wore them in life—especially in times and places where people had only a few articles of clothing of their own and owned at most one good set. As with a body, clothes are the holder of the person they envelop. Like names, bones, and photographs, they can be vestiges of the persons they indicate. In loss, people so often want something tangible to hold onto, to replace what has been lost.

People often consider the resting place to be inhabited, silently and casually, by the consciousness of the recently deceased family member. "While keeping malsa, we should not close the door to the house, or leave the malsa alone," Dawa Jyaba Hyolmo told me. "Because if we do this, the malsa gets upset and returns back. Mostly people tell the malsa that they are going out for some work: 'You stay here and I'll return back soon.'"

For many, the malsa localizes and materializes the deceased in a new but transient, substitute form. The logic of this siting coincides with Buddhist rituals more generally, in which deities, bodhisattvas, and other supernal beings take the form of icons and consecrated images. As Robert Sharf explains, "Buddhist ritual, both monastic and lay, bears a family resemblance to Hindu darśan, wherein the supplicant ritually invokes the presence of a deity, and both supplicant and deity behold one another. Darśan, for both Buddhists and Hindus, involved the use of consecrated images that served as the locus of the deity, the focus of veneration, and as a source of the rite's efficacy. The image was viewed not merely as a representation of the deity but as its animate corporeal embodiment."[1]

As the weeks march on, the malsa clothes stand in as a bodily locale for the deceased. The deceased's consciousness requires a mooring, much as a living consciousness does. The dead are localized. A concrete image replaces the unimaginable image of death. Family members and lamas relate to the bundled consciousness much as they would other spiritual beings hosted in their homes. They offer foods, treat it well, and communicate formally and informally with it. The dead and the living are less anguished, less lonely and adrift, for it.

These and other acts of concerned relation point to the ways the funeral rites involve a continuation of familial care and connection. The ethico-figural gestures evident in the everyday lives of Hyolmo people—hosting, supporting, befriending, consoling, guiding, nurturing, honoring, respecting, listening, caring for—take comparable form in the funeral rites. People try to relate to the dead much as they do to the living: in caring, compassionate ways. The catch to this after a person has died is that his vacant, intangible presence implies a situation in which the living cannot relate directly. A lacuna, a gap, roots how the living communicate with the dead. There's no tangible response in the face-to-face, call-and-answer acts of offering foods, speaking soothing words, or engaging visually with another. It's like talking to a person in another room, voicing kind words to a remote loved one but without ever hearing that person's voice in return. People do not know to what extent the other is there, or in what ways, or what kind of spectral consciousness is precisely involved. Mourners have to proceed in the faith that their caring efforts work to good effect. The relations involved are tentative, approximate to a patchwork of convictions, reckonings, and ritual know-how. The sharp limit marked by death— the living cannot go beyond it, they cannot know beyond it—unsettles the idea that intersubjective relations can proceed in clear and continuous ways. Engaging with the recently dead is like walking down a darkly lit stairwell, missing a step, and bracing in the dark. People grasp for what they know to be there and try to hold on.

The ways in which families relate to their absent dead bring into relief how they and perhaps all other peoples rely on ethico-figural gestures in relating to people in everyday life. And yet the gist of those gestures hints at this question: are we truly relating to our neighbors as much as we tend to think we are, in a strong field of connection, or are our relations to them much like relations to the dead, with our communications and gestures extending outward into a shadowy realm of tentative, ghostly presences? What range does the gestural have? We think we know those we relate to, but how much do these presumed connections involve a patchwork of tentative guesswork, social conventions and know-how? The ways in which we relate to the living might not be all that different from how Hyolmo people relate to the dead. Are we trucking all along in faint connections and phantom gestures?[2]

For me, sitting close to the bundle of clothes was unsettling, entirely new. This was a visual jolt to my conventions. The bundled clothes stood in for a person, much as a corpse could. The resting place spoke to the man's continued presence in the world, but that presence had irrevocably changed, a delicate, dimming form. The man was at once there and not there. My companions that day did not seem troubled by this shadowy presence beyond the overwhelming fact that someone they knew dearly had shifted on. I kept returning to it.

A few more people arrived at the home that morning as the rites sounded on. Mostly close relatives and lamas known to the family, they had come to support the family and help with the rites to be performed that day, the fourth day after the death. I felt like an outsider included within this small span of families.

We were there for the *ne par*, the first major ritual performed on the dead man's behalf, now that his body had been extinguished.

The ritual draws its name from the fact that, at the crux of the proceedings, a lama summons the consciousness of the deceased and transfers it to a piece of paper known as a *jhang par*, or *ming jhang*, "name card." The lama burns the print just as he "elevates" (*par*) the consciousness to the Pure Land of Amitābha. The rite is known as *ne par*, "dwelling-elevating." The consciousness is elevated, lifted up, and transported to a purer, more enlightened realm.

The ne par is usually performed in the home of the deceased or in a Buddhist temple (*gompa*). The rites commence in the morning and conclude in the early evening of the day chosen. This is not a particularly social event, like the procession to the cremation ground is, and few people are invited to attend. Present mostly are family members, close friends, and relatives, and the lineage lamas who perform the ritual. The purposes of the ne par rites are essentially fivefold: 1) to send the consciousness of the deceased to the Pure Land; 2) to enhance the understanding of the deceased that she is dead and needs to leave the world of the living and seek a good rebirth; 3) to further reduce or "cut" any attachments the deceased might have for the world of the living; 4) to explain to the deceased what will happen during the intermediate between, and what funeral rites are being performed on its behalf; and 5) to augment the deceased's store of positive karma, while lessening his share of sins and negative karma.

Transfer, enhance, reduce, detach—and explain, ritually so. "Ne par is done," said Goser Lama, "to make the dead person's consciousness aware that he is already dead, so that it doesn't have any confused ideas that it's still alive in the human world. It's also to send the consciousness to the Pure Land."

A ne par rite is often performed on a weekly basis until the final funeral ceremonies are conducted seven weeks after the death. Most families nowadays perform the first ne par for a deceased family member "three and a half days" after the death. In effect, the rite is usually performed on the fourth day after the death. One reason for this timing is that it's thought that a recently deceased person is likely to become aware that she is dead around this time. By performing rites on her behalf then, the living can communicate effectively with her as well as help the consciousness to reach the Pure Land.

Some contend that the recently dead sense the flow of time in ways different than the living do: one week for the living is perceived as one day by a dead person. Since a recently deceased person, unaware that he is dead, would return home half way through his day to eat with family members, if the ne par ritual is held three and a half days after the death, there is a good chance of catching the deceased at home, as it were. Foods offered can alleviate the dead person's hunger, while words can advise him of his status.

Family members often find a grain of solace in these gestures of support and connection. With the loved one's embodied presence no longer existent, they can still act in the name of that person. They can dedicate merit on his behalf and assure a good rebirth. They can offer foods and talk some. The separation is not so sharp or final. How do we maintain relations with the dead?

When people came to the home that day they placed foods and drinks on the table set before the resting place, along with sur. The foods were dedicated to an array of deities and to all sentient beings. The abiding idea was that this dedication accrued karmic merit for the deceased. The foods also served as an offering to the deceased, one which could satiate his desire for food. I was later told that the dead man was unable to eat the existing food and drinks as they stood; he could only consume them through their smell and vapors. Yet by taking in the aromas produced by the sur, "the best food for the consciousness of a dead person," he could satisfy himself.

Family members performed prostrations on behalf of the dead man. They conceived of the dead man as a buddha and performed prostrations to that deity. The prostrations generated karmic merit, dedicated to the deceased. This act supported the dead person's efforts to reach the Pure Land.

Close relations offered foods to the deceased. They took some of the foods in their hands and held them out toward the resting place, but with arms crossed.

I asked about the crossed arms a few days later. No one was certain as to why the foods are offered with arms crossed, though some thought it might be done to signal to the dead person, in stark and conceivably offensive terms, that he is dead and so further "convince" him that this is so. The act makes certain matters known to the deceased and so shapes his consciousness in death.

Yet it's also thought that this how the transaction must be done, for only in this way can the dead consume the foods being offered to them. "Dying is the opposite of living," one man mused. "If the dead were offered foods in the same way the living are, they wouldn't be able to have them. So in order to make it possible for them to have the foods we have to offer them in a way opposite to how food is offered to living persons."

Wrist marked against wrist, the crossed arms clarified the terms of relation in death and the necessary divide between the living and the dead.

Ritual Poiesis, in Time

Perform a series of echoic, polysensorial rites on behalf of the deceased. Seek a measure of comfort in these ritual gestures.

After a death, then, and the elimination of the corpse, the family sponsors a major ritual each week, up to seven weeks, with an array of ceremonial efforts and mournful sentiments. To understand well what's going on with these rites, it's necessary to give thought to their phenomenal form and so appreciate the ritual practices in the concrete *phenomenality* of their terms. It's important, that is, to consider these rituals "in their own right," as anthropologist Don Handelman and his colleagues have advocated for the study of ritual more generally.[3] Rather than assume that the rituals serve as "texts" that comment allegorically on the nature of sociopolitical life, as several well-known theories of ritual advocate, their phenomenal form and experiential force must be taken seriously, from the start.

The funeral rites are practical and polypurposeful; they invoke multiple, overlapping purposes and rhythms, like a work of polyphonic music. The methods and modalities of the rites cannot be fully traced out; they go beyond any clear reading or interpretation. The ritual strategies are concerned primarily and most overtly with the fate of the deceased. "All of these rites are dedicated to the smooth transition of the deceased," said Karma. One has to take the deceased *seriously*. Their concerns and destinations shape how survivors relate to them. The dead person has a kind of subjectness, a consciousness with needs and desires, even if all this is imputed. People undertake the rites not so much to facilitate their efforts at mourning the loss but to aid the consciousness of the now-gone self. With those efforts come a gamut of ritual techniques—cleansing away sins, generating merit, satisfying desire, reducing attachment, clarifying the terms of death, saying goodbye, extinguishing the

Table 1. Hyolmo Death and Funeral Rites

Ritual and Social Actions	When Performed
consciousness transference (*phowa*)	usually in the first hours after a death
cleansing and preparing of the corpse	during the first days after the death
reading of the *Liberation upon Hearing in the Between* (*Bardo Thedol*)	during the first days after the death, and often after that as well
consoling the bereaved family (*sem so bheke*)	during the first days after the death
prayers (*mani*)	during the first days after the death
burnt offerings (*sur*)	during the first days after the death, and often after that up to the 49th day
dedicating the five sensual pleasures (*doyen ngogen*)	sometime during the first days after the death
cremation; "eliminating the corpse" (*phungbu jhanghe*)	usually 2nd or 3rd day after the death
collecting the ashes and the burnt bone; identifying any relics (*ring sel*) found among the cremated remains	the morning after the cremation
"residence-elevating" funeral rite (*ne par*)	often on the 4th day after the death, and on a weekly basis after that, up to the 49th day
"merit-generating" funeral rite (*ghewa*)	between the 4th and 7th weeks after a death
"period of seven" funeral rite (*dhinda*)	on the 49th day after the death
making of religious figurines (*tsha-tsha*)	after the funeral rites are completed
anniversary memorial rite	one year after the death

sensorial grounds of its existence—that modify the status of the dead person. A transmutation of life is at stake. The rites might well be thought of as a "technology (*techne*) for bringing forth, or *poeisis*," to quote anthropologist Bruce Kapferer, who advocates such a take on ritual more generally.[4] "Ritual, or at least some events defined as rituals," Kapferer contends, "can be grasped as technological apparatuses . . . as artifices or technologies designed to work within the elements and fabric of human constructive existence (physical, mental, material, relational, etc.) so as to (re)generate their personal, social, and cultural continuities and possibilities."[5] Hyolmo funeral rites consist of technological apparatuses, of a decidedly tantric sort, that refashion the existence of the deceased.

The rituals aid the deceased in his journey, people say. That's clearly how most perceive the rites and their progress in time. "The mourning rites are not for the mourners," Karma once told me. Still, I have found that the rites bear within their reach certain imaginal, sensorial, and cognitive-emotional operations that might aid in the attenuation of grief. Specific modulations in the chemistry of memory, sorrow, and longing recur in diffuse and quiet ways as the weeks of ritual striving jog on. A shadow technology is at work in the rites and in the lives and consciousnesses of the bereaved.

The architecture of the rites is modular and recombinative. As is the case with Tibetan Buddhist tantric rituals more generally, they are composed of "distinct subritual pieces"[6]—visualizing a deity, cutting negative karma, transferring a consciousness—that cluster together in specific ways for specific purposes. Combined, individual rites form a larger ritual complex that drums on through a seven-week stretch. Rites performed on a specific day or week, consequently, must be grasped on their own terms and within the ongoing framework of the funeral rites as a whole. This ritual arc begins with the treatment of the corpse after the death and ends with anniversary rites conducted by the family a year later.

A narrative quality girds the rites. In commenting on the design of Tibetan rituals, José Cabezón justifiably argues that "the relationship between the elements, the relative positions of the parts vis-à-vis one another, and the relationship between parts and whole give rituals, I would contend, a *narrative quality*. Understanding this aspect of tantric ritual—its logic, or, perhaps more appropriately, its 'storyline'—is an important part of understanding such rites."[7] So it is with Hyolmo funeral rites: their consequential logic, their story-like structure, speaks to the transformation of the condition of the deceased and the transmutations of grief. The funeral rites pose a tale of loss and change through economies of memory, sense, and imaginative form.

The main figures within this story-like ritual complex are, along with the consciousness of the recently deceased person, a number of Buddhist deities, Buddhist priests who perform the rites, surviving family members, and friends and relatives of that family. These participants in the "ritual gatherings" play an important role in the efforts and transformations afoot.[8] The funerals prompt a rich field of relations and correspondences. Modifications in the deceased's post-life status emerge out of the ethics of care foundational to family and communal life.

That pervasive sense of collective care can also console the living in their grief. In talking with Karma once, I made note of the communality evident during the funeral rites.

"I've been struck," I said, "by how comforting it seems to be to have the whole community come together, in respect for the person who died and for family members. And I wonder if that helps people with the grieving process as well."

"Yes, it does."

"Because you see the care that people have for this."

"Yes."

The active responsiveness of the living to the needs of the dead offers the solace of ceremony. It also actuates ritual sequences in a time of rupture, which could possibly help mourners to get on with life. In his discussion of elegies in Western literature, Peter Sacks notes that "the emphasis on the drama, or 'doing,' of the elegy is thus part of the crucial self-privileging of the survivors, as well as a way of keeping them in motion, ensuring a sense of progress and egress, of traversing some distance."[9] The funeral rituals keep mourners in motion, nudging them on to currents of life that, in time, come to differ from those painfully at hand in the first days of a death.

The rites are echoic. Ritual motifs recur time and again. These motifs reflect aspects of life more generally, in ways both apparent and ghostly. The serial organization of the funeral rites builds on a poetics of difference-through-repetition and echoic recursiveness. Motifs repeat in variations fundamental to life and death. Images of presence and absence, form and emptiness, making and unmaking, and continuity and cessation circle through this ritual play. Ritual here carries the form of no-form.

The rites are polysensorial. Sights, sounds, scents, tastes, and textures weigh into how the rites proceed and how mourners and the dead alike experience their unfolding. Words printed on a page cannot do justice to the rich sensoriums of Hyolmo rituals. Those involved hear effusive lamaic music, they consume foods and aromatic scents, they speak to the dead person; mourners touch on the fabric of loss and continuity. It could be argued that, much as holding and viewing the body of the dead person helps to confirm the reality of the death in a mourner's mind, so the rich sensorial grounds of the funeral rites help both the living and the dead to realize the death. *Yes, it's death*, the senses sense.

The rituals prompt fields of attentiveness. Their dramatic, intensive features require notice. The rites get—and keep—a person's attention, be they any mourners attending the rites or a deceased person looking on, silently listening. It's like someone who says "eh, eh . . ." and gets you to look at the form and movement of his hand.

Crucial here is the fact that the rites occur in time. Not just some pure, timeless construct of thought and action, the funeral rites are grainy with time. Beaded together in the hours and weeks after and before a death, the rituals are of time, about time; they show time at work; they take time to perform; they keep time, the time of ritual process. They show how time necessarily includes elements of repetition, change, and difference. The ritual efforts nudge mourners and onlookers forward in time; they get the world going again. They return mourners to a flow of time—ritual time, calendric time, astrological time, karmic time, the time of family and social life.

Through all this is a driving, rough-pulsed beat of transformation. Nothing stays the same for long; everything tilts into something else. Time and again, image after image, the rites enact specific alterations of thought, awareness, perception, and sensation precisely required in the moment. Those undertaking the rites strive to "call" and "hook" a roaming consciousness, locate it, shelter and imagine it, feed and nourish it, move it along. They alert that consciousness and relate to it while ending the terms of such relations. They make the consciousness rethink the grounds of its existence, change the aggregate of its form, dissolve it, prompt its transcendence. Central to such shaping and reshaping is a creative making, a generative fashioning of sense and consciousness that serves to aid the deceased's plight while tending to grief and longing. Nothing remains itself for very long; one moment flows into the next. Verbs, not nouns, constitute the language of ritual. Mindful of this, I am tempted to take a pencil and write the word "change" in graphite marks cutting diagonally across the pages at hand—or encourage any readers to do so.

Dragging, Hooking, Naming

Hook the deceased's consciousness and drag it to the site of the funeral rites. Inscribe the name of the deceased on a card that serves as a material sign of the deceased's tenuous absence.

I sat and watched through those hours of ritual pronouncements and tea and quiet conversation. I did not know it at the time, but next to the bundled clothes, close to the foods set before it, was a small piece of bone. Retrieved from the ashes of the cremation, it was wrapped in a small silk scarf. This bonelet, a solid, fleeting remnant of the dead man, helped to draw his consciousness to the site of the ritual and anchored it there.

For the funeral rites to be carried out in an effective manner the consciousness of the deceased must linger within the vicinity of the place where the rites are being enacted. The consciousness, otherwise adrift in its wanderings in the between, must be summoned or retrieved—much as a spirit is called and "hooked" during spirit-calling rites performed by bombos and lamas.

The charred bone, retrieved from the cremated remains of the deceased, can aid in this endeavor. By placing the bone in the resting place, lamas can "drag" or "hook" the consciousness to the resting place and to the site more generally of the funeral proceedings. The consciousness, which is attracted to a physical locus of some sort, gravitates toward the residual, material grounds of its now-gone self. Its attention is now captured, summoned, like a lost soul being called back home. Spirit is linked to matter. "From that day on, we think of the consciousness as being there," said one man. The deceased's impurities are later washed away by pouring pure water over the bone through another act of purification.

"The bone is important to have," Nogapu told me. "If you put the bone in the resting place, next to the clothes, then the consciousness will come there. If a person dies and is cremated elsewhere, then they bring back the bone, and the clothes, so they can do the funeral rites."

The ritual sensibilities call for a material artifact or re-indication of the deceased's body. The object anchors the deceased's consciousness in a tangible, workable form. The dead person's image is ontologized, once again.

The bone serves as a stand-in for the corpse, which has since been cremated. "It's the same as the dead person's body," one man told me. The bone is a now-transformed, still-kept vestige of the person's life. But it's also different from the corpse in form; the body is reduced to a singular, crystallized element. The living person is now gone. Still, through the effectiveness of that bodily remainder, the bone can be used to lure the bodiless, wandering consciousness to the scene of the funeral. As the rites proceed, the bone serves as a "support" and material ground for the consciousness. By acting upon the bone, by washing it or placing it next to the bundled clothes in the resting place, one can act on the condition of the deceased.

It's not strictly necessary to have a rhiba bone. But some "remnant" of the person that was—be it his name, a piece of clothing, or a bone—must be used to attract the consciousness "like a magnet" and summon it to the funeral proceedings. Names, clothes, bones, or other belongings entail distinct, self-owned elements of the otherwise intangible now-gone self, which returns to the space of a home.

The bundled clothes and the charred bone were two in a series of objects that served as images of the dead man in a complex visual poetry of grief, memory, and ritual transformation. But these corpse-images were fleeting ones. Once they served their ritual ends, they were withdrawn. The resting place was dismantled, the clothes given away. The lamas ground the bone into powder and mixed it with clay to form the small religious figurines known as tsha-tsha.

The sun bore its way across the hill above Thodong. Children minded a band of water buffalo near a grassy bluff toward the trail to Gomden. The lamas read from their texts, sounding the words methodically, patiently. We heard voices coming closer to the house, their bearers not yet visible, coming closer, the rustle of shoes on stone and wood ever nearer in sound. I noticed the force of shadows and heard footsteps by the doorway, quiet talk. A man and woman stepped into the home. A boy stood by his father. An infant girl was held with a cloth on her mother's back.

The family served food to the dead man. We ate as well, using our right hands to draw from the potatoes, flattened rice, and ground chili that filled our plates. We drank salt butter tea. Two men sipped from glasses of heated raksī.

The lamas resumed their efforts by the altar. An assistant fixed a stick on a stand, rooted in some barley clay. Attached to the stick was a piece of rice paper with block printing on both sides. On one side of this paper, known as a *jhang par* or *ming jhang*, "name card," was an iconic image of a human being replete with religious objects: butter, lamps, food, gold, silver, ornaments, a mirror, a bowl of water. Sacred Tibetan letters were inscribed on the body of the person pictured. The image represented the body of the deceased. On the other side were a few lines in Tibetan script, with a series of ellipsis-like marks (. . . . . .) set in the text. These words stood as a prayer.

The name card is a semiological device. The word *jhang* relates semantically to the Tibetan words *byang* and *byang-bu*, which carry meanings of "tablet," "piece," "label," an "index" of something more general; *byang-bu* is "a bit or piece that indicates something else." Janet Gyatso has observed of the signification of *byang-bu* as a label: "Here the piece acts specifically as a tag or a codicil, whereby a section of an object serves as a marker, carries some sort of identifying information, and points indexically to the object as a whole."[10] Gyatso also notes that, in Tibetan Buddhist societies, a *byang-bu* can serve

Figure 21. The two sides of a name card.

as an identifying label which is separate "from what it signifies and becomes its functional substitute": "This occurs in ceremonies for the dead, where a *byang-bu* acts as an effigy, a substitute for the deceased, at which are directed prayers, instructions, and other ritual acts to guide the soul and purify the deceased of sin. . . . In yet other death rituals, a *byang-bu* card is used that has an iconic image drawn on it, in addition to an inscribed name."

In Hyolmo communities the name cards used during funeral rites likewise imply an index or simulacrum of the deceased. When such a card is employed during the funeral rites, the name of the deceased, "the passed-life one," is written in the elliptical space given in the card. Once the name is inscribed, the card serves as a material sign of the body and the worldly aspects of the deceased's now-gone life. The card gives a tangible, textual presence to a figure no longer capable of being present.

Subsequent ritual actions work to "purify" the sins and impurities of the deceased, with the petition for that purification spelled out in the prayer inscribed on the paper.[11] The prayer on one name card translates as:

> The one who passed away, from this impermanent world to the other, the passed-life one, ..., may all the sins and impurities, accumulated from his first life on, be dissolved.

Another reads as:

> Prostrations from the passed-away one, the one who passed away from the impermanent world to beyond, ... ; with prayers and offerings, may his sins go away; protect him from sansara, and grant him refuge from the three lesser worlds; wipe away all sins and impurities; burn the receptacle toward Bodhicitta; may he immediately obtain enlightenment; Rinpoche make sure this is obtained.

It makes sense that a set of graphic marks comes to signify, embody even, the gist of a person. Textuality for many people is on a par with bodiliness. Both texts and human bodies entail graphic traces. Both can be "written" on and read and interpreted. Text and bodies alike hold the spirit, the "consciousness," of that which they incarnate. Both mediums carry elements of the sacred. Texts as well as bodies can be incinerated, with their more immaterial aspects moving on. A body is a corpus of echoic signs. A text is an aggregate of graphic traces. The name card simulates, much as a corpse does, the provisional emanation of a subject no longer present.

"Images were first made to conjure up the appearance of something that was absent," writes John Berger.[12] Berger's chronicle has relevance for Hyolmo funeral images: they conjure up the presence of someone who is absent, someone who no longer has on his own the capacity for bodily presence. The images indicate something else, something that cannot be indicated otherwise than through images. A person needs to be pictured in death. Mourning, Jacques Derrida contends, "consists always in attempting to ontologize remains, to make them present, in the first place by *identifying* the bodily remains and by *localizing* the dead."[13] Some tangible remnant or semblance must be used to allow mourners to relate to the deceased, visualize him concretely, and perform ritual actions on his behalf. And so there is a bone, or a resting place, or a name card.

The name is written by the hand of another. The deceased can no longer sign his name. A radical alteration of language and agency occurs in the time of death. The once, now-gone singularity of a person's speech takes the form of a single written name, inscribed by another. The fact that a person's name will be inscribed in this manner, after the death, by the hands of others, undercuts the permanence and stability of a person's name through a lifetime. Through the course of a life, one signs one's name with the implicit knowledge that that name will be taken away at some point, that the name, in death, will no longer be signed by the bearer of that name; and then it will cease to be written altogether. A name is provisional, fleeting, impermanent in its terms. It's as though the ellipsis that designates the space-holder for the person's name, on the name card, in the time of death, follows the name around in life, like the fiery tail of a comet. The elliptical space, vacant, hollow, is a portent of events and signings to come. From the first days of its worldly existence, from the first naming in life, the self is elliptical, already empty of inherent, lasting existence. Any name is elliptical: ellipses are built into the structure of a name's articulation and reception.

The ellipses, in the space and nature of their marking, suggest the form of a life or a sequence of lives: a series of moments and the spaces in between. Ellipses likewise constitute the forms of a ritual.

The dead man was named, formed, and dissolved during those transformative moments. Signifying here was a gesture of care. To picture the man in image and name was to sustain relations between the living and the dead in increasingly altered forms.

Name someone until that person no longer has a name, or needs one.

Explanations, Face to Face

Communicate indirectly with the dead person, who remains silent. Explain to him that he is dead, that he can no longer dwell amongst the living. Detail what is being done to aid in his plight.

The rites built in intensity as the day shaded into late afternoon. The head lama drew from prayers and mantras in calling the itinerant, bodiless, consciousness of the deceased. He summoned the consciousness and hooked it to the location of the room where the rites were being conducted. He established this soul-like presence with the name card. By fusing it so, the simulated body was conjoined again with the consciousness associated with it, body and soul. The lama engaged in a meditative visualization that enabled him to imaginatively construct the physical features of the dead person.[14] He skillfully rendered the man's body, face, voice, laugh, and gait. He invoked the image of a person in order to relate to and transform that person.

The lama reconstituted the body of the deceased, with consciousness intact. But he did so in a provisional, makeshift way. The name card was one of several material images of the deceased that were invoked and then dissolved during the funeral process.

The lama's assistant held a mirror up to the deceased's resting place, such that its reflection appeared on the surface of the mirror. A pure, sacred ambrosia water known as *dhi-tsi* was poured from a vase just before the mirror. As the water streamed over the image of the clothes—and over the image of the dead person—the sins and impurities of the deceased's consciousness were "washed away." This purifying process, known as *thi-sel* (the same term is used to depict the act of purifying the cremation ground after a body is cremated), made it more likely that the deceased's consciousness could reach the Pure Land.

No images of any living persons should be cast into the mirror. If that were to occur, the person reflected in the mirror could risk harm through the mirror's association with death. Such are the perils of certain kinds of simulations, as real as ghosts.

With the consciousness of the deceased summoned to the room and fused with the name card, the lama began to speak to it. He read a set of sacred texts that detailed what was happening in death. He looked toward the name card and spoke to the dead man. He informed him that he was dead and he invited him to remain for the duration of the rite. He described what was taking place, and he explained that mourners were reciting mantras and prayers on the dead man's behalf. "Foods and sur are being offered to you," he said.

"You are dead now," the lama told the man. His words hung like a cold fact in the air. The lama explained that the man could no longer remain among the living, that he was roaming within the intermediate state between one life and the next. He instructed the consciousness as to what could be expected to happen to it while it drifted about in the bardo "between" in the days and weeks to come. From texts he read and spoke of paths to be taken or avoided, what deities would be encountered during the between, and to which deities the man should pray. The lama described the sufferings to be found in the six realms and he advised the consciousness to seek enlightenment so as to avoid a rebirth in any of these realms. He encouraged the consciousness to not think about the world of the living, nor to give thought to relatives or to any activities or transactions it engaged in while alive. He advised that it should contemplate only its current situation, the grounds of its existence, and how to achieve enlightenment.

Through this process of *ngo te*, "introduction" or "explanation," matters were made clear to the passed-away one. In effect, the words introduce the dead person to the fact of death and explain his current condition and situation in clear terms.

The term *ngo te* relates to the Tibetan verb *ngo sprod*, which carries connotations of "to introduce, to explain, to lay open the features, to show the nature of a thing."[15] *Ngo* literally means "face," while the verb *sprod-pa* in Tibetan means "to bring together, to put together, to make to meet." *Ngo te* apparently means in a more concrete sense bringing two faces together, or having them meet in some way, hence the idea of an "introduction"; it can also entail the sense of showing or revealing the face of something to another. The words bring the dead person face to face with the reality of his death.[16]

Most of the lama's explanations occurred while he was reading pages of sacred texts, including the *Liberation upon Hearing*. But toward the end of the funeral rites, before the name card was burned, he spoke directly and informally to the man imaged by it. The explanations clarified what was happening to the dead man and what needed to be done on his behalf. They helped the man to "concentrate" his mind on his present situation and streamline his thoughts.

The lama's explanations worked to satisfy the deceased's consciousness and prepare it for the journey to come. They reduced the dead man's longing for his former life.

Late in the afternoon the lama concluded his instructions and caught his breath. He asked for some water. A young woman walked over to him with a vase and poured a cup. He drank from it and placed it on a small table. He spoke to the dead man's two sons.

The first son picked up the name card and held it in his hands. He looked toward the bundled clothes. He spoke, at first slowly, hesitantly, and then with strained emotion. He was talking to his absent father, explaining that he was dead and could no longer stay with them. He brushed away tears with the shirt sleeve covering his right arm.

"We're doing everything for you now," he said. "We're doing the ne par, and the ghewa [funeral rites]. You can't stay with us. Don't leave any semjha [attachment] with us."

His brother suggested a few words. The first son repeated them.

The man paused. He began to say more, but stopped. He handed the name card to his brother. The first son stood up, stepped back, and found his footing. He held his hands together and performed a set of prostrations while facing the bundle of clothes.

The younger man sat for a moment. He took a breath and uttered statements similar to his brother's. Once empty of words he put the name card down. He lowered to his knees and laid his body in front of the resting place, hands flat on the floor. He stood up clasped his hands together and prostrated again.

The lama asked the dead man's widow if she wanted to speak. She shook her head no, tears in her eyes. Her face turned away.

Others spoke in turn. The room filled with unbearable sadness and a sense of parting, with all quiet save for the strain of words.

The statements and pleas of each turn churned within me. I felt for the man who had died and for the family who missed him. I sat quietly, looking on, and felt cheap in my desire to watch and listen for the sake of research. I put down my pen and notebook and looked at the ground and stared into the amber glow of a candle reflected in a mirror on the altar and thought myself to be far from home while keen to take in all that was happening around me.

"People sometimes cry while undertaking the explanation, because of the love," someone later told me.

The lama's explanation consists primarily of a guide to the between states and instructions as to what the deceased needs to reach the Pure Land or a good rebirth. The explanations of family members, in contrast, are concerned primarily with detailing what sorts of funeral rites are being conducted on behalf of the deceased as well as any business or financial transactions that need to be done in the wake of the person's passing. By doing this, any attachment, desire, or "interest" which that person might still have toward the world of the living can be diminished. Family members also advise the deceased to refrain from any attachments to anyone or anything in the world and to focus his thoughts on the task of arriving at the Pure Land. Much of the lama's explanation derives from sacred texts written centuries ago, whereas the family's words are produced on the spot, making for interplays of text and speech, past and present, prepared statements and spontaneous utterances.

I have never recorded an explanation uttered by a family member at a funeral rite, out of respect for the dead and the bereaved. Several friends have summarized the recurrent gist of these instructions, however.

Temba: A family member sits, takes the name card and holds it in his hands, and he talks about everything, all the processions that are being organized for him. And also if there are any kind of transactions that have gone unfulfilled or unresolved, then he says, "Okay, I'll do this, I'll do that, I'll take care of all these things. Don't leave any attachment with anyone or anything. Just think now of your next life. Just pray to your lama and to your deities and try to get to the Pure Land. Don't leave any attachments on the relatives, don't leave any attachment."

Nogapu: They say, "When you were alive, we sometimes had arguments. Please don't give thought to those arguments. And you said you were going to do this thing, but you weren't able to do it. But now that you're not here, we're going to do it for you." That kind of thing is said. And some people say, "We're going to do another ritual for you next year, on the same day that you died. And we say to the person, "Please don't stay around here."

Don't stick around here. The family tries to induce "satisfaction" for the deceased, and so diminish his yearning for aspects of his former life. Everything is resolved, completed, the speakers' words promise. You have no worries to speak of, no hindrances or deeds undone on which your mind could stay hooked. This is ritual as communication, as satisfying explanation—language and ritual as the reduction of desire and the elimination of sensate connection.

The explanations entailed a strong scene of communication. They implied a face-to-face dialogue. But the dialogue was partial, one-sided, with one party speaking and the other listening. The living spoke to a presence not fully apparent, as though talking to someone in the dark somewhere or in another room or locale. The person remained invisible and unheard but presumable he was still conscious, attentive, capable of listening.

An explanation stands in counterpoint to the oral testament transmitted from a dying person to his or her family members. Both speech events entail acts of clarifying statement, advice, and farewells. Yet whereas an oral will implies words transferred from the dying to the living, an explanation implies words transmitted from the living to the dead. In death, a person moves from the role of speaker and actor to one of listener and reactor, subject to death and the ritual efforts of others. The system of relations has changed valences. After a person dies, the transactive flow is from the living to the dead, from life to death. If something goes the other way, from the dead to the living, it's usually taken as problematic, unhelpful, and harmful.

"No Form, No Sound . . ."

Clarify that life is emptiness only, that all composite forms are void of intrinsic existence. Tell the deceased that he no longer exists, that he no longer has any sensorial or phenomenal means of engaging with the world. Perform this existential dissolution ritually, making it so. Nullify desire.

You are emptiness only. Consider the implications of this profound and serious scene of communication: one person tells another that he no longer exists, that he no longer has any physical basis to act in or engage with the world. He tries to convince him of this. He voices words that announce the process of dissolution, simulates it, and realizes it. There is an erasure of the self, of the person as a living, sentient being in the world. A few select words produce the emptying of self required here. Language and ritual work to inform a person that he is truly dead. They describe, transform, and, ultimately, dissolve. The funeral rites subject a person to death.

The recently dead are, like the living, desirous, engaged, invested. To assure the proper transfer of the deceased's consciousness from the world of the living to the Pure Land or to any new rebirth, it's necessary to diminish its attachment to, and interest in, that world. Lamas and mourners act to persuade the consciousness "to not think about the living world . . . about any transactions or activities." Their aim is the nullification of desire.

The lama's explanations on the day of the ne par contributed to this goal, for words were used to eliminate any longings for the world. A mantra performed toward the end of a funeral rite worked along similar lines. After the lama had completed the last of his explanation and other ritual acts, and the family members had offered foods and performed prostrations on the dead man's behalf, the lama took the name card and set it on a table before him. He voiced a mantra sudden in its force and power which culminated with these words:

zug mhe	There is no form,
dha mhe	no sound,
dhi mhe	no smell,
rho mhe	no taste,
rhecha mhe	no texture,
chhe mhe do!	no mental phenomena, period!

This "litany of negation" comes from the Heart Sutra, one of the most famous of Buddhist scriptures.[17] Dating back to the Buddhism of ancient India, the Heart Sutra belongs to an important and well-known set of Buddhist scriptures known as the Perfection of Wisdom sutras. The sutra offers profound perspectives on the contingent, impermanent nature of existence, including its cryptic, Koan-like adage that "form is emptiness, emptiness is form." The sutra has been recited for centuries now, by monks and laypersons alike, in many Buddhist societies. "Therefore, Shariputra," reads a central passage, "in emptiness there is no form, no feelings, no perceptions, no mental formations, and no consciousness. There is no eye, no ear, no nose, no tongue, no body, and no mind. There is no form, no sound, no smell, no taste, no texture, and no phenomena. . . ." All composite phenomena, including emptiness itself, are "empty" of and devoid of inherent existence. In reciting the Heart Sutra and contemplating its meaning, practitioners can better grasp the interdependent and transient nature of all phenomena. This cognition of emptiness brings them closer to achieving enlightenment.

In drawing from the Heart Sutra, Buddhist lamas strive to convey a similar message to the deceased: that, since there is "emptiness only," it is pointless to grasp for the stuff of life or an enduring, substantially real self, and by directly perceiving emptiness alone, enlightenment can be achieved. The "therapeutic thrust" of the chanted words is, like many Buddhist teachings on emptiness, "to get the listener to abandon attachment to inappropriate modes of thought and to gain the liberation that comes with freedom from clinging."[18] Here, the deceased happens to be the main recipient of this message. Specifically, the litany of "no form, no sound . . ." clarifies that the sensory basis of form, sound, smell, taste, texture, and mental phenomena do not really exist in any permanent or foundational way. All is emptiness only. The dead person's lifeworld is emptied of its apparent significance.

At the same time many Hyolmo people understand the "no form . . ." incantation of negations to make clear that the deceased no longer has a physical existence and thus has no means to engage with world through the mediums of sight, sound, smell, taste, touch, or intellect. When voiced, the negations at once depict and confirm this situation and make it so. The words coax a subject's calm and sensible fading into the quiescence of death. They also appease the grasping of the grief-stricken for a lost loved one.

Without the ability to engage in the world, the deceased is no longer a person. What remains is a consciousness characterized by luminous emptiness.

"'You are emptiness only,'" Goser Lama said in conveying one thread of

Figure 22. Burning the name card. Thodong, 1989.

sense here. "'Nothing exists now, so now you have to realize yourself, you have to think of yourself and prepare well for your new journey to a better place.'"

A fading of the qualities of personhood, of the subjectivity of a human being, occurs in the days following a death. "'You've lost the qualities and features of a human being,'" Goser Lama once said in paraphrasing the message conveyed in the "no form . . ." chant. What are those qualities and features? A physical form. Speech. A field of desires. A tracework of thoughts, habits, memories, and attachments. The ability to engage with others, to leave marks and traces in the world. The ability to act in consequential, traceable ways; to love and care for others. This is what a human being is, in his or her fullest expression. Bereft of those qualities, it's only an intense spiritual force with the potential for consciousness but devoid of physical form and the ability to interact with an environment. *You have to realize yourself as less, and as more, than a human being, you have to realize the Buddha nature in you.*

Yet there is apparently still a "you" there. There is still a consciousness that is listening, receptive, in some way. What kind of spectral subject is listening or can be listening here? What kind of "you" or "I" can perceive its own emptiness? We can't say. The logic short-circuits. As I imagine it the rites proceed

until the "you" dissolves, until the self is extinguished into its own luminous emptiness.

Tongba nyi. Emptiness only. Soon there was no sound, no taste, no texture. The head lama spoke quietly, with eyes closed. He had just voiced the "no form . . ." chant. His right hand held a wood stick wrapped in a small cloth. Like others, I was riveted to the scene. The lamas read from their texts. The man was as though entranced, his mind altered, elsewhere, tuned to the tantric contemplations employed in this most crucial of moments.

He was transferring the dead man's consciousness from the sansaric world of *khorwa* to a realm above and beyond that world. He was sending it to the Pure Land, like an arrow shot from a bow.

The man held the stick to the flame of a candle before him and set it on fire. He brought the flame close to the name card. He moved it closer, eyes still closed, sounding tantric words to great effect. He mouthed a quiet "phet," a forceful hiccup of a sound alone in the silence of the room. He circled the flame three times around the name card, the flame touched the base of the card, the paper ignited on fire. Flames swarmed the paper, shooting upward and engulfing image and word in a fiery glow. Flames burnt the paper seared to red black heat, turned to gray white ash.

Within seconds the name card had dissolved into a pile of sooty ashes, black and gray. They had burnt the dead man's name and thus eliminated his current existence within the world of humans.

The act of transference here was known as *da phang*, "arrow shot." The dead man's consciousness was released from the world of the living and delivered, like an arrow, to Dewa Chen, the Pure Land of Amitābha.[19]

Goser Lama explained the process, as he learned it:

> In the course of sending the consciousness, the lamas do not send it directly
> to the Pure Land. They are not capable of doing that. So they submit the
> consciousness to Phagpa Chen Rezig, or Amitābha. While performing this,
> the lama should spiritually convey to the consciousness that "the human
> world is no longer suitable for you, and you have already lost the qualities
> and features of a human being. So now your destination is in front of Phagpa
> Chen Rezig, where you'll find only peace, happiness, a place full of flowers
> blooming, where there are no more sorrows. This is the world of gods and
> goddesses." After these sentiments are conveyed to the consciousness, the
> lama voices the "phet" and the consciousness is submitted to Phagpa Chen
> Rezig, in order to send it to the Pure Land.

The "arrow shot" promoted the transfer of the deceased's consciousness to
the Pure Land and thus "elevated" the consciousness to a new dwelling place.
Yet since the physical grounds and features of the deceased's life had yet to be
fully annihilated, the head lama acted to make this so as well. He achieved this
annihilation by eliminating the deceased's sins and worldly existence through
a set of forceful mantras and visualizations.

The lama demonstrated this radical conversion into emptiness by circumambulating a small flame around the print, then setting the print on fire. The
burning of the name card conveyed the elimination of the deceased's negative
karma and the end of his material existence in the world.

The lamas recited additional prayers and mantras to help the consciousness to reach before Amitābha in the event the consciousness had been unable
to arrive there due to some remaining, unwashed sins. "These mantras and
prayers are done as much as possible," one man told me.

The name card presumes its absence. Those attending a funeral know it
will not be around for long. The card's ritual purpose is to be immolated and
purified in flames. Its disappearance is already there. The same holds for any
of those observing the funeral rites, a fact made clear by the show of disappearance at hand.[20] The scene always yields "a foretaste of mourning," to use a
phrase of Freud's.[21] Those who attend the funeral rites know that the lost one
will be re-created in a substitute form, only to be eliminated once again.

The name card signs the deceased, while the incineration of the print simulates the annihilation of the dead person's worldly existence. For many this
is a simulation only. Some understand that the dissolution of the person's sins

and worldly existence occurs with the burning of the print. Others, learned lamas especially, hold that it is achieved through the mantras and visualizations enacted by the lama. As they know it, the act of burning the name card is to "show" or "demonstrate," in a graphically dramatic way, the physical abolishment of the deceased. The real changes result from the lama's tantric practices.

"It's a concrete prompt," Karma said of the name card. "It's easy to visualize. When it's burned, people can visualize well the dissolution of the dead person's existence."

With this theatre of emptiness, the burning of the text drives home the fact that the physical form and worldly existence of the deceased no longer remain, that the dead person is no longer alive as a fully formed, flesh-and-voice person.

The name card is a corpse-image. The text resembles, and in some sense simulates, the corpse of the deceased. A ritual "transference of consciousness" is enacted upon it, just as it is performed on a body after death, to elevate its resident consciousness to an enlightened realm. The text undergoes an incineration similar in means to the burning of a corpse. The deceased's *corpus* is eliminated, subtracted, wiped out.

The burning of the name card is exorcistic in form. At times, if a ghost afflicts a Hyolmo household or family, the members of that family will ask a lama to undertake a ritual whereby he writes the name of the haunting spirit on a piece of paper and burns the paper while reciting an appropriate set of mantras. The incineration of the ghost's "name" can drive the ghost from the household. By immolating the name card, the living expel the deceased's unwanted sins and impurities from its post-life form. They erase the material grounds of its existence and undercut its potential to haunt the living.

"They burn the dead man's name," people say of the act. To incinerate a person's name is to obliterate his social identity. When a child comes into the world, bestowing a name upon him works to establish his identity as a person and social being. Taking away a person's name accomplishes the inverse. That a life has ended is the lasting message here. For many, the incineration of a name card, whose inscriptions embody a graphic trace of a person's life, a bio-graphy in the strict sense of the term, the inscription and naming of a life, spells the social death of the deceased, the cutting away of a singular identity, and the end of a vital public life.

When speaking of a deceased person, Hyolmo people will often mention the identity of the person—so-and-so's father or sister, for instance—

and then add the word *tongba*, "empty" (much like Americans might use the phrase "late" in speaking of someone deceased; the late Johnny Carson: *Johnny Carson, empty*).

"The person does not exist anymore," one man told me in speaking of this designation. "And even if his belongings are still around, there's no connection to him now. It's gone. It's empty."

Name, empty. This grammatical structure entails an existential one. Each name in the world, of a "who" or "what," foresees that future modifier, *empty*, such that the subject carries a trace of emptiness in each moment of its naming. A name is undermined by its future designation, haunted by its destiny, its inherent emptiness. In life, as in death, a name carries a spectral presence. A name is part tangible, part ghostly. Any memory, any image-name, is like this as well, at once vivid and spectral, tangible and absent of tangibility.

The person was gone, the connections emptied out. The dead man was de-named, defaced. Rendered signless. To transform someone, you have to take away his name. One has to name the dead person as dead, as being within the name of death, and then one has to take away the name of the dead, such that the person, no longer a person, is fully within the name of death, which, ultimately, cannot be named.

Generating Merit

Perform public funeral rites on the deceased's behalf. Increase his karmic merit. Pay back any debts the deceased might have accumulated during his lifetime. Construct an effigy that represents the deceased and place foods and the name card close to it.

The name card burned into ash shortly after nightfall. The room was quiet. The main work was done. The lamas performed a series of concluding rites and offerings to the deities at hand. They sat back, rested. They placed their texts and bells, conch shells and cymbals, in the cloth bags with which they had come. A boy took down the drum hanging from a rafter and set it on the floor. The family served another round of foods. Tea lined the rims of cups.

I left with several men and women returning to our village. We walked down the winding path toward Gulphubanjang in the night's stillness. The beams from our flashlights flitted against the rocks and sods of grass that came before us. Once alone, I looked up and gazed dumbfounded at the creamy stretch of the Milky Way that banded the sky high above.

The family remained at the house, the man's bundled clothes still intact.

Back in the cabin I found folds of comfort in my sleeping bag. I could hear the gurgling of cold spring water running from an open tap yards away. Fiery dreams lit up my thoughts as I drifted to sleep.

The family performed a second ne par a week later, and a third and a fourth after that, at weekly intervals. I did not attend any of these. I was not invited to do so and felt shy about asking. I was reluctant to disturb the intimacy of the family's grief.

Successive ne par rites can be performed every week during the seven-week period that follows a person's death. There is a lot of variation here. Some families perform only one ne par, three and a half days after the death, while others perform five or six ne par, each held on a successive weekly anniversary of the death. Any ritual repetition here is not redundant so much as it is additive. The recurrence of the rites adds to the deceased's growing realization of his death, furthers his store of karmic merit, and increases his chances of a good rebirth.

Most families hold a final major ritual sometime between the fourth and the seventh week after a death. While similar in form to a ne par, this rite goes by a different name. It is called a *ghewa*, primarily because one of the main purposes of the rite is to increase the ghewa (Tibetan *dge ba*), the karmic "merit," of the deceased person, through rites and actions. Other aims of a ghewa are:

a) to pay back "debts" that the deceased owes to living persons by giving them food and drink on the occasion of the ghewa;

b) to provide a public opportunity where guests can further console family members of the deceased, especially by giving them money to help pay for the funeral rites;

c) to separate any remaining sins and impurities from the deceased's consciousness;

d) to enable the living to envision and talk to the deceased one last time;

e) to clarify further to the deceased that he is no longer alive;

f) to communicate what needs to be done in order for that person to achieve a good rebirth or transcendence altogether; and

g) to send the deceased's consciousness to the Pure Land.

In form and spirit, many ghewas are similar to the "mortuary feasts" held in many societies. These final funerary rites usually occur once the "soul" and

Figure 24. Arriving at a ghewa. Thodong, 1988.

"body" of the deceased have taken on new, altered forms in life and mourners are set to return to lives not entirely marked by the shadow of the death.[22]

The ghewa must be held within forty-nine days after a death. If it were to occur after the forty-ninth day, any rites performed at the ghewa to help the consciousness to reach the Pure Land or to seek a new rebirth would prove ineffective, and the consciousness would have to remain roaming in the between. A ghewa usually takes place, therefore, sometime between the third and the seventh week after a death.

A ghewa is typically a three-day affair. People arrive the first day and leave at the end of the third day or the morning after that. The main funeral rites take place during the second day. The ghewa's main ritual activities usually take place in a Buddhist temple. If the person lived in a village without a temple, a temple-like setting can be improvised by setting up a temporary structure adjacent to the house.

A ghewa can be quite crowded, with a number of lamas and assistants seated within the temple, performing the funeral rites; relatives, friends, and neighbors of the deceased and the deceased's family seated and milling about in open areas outside the temple or the home of the deceased; and close family members working constantly in makeshift kitchen areas, where food is prepared for the lamas and the guests. The large number of guests attending a ghewa make it different in nature than any of the ne par rites performed in the weeks prior to the ghewa.

"A ghewa is just another ne par," Karma noted, "but in a form where all the people are invited."

The family invites many people to a ghewa for two main reasons: to increase the deceased's store of karmic merit, and to pay back any debts to others that the deceased might have accumulated in his lifetime. The event gets its name from the fact that those attending it work to augment the ghewa, the karmic "merit," of the deceased, through select rites and actions. Primary among these are collective performances of mani prayers; when people voice these prayers in this context, they are doing so in the name of the deceased. Any and all merit that results from these actions goes to that person. That additional merit can help the person to achieve a better rebirth than he might otherwise be able to. In a spirit of communal support often found in Hyolmo communities, others help out on behalf of the deceased. "Everyone is working together to improve the merit of the dead person," Karma told me.

One implication of this ethos is that the more people who participate in the voicing of mani prayers, the more merit that goes to the deceased. The number of people attending a ghewa is therefore of importance. Those well respected by others can be expected to generate large crowds at their ghewa. At the same time, wealthy families have a better chance of assuring a good turnout, since they can afford to invite a lot of people to attend. Poorer families do not possess the means to pay for the vast amounts of food, beverages, and liquor that are required if a large ghewa is to be held.

The foods served to the guests at a ghewa are also a means to improve the karmic status of the deceased. The logic in this idea is that, since a person becomes indebted to so many others during her lifetime, not only for any monies borrowed but also because of the many ways that others have helped her, there is value in attempting to pay back these "debts" by giving food and drink to those attending the ghewa. People in fact distribute these foods with the unselfish aim of "giving back" more than the deceased actually received. Since any debts owed to others detract from a person's store of karmic merit, the reduction of the deceased's debts, or elimination of them altogether, increases his karmic merit in general.[23]

The cost of hosting a ghewa and other funeral rites can be considerable, especially in Kathmandu of late, where wealthier families sometimes try to outdo one another by providing a bevy of tasty foods and drinks to their guests. Families do sometimes fall into debt because of the expense of the fu-

neral rites—as they do with the expense of weddings. To help defray the costs
of the funeral rites for a bereaved family, the other families attending a ghewa
usually give a compassionate gift of money to the bereaved family. The gifts
are given at a certain time during the ghewa, with people lining up to give their
family's share and a representative of the bereaved family writing down the
name of the donor and the amount given in a notebook. The record helps the
family to keep track of who gave what. People tend to give the same amount
when someone in a corresponding family dies.

These practices count for a precise and balanced calculus of reciprocity.
Debts and obligations are leveled out, further annulling the deceased's ties to
the living. Longing and connection are reduced, ideally, to a degree of zero.

The time of mourning was held within the workaday affairs of the villages there, and as the weeks went on the sadness of loss was not far from
the thoughts of many as they farmed or traveled or ate with family. Mheme
Mingmar's family held a ghewa for him in the seventh week after his death.
Guests began to arrive the morning of the first day. Several cousins undertook
the day-long trek from villages along the eastern ridge of the Hyolmo region.
Two men had made the journey from India. Others came from villages close
to Thodong. Some brought bags of uncooked rice. Relatives and neighbors
pitched in with the work to be done. Women helped to cook meals and brew
teas; men prepared firewood and cleared rooms for sleeping quarters.

I hiked up to Thodong early that afternoon with families from Gulphubanyang. Once we arrived at the house I stayed outside, to be among those
gathered there. I stepped to the back of the house to check out the stable-like
area that had been renovated into a temporary temple for the rites to come.
A blue plastic canopy had been draped over the roof, to prevent rain from
leaking down. Two young men were molding the shape of numerous deities
from freshly cooked rice. Three others were putting the finishing touches on
the altar established close to the far wall. Their senior, the same lama who had
led the proceedings at the ne par, sat close to the altar, a cup of tea in his hands.
He gave instructions, when needed, to his assistants.

I walked to the front of the house and stood by the door frame. "*Sho*," a
woman's voice invited me into the main room. I stepped inside and sat beside
the door, close to other men positioned with legs folded neatly, lotus-style.
I tried to emulate those compact arrangements but my knees couldn't keep
from sticking out at odd angles. I looked around at the faces in the room and
nodded to the men I recognized and to those I did not. My gaze tarried with

Figure 25. An effigy of the deceased. Thodong, 1988.

the most striking presence in the room. Close to the altar, where the bundled clothes once lay, stood a life-size simulation of the dead man.

This was the *ghur*, a word that literally means "tent." The effigy would soon become a central locus of the ritual actions performed at the funeral rite. In a sense, the ghur *was* a tent, a canopied structure which could house the dead man's itinerant consciousness. A tent is a temporary abode, a way station, possibly empty or full, designed to provide shelter or a space for storage. It can be set up quickly and disassembled quickly. Often "skin-like" in appearance, a tent is a thin architecture, a container for something else, almost vacuous of substance itself.

"When did they make this, brother?" I asked the man seated to my right.

"They made it this morning," he said.

"The family made it?"

"Ho. Yes. They had someone make it for them. These two did it."

He nodded toward two young men seated in the room. Related to the widow, they lived a few houses down from her.

The builders of the effigy had put maize in a *pathi*, a bucket-like vessel used for measuring grains. They stuck wooden sticks firmly in the grain and tied other sticks to that stand. Combined, the sticks formed a sturdy cross. The men wrapped clothes once worn by the deceased around the sticks until the bundled structure resembled the head and torso of a body. They wound white cloths around the head, forming a pure-white face, pure and untainted. They dressed the effigy in clothes and placed a rig nga crown atop its head, much as it might rest atop the head of a corpse. A rhiba, the charred bone retrieved at the cremation site after the man's body was cremated, was placed in the "arms" of the effigy. Once the effigy was fully adorned and set in place the family placed fresh tea, liquors, curd, rice, and eggs on a small table positioned before it.

An effigy simulates a corpse. "It's just like the dead person," people say. The effigy is a *tshap*, a "representation," of the *zuk*, the "visual image/appearance," of the body of the deceased. It's an image of an image, an apparition squared. As Goser Lama explained it, "The lama should make the effigy as though it is the real person who has come alive for a few moments." In reconstituting the deceased in this ritually temporary form, "all the features of the deceased" should be established. A precise tantric mimesis is called for.

It's clear that the effigy does not simply represent the dead person in an abstract symbolic way. For many of those attending a ghewa, the effigy effectively becomes the person once the consciousness returns close to it. "The effigy is the same as the dead person."

When conducting fieldwork in Hyolmo for the first time in 1988, I attended several funeral rites before I saw a cremation performed. At the time, I took the effigy to be a representation of the deceased person when she or he was alive. It was only after I attended a cremation, and saw how the corpse was, like an effigy, wrapped up in the white cloth and adorned with clothes, ornaments, and the sacred crown, that I came to understand that an effigy resembles a person as dead, not as alive. And a corpse resembles an effigy.

"And then the body was set upright," I wrote in my notes after visiting the home of a person who had just died. "When it was positioned like this, it didn't look like a corpse any more but something transformative, transitional, so very much like an effigy. Now I know why the effigy is constructed in the way it is and why it's so significant and so evocative of emotions."

Note that the effigy is not the same as a living person. The effigy, hollow, stiff and empty, mute, and unresponsive, is a representation less of the living person than of the person as the passed-away one, beyond the point of death. The effigy stands as a material reminder of the fact and reality of the death. It's like an image encountered in a dream, or a reflection in water—not the true person but an echoic image of the person.

Although the effigy functions as a material base for the consciousness, unlike a living body it does not involve an active, willful, agentive being, one that can act and feel and move about and respond communicatively to others. There is an artificial, textual quality to the effigy. It is appropriately deathlike, something between life and death. The effigy is a second corpse.

Still, by interacting with that later image, mourners can affect the karmic and spiritual condition of the deceased. The use of an effigy during the funeral rites fits with a common structure evident in Hyolmo engagements with death: by simulating the form of the deceased in some object or image–a bone, an effigy, a name and figure inscribed on a piece of paper, an image cast into a mirror, the corpse itself—and then engaging with that object or image in some way, working on its construction, relating to the image, undermining its features, the living can effect changes that pertain to the status of the person invoked. Apparently there is a need to present the dead person through material and mimetic images of this sort. Then again, there is a profound need for images in life. We couldn't get by without them.

Blank White

Encounter the effigy and its field of ghostly energies. Look at the white
face banded there and try to perceive what can, and cannot, be seen
there.

Only recently have I come to appreciate that the design of a ghur effigy contains a spectrum of different valences, energies—realms of life amid and
beyond the sphere of the human. There is the ground itself, the terrain of the
earth, and then set on its surface are the incense, foods, nourishing drinks,
gifts, monies, and anything that the deceased person particularly liked and
desired while alive, such as a pinch of alcohol or a box of cigarettes—in short,
this is the worldly, material, affective matrix of a life. Above that corpus of
energies stands the torso, simulative of the deceased's body, arms and hands
included, all of this clothed in shirts, coats, and adorned with the jewelry and
prayer beads that the deceased wore while alive. The clothes carry a fabric
of traces related to the singular identity of the deceased, a sense of his or her
recognizable biographic, corpographic stance in the world. Above the torso
rests the face of the deceased, conveyed in the blank features of a white wrapping of katha scarves. Atop the face and head rests the *rig nga* crown, emblem-
atic of the five Buddha families (much as it rests atop the head of the deceased
person during the cremation rites). The crown "empowers" the deceased, once
again, by activating and demonstrating the inherent Buddha nature. Beyond
the features and nature of the person is the immaterial space "above" the figure
of the dead person, a realm of purity and transcendence.

From the ground of the earth to the life of the person and his singular
biographic identity, onto realms more spiritual and transcendent, the effigy
carries the valences of different energies in life, from low to high. The person
is configured as being multiple, as holding the capacity for altering possibilities
in life, with each potentially in a state of flux. The effigy entails a force field of
differential energies and alterity as much as it simulates a singularly coherent
assemblage in the world. There is a play of forces at work here, a play between
forces; between the identifying marks found in the clothes and the absence
of biographical features with the face; between the relatively known terrains
of the earth and sensate existence and the unknown realms of transcendence;
between the viscerally human and the spiritually transcendent. The face itself
might be conceived as being on a par with the bardo realms "between" one
life and the next, for in its blank white spacing the face suggests an indistinct

interval of in-betweenness, intermediate between the life of the deceased and the spiritual realms beyond that life.

The face is, arguably, the most enigmatic aspect of the effigy. Stone blank in its features, the face is composed of katha ceremonial scarves wrapped around the makeshift head; the fulcrum of the person is banded over in sacredness, blanketed in an auspiciousness of pure form. The white cloth here is consonant with the white sheet that is placed over a recently dead person, covering over the graphic nature of the death, its visceral, potentially disturbing reality; it is also consonant with the cloth that covers the face of a person while being brought to the cremation grounds, and while being eliminated through burning. The cloth also bears affinities with the katha scarves wrapped in oil and tossed into the cremation fire; with the long white banner that "shows the way" to enlightenment or a good rebirth; and with the katha scarves given to those leaving on lengthy journeys, or as a ceremonial blessing more generally. The face carries these associations. And yet the face carries a singular distinctiveness of its own, in its lone appearance.

The effigy's face is bereft of any details of identity. It's like a blank sheet of paper, unmarked, unsigned, with no names inscribed. It carries a monotone purity with little relief or variation to it. No history is encoded there; there's nothing singularly biographic. The face is empty of any overt markings, codes, traces, inscriptions. This is entirely fitting, for the deceased person is now (or should be) beyond worldly significance, beyond individuality, beyond the reach of traces and markings. One cannot see the face of the deceased any longer, if only because the dead person no longer has a distinctive countenance which one can perceive, embrace, or sustain within a field of memory. There is no face, no texture, no perception, no touch. No hunger, or thirst. No hardship, suffering. There is a face, and there is no face. The blank white face is as unknowable and unrepresentable as death itself.

The face is not imbued with the qualities of a mask. Although constructed, fashioned, and three-dimensional in form, its appearance does not hide, or reveal, anything. The face does not convey the countenance of any persona or extant actuality.

And yet the face is not purely blank. There is still a striated surface there; the seams and folds of the katha scarf are apparent in the wrapping. There is a texture to the face, even if it's a minimal, nonsignifying one, like a text that holds no recognizable, readable words. In effect, the white of the face is the visual and tactile font for something that can no longer be seen or touched. The face holds the remnant of an erasure. The white face is an image of imagelessness, a sign of signlessness. It entails a nonresemblance, or, perhaps, the most precise and minimal of resemblances; the face resembles nothing, the face resembles emptiness.

The face is an image nonetheless, with a potentially potent affective force. Its appearance can strike the heartmind. The white face is like so many effigial faces that have come before, simulative of those who have passed into emptiness. The face carries the trace of past deaths as well as of future ends.

The face has the qualities of a blank screen upon which images can be projected—somewhat like a film screen in a theatre, upon which the aura of moving images can be projected. Upon the screen of the face mourners can imaginatively "put" the face of the deceased. They can construe the face as being there, even if they can no longer see the actual face. The imaginary image of a person's face is placed back onto the visual font of the white surface. It is possible to imagine a face there and thus to recall, imaginatively, a life. Others attending the funeral, supportive family and friends, might also envision the faces of lost loved ones within the blank screen of the effigy's face. One can imagine a life within the blank screen of a face. What is imagining but writing—drawing, projecting—on the face of the world?

All told, the blank white face suggests the many ways in which images can work in the world, through concrete acts of signification or moments of non-signification; through association or projection; presence or absence; through folds of history and time or the absence of time and history; through imaginative fabulation or an absence of the means to imagine.

At times, it seems as if it's not just the mourners who are involved with the visual regard of something. The face of the effigy stands in silent regard, as though looking at any viewers of it. It's a commanding, uncertain aura of a presence; a vague, unseen, unperceivable look.

Effigies of the dead have always struck me as eerie figures. Opaquely ethereal, this phantom simulacrum nicks at a sense of an uncanny doubleness. It suggests a liminal, nonfigurative figure at once dead and not-yet-dead. Effigies of the dead make me anxious. They are specter-thin, enigmatic. Unfathomable. Its disappearance is already there. An effigy is *almost alive*, and in that lingering almostness lies its spooky, hauntive quality. Strange presence, strange absence. The silence of an effigy is like the silence of death, a silence before and apart from any language, incapable of being heard or deciphered.

Most Hyolmo people tend to think of the effigy as a straightforward image of the dead person—much as a photograph might be in other settings—perhaps because they are more familiar with material simulations of people, deities, and demons. When speaking with me about it, Karma has referred to an effigy as a "dummy."

Worth noting in this context is the etymology of the English word "effigy," which relates back to the Middle French *effigie* and the Latin *effigies*, "copy or imitation of something, likeness, image, statue," a word that is itself from or related to *effingere*, "to mold, fashion, portray," from *ex-*, "out," and *fingere*, "to form, shape." An effigy in the European context was most often an "image of a person," especially figures made of stuffed clothing. An effigy is a likeness or copy of someone, of something "made" or "figured." The word is related etymologically to the modern English word *fiction*, which itself draws from the Old French *ficcion*, "dissimulation, ruse; invention, fabrication," and from the Latin *fictionem*, "a fashioning or feigning." All of these terms are related to the Latin *fingere*, "to shape, form, devise, feign," originally "to knead, form out of clay." The Hyolmo word for effigy—*ghur*, or "tent"—carries none of these semantic resonances in any overt way, and yet there is still something "fictional" and "figurative" within the simulative imitations of effigies. The effigy is a fictive figuration of the deceased, one that carries a powerful array of imaginative connotations. In some ways, an effigy eventuates in an all-too-real, all-too-fictional reappearance of the deceased in the lives and thoughts of the living. An effigy is a fictional structure, a tent of fictions. And so is a person.

I stayed for hours in the grieved home that morning, a few feet from the effigy. Nibbling on tea and tsampa mixed together with the fingers of my right hand, I spoke with those who ventured in conversation with me, answering questions such as "How much is the airfare to America, up-down?" I could not shake the looming silhouette of the effigy. It sat there, primed for interaction, for continued engagements in the world. And yet its ghostly, vacant form was removed from the talk and doings of everyday life. I was in my own private uncanny valley.

Guests invited to the ghewa arrived through that first day. They drew near to the house and greeted friends and relatives. They rested in the house or with their backs against a low wall outside and welcomed drinks and foods served to them. At night, they found places to sleep in the house in the newly fashioned gompa and in neighboring homes.

I tried to take in all that was happening within the crowd of people and movement. Men sat together in a clearing, trading news and stories. Children played near their parents. Girls clung close to their friends, eyeing boys and eyed by boys too shy to approach on their own. The family remained subdued in mourning. Late in the day I watched the lamas and their assistants complete the altar, replete with the proper images of buddhas and bodhisattvas. I saw them commence the preliminary rites. Tired out by nightfall I left for home accompanied by a boy with an oval face returning to his family's home. We made our way through the dusk-lit landscape, tramping down a sequence of bluffs. The boy swapped queries with me. "What are the schools like in your country?" he asked, leaping from a boulder to the sandy trail.

I came back late the next morning, joined by members of several families. I had my camera with me, but I wasn't sure when to use it. I stood with the guests waiting about the area outside the house. Others were by the doorway, facing within. Still others hovered beyond the threshold. Someone told me that the lamas were inside, close to the altar, along with the widow and family members and close relatives. The lamas performed a set of ritual offerings in anticipation of the transfer of the effigy to the temple. They were getting ready to leave the home and make their way to the gompa. We watched and waited. When would they leave the house?

Showing the Way

Carry the effigy respectfully from the home of the deceased to the place where the funeral rites are to be conducted. Demonstrate the way to the Pure Land and to a good rebirth, while saying goodbye to the passed loved one. Express grief at this ritually acute time.

A stir trembled from inside the house to those clustered by the door to women and men waiting outside. The lama's music soared in full, the bleating blare from a *kangling* trumpet and conch shell thrilling the air, their deep, plaintive tones pulsing through a body. The head lama stepped from the house in deliberate, formal, slow-stepped motions. He read from a text held in his hands, learned authority in his rasped voice. Other lamas and several men holding the lam-den cloth followed. The banner uncoiled into a flowing white banner as the men strode further from the doorway and people tarried for a glimpse of the action. The effigy appeared in the shadows. Held by three men, affixed to the banner, this silent, watchful figure passed rockily through the threshold like a ship righting itself in stormy straights and emerged into the crowded clearing before the house.

I thought of how mourners carry a corpse to the cremation ground in much the same way.

The man's loved ones came close to his clothbound apparition. The widow

Figure 26. Procession to the site of a ghewa. Thodong, 1988.

walked with her sister, who supported her with an arm to her back. Tears crossed their cheeks. They were parting from him, seeing his face for the last time.

The lamas led the way around the north corner of the house, toward the gompa, the streaming white banner leading the effigy, the mourners close by, the banner and effigy searing a path through the crowd. Women carried the foods set out for the dead man.[24] A young girl with deep brown eyes carried an iron plate with charred ash. Women and men sang mani prayers, the lift of their voices fused with the crying of the saddened. A nephew of the dead man snapped pictures with a small black camera, crying as he turned the spool of film.

I took the Minolta camera from my knapsack and tried to hazard visions where I could get a good shot. The fleet pace of the procession along a narrow footpath round the back of the house and the overflowing force of mourners and their guests in motion kept me from framing the scene well. I lost my footing walking backward and fiddling with the lens. I dropped to one knee by a ridge. Boys giggled at my missteps. I smiled back at them, brushed the dirt off my pants leg, and stood on level ground to refocus. Everyone was in motion; they were sending the dead man off, saying goodbye, their thoughts cued to memories of him and to others lost, one year or another.

The lamas came to the makeshift gompa, renovated from a shelter for goats and water buffalo, and stepped inside. The men carrying the effigy held it low and rickety in approaching the cropped doorway. We watched their passage. They paused to get a better grip on the structure and carried it inside and gripped it anew. They brought it to a sound, level place before the altar and set it down.

The music halted. The family positioned before the dead man's torso foods and provisions he enjoyed while alive. A pack of cigarettes lay to the left of the foods, a bowl of chang to the right. The charred bone fit snug in the long-sleeved arms.

The effigy sat squarely by the altar, silent and still. People found places to sit in the crowded room. I wasn't sure where to sit or what to do.

I later gave thought to the anticipation so palpable and the shared sense of loss and expectation that came with the transport of the effigy from house to gompa. One memory that recurred was what a boy (now an adult, with children of his own) told me at the first ghewa I attended. We were standing close to a stone wall outside the home and the clearing before it, filled with guests and mourners.

"What happens now?" I asked, leaning an elbow against the wall.

The boy nodded toward the house and said, "Now they bring the dead man out and the people cry."

Minutes later they bought the dead man out and the people cried.

"It's all due to the affection that they cry," Goser Lama said when Temba and I asked him about this one day as we sat his home in Boudhanath.

Because their loved ones, people were close to them and with whom they spent their lives with, have died. When a mother dies, then her daughters and sons cry. It's normal in Hyolmo society—not only in Hyolmo society, but in the whole world. When someone dies who is dear to his friends and family, then the affection, and the thought that they won't be able to meet him again, makes them cry.

The simulation of the deceased can prompt sentiments of pain and sadness, connection and loss. The presence of an effigy can sharply resemble the dead person it represents; "people come to think the effigy is the same as the dead person"; "when the family members see the effigy, they think that the dead person is right next to them." The person's sudden reappearance can bring "a certain kind of satisfaction," as Goser Lama noted. Mourners can show their respect to the dead person, prostrate in front of him, voice prayers on his behalf, and offer foods to and talk to him, all the while "feeling as though the dead body is really standing there." The re-enacted presence of the "visual form" of the deceased appears to fulfill a desire among some to engage once again with the person lost.

Goser Lama once suggested that the making and viewing of an effigy was a "compulsion" for some. This compulsion, I take it, relates to a desire to give continued form to the dead person and to communicate tangibly with him. People need images, something tangible to hold onto, to work with, make and remake, particularly in times of distress.

And yet it can be painful to encounter the dead person again. The life-like form of the dead person induces sentiments of love and longing for the deceased. The ritual passage of the effigy from house to gompa, where it will soon be dismantled, leads family members to feel that the loved one is now leaving them for good. "It's because he has only a few more minutes to stay with us," Lhatul Lama told me when asked why people cry at this time. "And after those few minutes he has to leave us, and go to some other place. While he was inside the house, it was his house. But once he departs from the house, he doesn't come back. . . . That's why people cry then, because he is now being separated from all of them."

The visual image of the deceased induces a stream of recollections of that person as he was when he was alive; "If you make it exactly like the person, many memories will come again"; "There's pain, and in the mind all the mem-ories come, from very early on." One image brings other images, and people can relive, to an extent, how they once engaged with the dead.

These recollections are memories only. No further living engagements can occur. The sudden reappearance of the dead person can remind the mourners that the person is dead. Mourners face a second corpse several weeks after the first one was cremated. There is comfort and value in seeing the body of the deceased again. And there is heartache.

I took the photograph printed here back in 1989, at a ghewa in a village to the southeast of Thodong. Mourners are leading the effigy, protected by a black umbrella, from the dead person's house to the site of the funeral rites, the long white banner showing the way. When I showed the image to Pasang one afternoon in 2012 he looked at it and said, "Oh. There's a lot of emotion there. The feeling is right there, in a strong way." He held his hand close to the photo and drew it close to his chest. Pasang and I could have cobbled together an affect theory right there: certain images, crystalline of moods and moments,

Figure 27. "Showing the way." Dhupchugang, 1989.

can hit the heartmind, putting the feeling right there, the affective force leaping from image to body.

An effigy occurs in the lives of the living much as mournful memories do. Effigies of the dead, like memories of the dead, can be unsettling. Their full-blown appearance causes grief. Many feel that they are best avoided, done away with, left unconstructed or kept in a more diffuse form. Much the same could be said of memories. People have ambivalent relations to both memories and effigies. They long for them, have a "compulsion" to construct and relate to them, but they are aware of the distress they can cause.

Effigies wound. Names wound. Memories wound.

The charred bone snug in the effigy's arms enabled the head lama to summon the consciousness of the deceased to the site of the funeral rites. Once the consciousness had been localized in this way, and the body imaginatively depicted, the lamas and mourners took the effigy to be the dead person, complete with the awareness that the consciousness afforded, even in death. They acted toward the effigy as though they were acting directly toward the deceased.

Goser Lama:

First the consciousness is called and established on the name card, and through the print to the effigy. In the course of establishing the consciousness in this way, it should be called in a calm and smooth way. After the consciousness is summoned and established, the effigy is regarded as the dead person returning home and served like an important guest. The lama serves the consciousness food and satisfies it well by performing mantras. He then explains everything about what has happened to the dead person, what is to be done and what needs to be considered.

Mourners met their loved one face to face one last time. The head lama undertook an "explanation," much as he did during the earlier funeral rites, to clarify to the deceased what was happening and what was being done on his behalf. Family members, the widow included, followed with their own explanations. They held the name card in their hands and told the lost loved one what funeral rites they were sponsoring and which debts were being resolved. They advised him not to stick around the world of the living. Family members made these pleas one by one while looking at the effigy's face, opaque and expressionless in its blank whiteness. They saw his face envisioned one last time.

A dead person remains silent at such moments. It wasn't necessarily always that way, some say. "They speak as though the person is right there," Temba once said of the explanations performed by family members.

It's also said—I heard this as a young boy—that many years before the effigy also used to converse with the person speaking to it. It was the time when the bombo [healer] used to do all the funeral works. I don't know how true this is, but it's said that at that time the effigy used to talk back and ask questions and say what things had to be done and resolved.

What are we to make of the idea that in earlier, reportedly more shamanic times, the effigy used to talk back to the living? The story points, for one, to a sense of the potential invested in the effigy, how it's so close to being a fully realized person, for a material form can be inhabited, animated, and come to life in some sense. An effigy, the story goes, used to converse in full, dialogical terms with the living (just as deities and animals once fully conversed with humans, other narratives relate). But the story also notes that the effigy no longer does this. A limit to communication divides the living and the dead. Any communication between the two is one-sided, cut off. The story can also be heard as an allegory of how the actual, individual person used to converse with family members, but the dead can no longer do that. Death is silent. There is a shift, both in history and with any given death, from tangible affiliation and engagement to removed and distant contact. With a death language withdraws from us.

The effigy is like a corpse, a dead, vacated body, used as a temporary abode. If it were to come fully alive it would be a zombie, a *rolang*, "corpse-arisen," unnatural and unwarranted. These days the division between life and death is — and necessarily should be — a sharp, uncrossable one. The story points to the present limits of engagement with the living that occur with a proper death. There is a muteness to death, a silent emptiness. The face of death is a pure white blankness. A dead person never returns directly to the world of the living but only in some kind of associative, apparitional, simulated manner. The communication is never direct, never completely relational, never fully traversing the divide between the living and the dead.

Yet the person is still there, in some way, for the last time. This is why family members find such value in the funerary explanations.

"It's the last time," said Karma. "It's the last time that people can talk to the person who died. It's the final time that family members can communicate, and convey messages."

Those Dangerous Supplements

Dismantle the effigy that stands in for the deceased. Re-enact the death, ritually and mimetically. Mind the ways that love, memory, and simulations can disturb, disrupt. Conclude the funeral rites with a collective, spirited participation in sung prayers that continue through the night.

Forms appear and then disappear. Many events performed on the second day of the ghewa paralleled those that took place at the ne par. The name card was prepared and the lamas summoned the consciousness and established it within it. The print was burned immediately after the consciousness was transferred — shot like an arrow — to the Pure Land. The paper vanished to a dramatic charge of lamaic music. Family members collected and took away the foods. The assistants removed the crown from the head and they unwrapped the white cloth that composed the face. They unbundled the clothes that made up the bulk of the body just as the head lama performing the rite abolished the physical appearance of the deceased as he imagined first its appearance and then its disappearance through contemplative visualization. The effigy disassembled into a pile of loose clothes, and then there was no face, no arms, no body, no person.

Figure 28. Dismantling the effigy. Thodong, 1988.

The dismantling of the effigy (*ghur shyuge*) coincides with the end of the palpable, relational presence of the deceased in the lives of the living. The breakdown of form marks the end of tangible, actionable traces of the person that was.

"That completes the whole ghewa process," Karma said of the effigy's dismantling. "It reminds me in a graphic way that the deceased person is no more. Up to that point it was so important that the lama was performing rites directly linked to the deceased person. After that, there's nothing you can do directly for him. There are other rites, of course, but they don't affect the concrete existence. So that's the end of it."

The dismantling marks the end of the social process of death that began (but began only) with the demise of the body weeks before. If death for Hyolmo people is a lengthy process, which begins with the cessation of breathing, then the dismantling of the effigy signals the completion and terminus of that process. Before and after the consciousness left that body the living could relate to and act directly on behalf of the dead person. The dismantling signals the moment when death became securely nonrelational.

The effigy's sudden dissolution suggests an object lesson in the methods of life, death, and impermanence. The presence-then-absence of the effigy displays once again the constructed, relational, "empty nature" of all reality.

The act of "dismantling the effigy" reflects a second cremation: the deceased's body is eliminated once again. Gone in a matter of seconds, it is torn asunder, disaggregated. Images of the deceased are made and then destroyed time and again throughout the funeral rites. While it's difficult to say for sure why this is the case, it's evident that the making and unmaking of corpse-images models, in a temporally abrupt form, the flow and ebb of life as known by Hyolmo Buddhists. Composite forms arise, exist, and cease to exist. Something once constructed is soon deconstructed. Persons are made and unmade. A series of minor, fleeting rebirths and sudden, dramatic redeaths course throughout the funeral rites. Apparently, there is a need to enact the death of a person, time and again, for that person's benefit and for the benefit of the living.

Spouses in particular can become distressed upon witnessing the demolition of the effigy standing in for their lost loved one. Often, before the name card is set on fire, the widowed wife of a dead man is taken from the room after speaking to her husband as conveyed by the effigy. The fear is that if she directly perceives the act of "stripping off" of the clothes on the effigy, which she takes to be her "own deceased one," she will be greatly distressed and she will no longer be able to maintain control of her emotions. If it is a wife who has died, her husband usually stays, but only if he can control his emotions. Any emotional outbursts could jeopardize the proper transfer of the deceased's consciousness to the Pure Land and hinder the elimination of any remaining defilements and physical qualities.

The practice of constructing an effigy at a ghewa, carrying it from the house of the deceased to the temple and then dismantling it at the climax of the rites, has become increasingly contested and debated in Hyolmo communities. Some communities no longer use an effigy during funeral ceremonies. On the western side of the Hyolmo valley, where I conducted fieldwork in the late 1980s and have returned infrequently since, effigies are still commonly built and used at ghewa, to stand in for the dead person. On the eastern ridge of the valley, and in Kathmandu of late, families tend not to make an effigy. Most of them have stopped using one for two reasons: because they find it's not really necessary to prepare an effigy of the deceased in this way, and because the use of an effigy at a ghewa is known to induce displays of severe grief among mourners. These displays are thought to disturb the deceased's consciousness and trouble its transfer.

People are known to become distressed by the sight of the effigy being carried from the deceased's house to the temple, and any expression of grief at the ghewa is thought to give trouble "time and again" to the dead person: he encounters tears as rain, sobs as storms, and shouts as thunder. A mourner's distress can be detrimental to the ritual aims of a ghewa. "The less we have the effigy, the less we mourn and cry," Goser Lama explained. "The less we cry and mourn, the more the consciousness benefits."

Given this, some families and communities have decided not to use an effigy at ghewa, especially if an effigy was made at a ne par rite. If they do make an effigy, they do not perform the lamden procession wherein mourners carry it from the dead person's home to the place where the main rites take place.

People feel justified in not using the effigy for two reasons. One is that the use of effigy in funeral rites does not appear to be a "real tradition" of Buddhism; there is no mention of its use in the ritual texts they use, and it appears to be more "shamanic" than lamaic in form, in the sense that the use and nature of the effigy is like the many effigies used in the healing rites and exorcisms performed by bombo.

The second reason is that it's not necessary to use an effigy to summon the dead person's consciousness, extinguish any remaining sins and defilements, and dispatch the consciousness to the Pure Land. All of those acts can be accomplished with the use of the name card. There is a growing understanding that the effigy is *supplemental* to the rites being performed; it serves only to demonstrate in vivid and dramatic terms what is taking place. As Karma put it, "People understand more and more that the effigy, as a material thing, is not necessary. . . . It's really like a drama for people to understand what is happening."

These days, members of the same family sometimes are of different opinions as to whether or not to use an effigy at a ghewa for a lost family member. Dawa Jyaba Hyolmo spoke of how he and his brother took opposing sides on the matter in the wake of their father's death: his brother wanted to make an effigy, while Dawa did not. When Temba and I asked Dawa if an effigy was made at his father's ghewa, he replied, "Yes, we made the effigy." He continued:

When my family and I met to discuss how the ghewa was to be held, I said that I didn't want to make the effigy. But my brother didn't agree with me. What I told them was that, "If we make it or if we don't make it, it won't make any difference. Because if the lamas do all the rites properly, that's what will help the dead person."

When a person dies there's love. There's love. If you make the effigy exactly like the person, many memories will come again. Some faint even. If it's made exactly the same, they feel as if it is alive, with the hands set like this.

I said, "Don't make it." I also said to the lamas, "If it's really necessary, then show me in the lama texts where it says this. Otherwise, I won't
make it."

At first I refused to make the effigy, but after an argument with my
brother I realized that if I don't make the effigy, then people will say, "He
abolished the custom of making an effigy at his own father's funeral."

While making the effigy the people feel so much pain. There's pain, and
in the mind all the memories come, from very early on. And then from that
people cry. It's just like children playing with toys, it strikes me. It's made so
that it's just like the children playing.

For some, the effigy is a prompt, a theatrical device. Its imaginal basis can
be likened to the make-believe, pretend qualities of toys. Seen as such, this
theatrical play is a burden on mourners and gives trouble "time and again" to
the deceased. It's better not to have a concrete visual image of the deceased,
and it's better to reduce the degree of grief and sorrow. As Karma told it,
"More and more people tend to think that the effigy is a 'dummy' of the person, which has nothing to do with the physical existence now. The deceased's
existence is more spiritual in nature, so why even bother to make a life-like
thing? It's just a representation."

"Now the tendency is to make it as minimal as possible," Karma continued. "It doesn't really resemble the form of the person. It's just the clothes,
tidily folded clothes, and on top of that the rig nga crown is placed. It's a malsa
[resting place], in other words."

One line of mourning involves giving image and voice to memory and
sadness, to play out the loss in imaginative and dramatic forms in a moving
show of grief—shouts, cries, the terrifically felt image of the dead one. Another seeks to make the sentiments involved more refined, less theatrical, less
aching in their formations—purification into luminous emptiness. In the past
few decades most Hyolmo communities have been moving toward the latter
strand of mourning, suggesting a historical shift from more dramatic, "shamanic" sensibilities to more contemplative Buddhist ones.

The ghur effigy is characterized as a "dummy," a child's plaything, a theatrical device, unnecessary and superfluous to the spiritual work involved. In one
line of reasoning, an effigy is a supplement to the rites proper, and a "dangerous" one at that, much as writing has often been understood in European philosophical discourses as a "dangerous supplement" to speech, to full, direct, and
properly authentic communication, as Derrida has shown through a number

Figure 29. A malsa-like effigy. Kathmandu, 2002.

of writings. From Plato to Rousseau to Saussure to Lévi-Strauss and beyond, speech has been taken to be the immediate expression of living presence. Writing, in contrast, is constituted as merely a technical, auxiliary, and extrinsic form of communication, an "artful and artificial ruse," a set of "representative images" which can entail, at times, "a dangerous, almost maleficent technique."[25]

A parallel construction is at work in some Buddhist assessments of the use of effigies during Hyolmo funeral rites. The lamas' performance of the rites, drawing from Buddhist texts, advances a set of spiritual transformations which attend to the spiritual status of the deceased. The use of effigies is currently seen as unnecessary for the proper functioning of the transformations undertaken through the rites. There is no mention of them in the Buddhist texts recited during the funeral rites. The effigies and a few other processes are thought to be marginal to, exterior to, and superfluous to the rites proper. Many now take them to be a kind of non-originary, inessential technique, a shamanic add-on to the true and necessary spiritual processes required.[26]

The effigy is a dangerous supplement, a made-up device that shows in a graphic way what is happening to the deceased; a fictive figure that resembles the dead person, one last time. That life-like, corpse-like display can readily provoke strong emotions among the mourners, sentiments which can disturb the proper course of ritual and mourning. The emotions relate to vivid memories of a lost loved one. As Dawa put it, "If you make the effigy exactly like the person, many memories will come again. Some faint even."

Memories are a dangerous supplement to the funeral rites. They can flood a person in an anguish of pain and grief, and that torrent of emotions can trouble a smooth flow of ritual practices; it can disturb the journey that the deceased is presumably undertaking, to a buddha field or to a good rebirth. Memories are inherently dangerous. They can irrupt, stir, haunt, disappear, throw things into doubt, or take on new forms at any moment. As active as unruly ghosts, memories are never settled. They cannot be. Memories are largely wild, untamed; free radicals in a system of spiritual becoming. Specific memories can cause trembling in any ritual of remembrance or forgetting.

In effect, memories are like effigies: they are a secondary image and presence, a double of life and experience; they are built up after the fact; memories are fictive constructs, life-like "dummies" similar to the moment or person recalled. They embody a force field of differing energies. They involve the mark, the trace, of something no longer there. Memories are echoic, at once substantial and ethereal. They entail a ghostly presence; they are somewhat "stiff," inflexible, looming up from the ground of the earth, into the depths of consciousness, like those effigial memories that come late at night. As with effigies, an air of mourning is built into memories. Memories can be too graphic, too affective, overly dramatic. Some recollections must be exorcised, if they prove to be too threatening, too demanding in their persistence, too disturbing to keep around. Any remembrance is a dangerous supplement to life itself.

The more minimal, the better, or so goes one line of thinking on the matter. This sentiment applies to effigies, to memories, and to feelings of attachment and affection.

> Better not to think,
> if I think my heart aches
> to work with one's thoughts,
> it doesn't help anything

Love is a dangerous supplement. "When a person dies there's love. There's love," said Dawa. The doubling of his statement suggests the additive, augmentative, supplemental, potentially excessive nature of love within the mixture of life and death. Love is a potential disturbance to the effective passage from life to death for both the mourners and the deceased. The intensity of love and memories can wreak havoc with the smooth flow of ritual transformations.

Figure 30. Performing mani prayers. Ghyang, 1988.

Don't make it. Don't construct it. Keep it minimal. It's a question of poiesis, in other words, of generative making, fashioning, and it's a question of which kinds of construction are to be preferred over others.

Some forms of poiesis are dangerous. Poiesis can unsettle; haunt; disrupt; devastate. A generative act can put things out of joint or boomerang back on any creators or perceivers of its forms. One person's creation is another's disturbance.

My memory of the final hours of the man's ghewa and the days that followed has now faded, having fused with the ends of other lives in those years. What I do recall is that on the last and third night the name card was burned and the effigy dismantled and many participated in mani prayers known as *mani chhepa.* Led by a lama chanting the main texts of the prayers in time with the clash of a pair of cymbals held in his hands, women and men stood and formed a large circle. Some joined in when they could or wanted to; others left the circle when they tired. Women formed one moving line from eldest to youngest and men constituted another. At first the two loosely threaded groups walked slowly in a clockwise direction as though circumambulating and voiced the mani prayers in response to the lama's words. The pace picked up in time, the tone of the prayers became lighter, less mournful, and the lines of women and men began to dance in formal dance steps while clasping their arms together and shuffling and stepping their feet in skillful gestures. The prayers skipped into folk songs that many took delight in singing. The singing and dancing continued into the night; mourners joined in or slept or rested when fatigue overwhelmed them.

"The purpose of the mani chhepa," Binod Hyolmo told me years later, "is to tell the people that now the ghewa is over. The feelings of grief are now over. It's time to put that in the past and to celebrate."

I remember a man from Thodong, in his sixties then and related in marriage to the dead man, sitting with a friend who had traveled from the eastern ridge of the Hyolmo region to attend the ghewa, and who would be heading back home the next morning. Friends since childhood, the two had not seen each other in several years. Cups of chang in their hands, they sat on a grassy mound close to a crop of dry firewood, within earshot of the dancers circling a bonfire a short darkness away. They sang with hoarse voices and gestured with their arms in half-drunken time, half-sober rhythm to the songs chorused by the larger group. By the look of things they were singing for themselves, reminiscing through the lyrics, their bodies tiding back and forth, happy to be there, together, singing songs in those brief hours.

On that last day the head lama purified and blessed a religious object made on the dead man's behalf on the second, main day of the ghewa.[27] Once blessed by the lama, this object served to lessen the bad deeds carried by the consciousness and thus helped the consciousness to reach the Pure Land. The blessed object was kept "with great honor" in the home of the family of the deceased.

And on that third day the head lama gave a "blessing" (ngo wa) to the bereaved family members by affixing a dab of butter on each person's forehead while reciting certain mantras. Along with working as a blessing to these persons, the act served to release family members from the state of mourning which they had been in since the death and from the restrictions that came with it.[28]

I was later told that a final, more private rite was held on the forty-ninth day after the death. It was called dhinda, "period of seven" or "seventh week." The word dhinda denotes the seven-week period after a death. This is the last day in which any rites performed will benefit the consciousness of the deceased. Since the consciousness is bound to find a new rebirth by this time, any rites performed after it achieves a new rebirth are of little consequence. The lamas advise the consciousness during the rite that, as Goser Lama put it, "this very day is the last day for it to get to the next world, either a better one or a worse one. So, even if the consciousness has been roaming within bardo until this date, it is instructed not to remain there any longer, and instead to try to get to the Pure Land or to take any other, better life."[29]

"This is all we do when a person dies," said Goser Lama after giving an overview of all the rites that take place during the seven-week period. The dhinda is usually the last formal rite performed for the deceased in the months after a death. Some families, however, do perform certain offerings after the forty-ninth day, with the idea that they might benefit the deceased. As Goser related, "Although dhinda is the last day in which family members and relatives can help the consciousness to wash away its sins and to reach dewa, some people nevertheless perform more processions and offerings in the name of the deceased. They do so in the idea that, if the consciousness hasn't been able to get to dewa and if it's roaming in the between, perhaps it could use some help."

This is all that could be done for the man with a taste for millet beer and a gentle, understated way about him.

PART V

After Life

Made for Forgetting

Drive away remembrances of the deceased while preserving mementos and relics of the lost one. Observe the ways in which remainders and reminders of a dead person transform in time, in line with the transmutation of the deceased's identity into more subtle, abstract, and collective terms.

So often it's a question of remainders—what sorts of remainders are good and valuable, which reminders are unwanted, unfortunate, or harmful, and how certain traces of the deceased alter in time. Two temporalities are at work in the treatment of the bodily remains of a dead person. There can be efforts to extinguish the body, to dissolve its elements and features and end its existence in time, and there can be efforts to preserve remainders of it. *You have to live within this tension.*

Material traces of the deceased are dispersed in several ways. A family member sometimes eats the foods set out for the dead person at the funeral rites. Others, however, take the food to carry impurities, and they feed it to dogs. The clothes that compose an effigy are sometimes given to a poor person of the same relative age as the deceased; others throw the clothes away. Any other clothes once owned by the dead person are often given to the poor, usually with at least some rice kernels placed in pockets; since anything empty is not good, passing on clothing with empty pockets would be unwise. Dispersing and discarding tangible possessions of the deceased help "to drive away the remembrance," as Temba once put it. Any image-memory lodged in a trace remnant or an article of clothing can bring back sudden reminders of the hard loss, and so it's best to reduce the chances of any impromptu memories.

The rhiba bone is ground into powder and, along with the ashes that result from the burning of the name card, mixed with clay to form *tsha-tsha*, the small conical figurines.[1] Other figurines are made from the other powdered bones, and some of the remaining ash, of the cremated body. Block-prints are then used to inscribe the prints of the eight different kinds of chhorten on the surfaces of the figurines. Lamas bless and purify the figurines and then place them in pure and sacred places—either in caves or on the tops of mountains, in places where people usually do not tread. Or they are set within the crevasses found between the stones in mani shrines. If a new mani is being built, then tsha-tsha might be placed inside them.

One idea motivating the construction of these figurines is that, if one is made in the name of a deceased person, then she or he can obtain enlightenment. Because the eight chhorten are imprinted on a figurine, the person receives the same amount of karmic merit as he would if he had constructed eight chhorten while alive. Since such a feat, which few individuals could actually accomplish in their lives, given the costs and time involved, accrues great merit, that additional merit vastly outweighs any misdeeds of the person and so enables him to achieve enlightenment. A secondary benefit of making the figurines is that it is also known to help the living. If a living person is sick, if his *tshe,* or "life span," is diminished, or if he has committed many sins (sometimes these hindrances amount to the same thing), the sins and debilities can be "washed away" by making tsha-tsha. Many hold that a remarkable transformative power is inherent in tsha-tsha. They can enable the dead to attain enlightenment and so transcend the samsaric round altogether, and they can help the living to recover their health and good fortune.

The figurines form "purely abstract and anonymous symbols" of the deceased, placed outside the habitat of the living.[2] No names are recorded on them nor are any other biographic traces inscribed. In time, the figurines, placed in mani shrines or in caves or on mountaintops, are seldom, if at all, associated with particular persons. Grouped together in a flat pattern, they come to signal the dead in general, in a post-liminal arena. "A book is a huge cemetery," Marcel Proust wrote, "in which on the majority of the tombs the names are effaced and can no longer be read." A similar repository of anonymities is on hand with a reliquary of tsha-tsha figurines. Through time, the name and identity associated with a person is often lost and the person's idiosyncratic visual form and remembered features are replaced by more abstract, anonymous images of the dead as a semi-collective, ancestral presence.

The funeral rites as a whole entail a process of *effacement*, in which the deceased person's "name" and "face" are gradually but decisively dissolved. Promptly after a death, people long to "see the face" of the dead person before it vanishes. The body is soon covered up in a white cloth. The body is cremated. No body remains after that. The effigy carries a pure-white face. The name card is burned, after which the deceased no longer has a proper "name." Bones and cinders are taken and molded into generic figurines. Like the rare funerary monuments mentioned in the Vedic texts of ancient India, the figurines are in many ways "made for forgetting rather than for remembering."[3]

The bones of some have a different fate. On rare occasions, certain patterns are detected on the surfaces of a few of the remaining bones of the deceased person. Hyolmo people understand these patterns to indicate considerable spiritual powers, a pure heartmind (*jang chub semba*), or both, on the part of that person. These qualities transfer to the person's bones when the body is cremated. There is a textual quality to some bodily remains; traces of a person's moral and spiritual character are inscribed on his or her bones. Unlike other remains of the deceased, these special bones and bone fragments are preserved as they are. Usually cleaned up a bit, then wrapped up in a katha and set on an altar within a home, they are quietly kept and valued by family members of the deceased, sometimes for generations to come. Traces of the dead recur.

In fact, the name these chalky archives go by, *ring sel*, points to their preserved nature: while *ring* is found in words that connote a long time or a lengthy duration of time, *bsrel* means something maintained, kept, or preserved.[4] Hence ring sel can be translated as "things which are to be preserved for a long time."[5] It is something long maintained. In general, ring sel are either relics of a Buddha or a saint, or the remnants of burnt bones. As Hyolmo people know it, whereas rhiba, "burnt bones," can be recovered from any cremated body, ring sel are found primarily in the remains of great lamas. "Rhiba are for ordinary people. Ring sel are for important lamas," one man told me. The nature of a person's cremated remains can both indicate and confirm that person's spiritual status. And whereas rhiba are eventually ground into powder to form tsha-tsha, ring sel are kept as they are. The remains of spiritually advanced people only are preserved as they are—in part to inspire people to live similarly devout lives.

The patterns detected in ring sel are usually vague, but evident in them are certain religious images: a lotus, a conch, the form of a deity. "Gangyu Mheme, who was your grandfather and mine as well," Goser Lama told Karma, "was a great lama, and it was said that, after his cremation, [images of] wheels were found on the underside of his foot, as well as white shells. Perhaps the relics are still with his sons and grandsons. Great lamas, as well as those people with very good heartminds, will have a greater possibility of forming ring sel."

The chances that any relics will be found are increased if great care is taken with the cremation process, such that the corpse is not contaminated by the gaze or touch of others.[6] With most cremations the body is set on the pyre such that anyone present can see it as it burns. With some cremations, however, especially for the bodies of important and respected lamas thought to be spiritually pure, the body is set within a *bhunba,* a "vessel" or container which acts to shield it from the potentially polluting gaze and touch of others, including any persons "with evil hearts and minds." The vessel usually consists of a furnace-like structure, made of mud and stone walls and a ceiling, with a few small openings through which air and smoke can pass.

In talking with Karma I learned that such a structure was made for his father's body when it was cremated. The cremation was performed by Mheme Amji, the Tibetan lama who lived on the ridge above Ningali. Karma's father and Mheme Amji were close friends, and so it was fitting that the latter would perform the cremation rites in respectful honor of his friend's importance to him and others. As Karma conveyed it,

> Our lama was also in retreat at that time. But he said he was going to break the retreat. He would be there. He would do the cremation for our father. So he came out of retreat and he was there when he was taken to the cremation place. He was the one who decided that my father would be cremated at a separate place, because he was an important person in the village. And not only that, he was a lama himself.
>
> The cremation was done in a different way as well. Usually you can see the corpse from the outside. But my father's cremation was done differently than that. The pyre was built and the body was placed on top of it. They placed enough wood and other materials over it. Then they hid it. They built a wall, made of mud and stone, around the pyre, so that nothing could be seen. They left just a small opening for smoke to exit. Then no one could see the body.
>
> Usually, when the fire is lit and the burnt offerings are being made, the lama does not put them on the fire himself. There are assistants who take the

offerings to the fire. But the lama was very near the fire himself, so he was doing everything himself. That showed great respect for my father.

One reason that the corpses of powerful lamas and other notable people are set within such pure cauldrons when they are cremated is that mourners are anticipating that they might find relics. If the bodies were simply set on a pyre, without any enclosure protecting them, the touch or visual gaze of less pure, less good-hearted people could contaminate the bodies and ruin any chance of finding relics once the cremation is completed.

When Goser Lama related to Karma what he recalled of the death of Karma's father, he told him that he and several other lamas found relics at the cremation pyre where the corpse was cremated.

> The next morning we went back to the cremation site. I myself was there, and I had picked some of the ring sel from the cremation ground. There were some round-shaped bones. Some were like that of the mālā prayer beads, and some were like the shape of a white shell. Actually they were not so clear or well-patterned, but they were quite extraordinary looking. In general, ring sel are not so well-patterned or realistic in appearance. They only resemble certain patterns, in a slight way. With some persons the shapes of certain deities are also seen.

In speaking with me of his father's death in 1998, Karma himself recalled that a ring sel was found in the remains the morning after the cremation.

> The lama thought that there might be some relics left, some very special signs, with his body. So they made it so that no one could see the body when it was being cremated. And then the next morning the lama went to see it. All of the body was just ashes. But his skull was still there. The bone of the cranium was in perfect form. So the lama himself, he thought there might be something in the skull, so he took it and placed it in some water. It was in perfect form, he said. I wasn't there. My brother, my uncle, and the lama had gone there. They took it in a bowl of water and he shook it. The bone crumbled away. Later on, they found something inside, like a small heart-shaped bone. And then the lama said, "I think this is something special of him." We still have that. We don't talk about it with anyone, but we still have it, in an altar at home, in a special way—wrapped up in a ceremonial scarf. It's a small piece. Still, we don't talk about this with anyone.

Figure 31. A chhorten by the cremation grounds above Thodong, 2011.

People sift through the cremated remains of some, inspecting their bones, in search of signs of their spiritual powers and moral purity. Any relics found in the remains are preserved as visually based artifacts. The relic is a lasting material remainder and reminder of the deceased's spiritual qualities, and, by implication, of his existence, practice, and teachings. Relics stand as biographic markers. They contain graphic traces of a life. A perfect form crumbles away, leaving a cherished image behind.

If a person is especially respected for his spiritual qualities, a chhorten or shrine might be made in his honor after his death, provided there are funds to do so. The shrine can recall the person in death. A chhorten is a dome-shaped Buddhist religious monument, also known as a stupa. Ranging from the great chhorten in Boudhanath to small shrines in wind-swept mountain ridges, they are found throughout South Asia and the Tibetan plateau. The monuments are erected to house relics, generate karmic merit, or commemorate the life or death of notable religious leaders or relatives. They can suggest simultaneously the presence and the absence of the Buddha or spiritual leader whose trace reverberates with the monument.[7]

After Karma's father died the community built a chhorten on his behalf, on the same hill-top where his body was cremated. An inscription on it, composed in artful Tibetan script, begins with the words, "Alas, such an unfortunate time has fallen on us." Mheme Amji, the Tibetan lama who taught Buddhism to members of that community and a good friend of Karma's father, authored these words. He was also the one who decided on that location for the cremation and subsequent chhorten. For one, that hilltop was a relatively pure place, never used for the cremations of others. It was also within sight of the lama's own home, such that Mheme Amji could look out from his window and light his gaze on the monument honoring his friend. As Karma told it, "He selected that place because he wanted to keep in contact with him. The lama's place is right across the ridge. He said he could see it from the window. He was even thinking at that time that, given that my father had done so much for him, that, after he himself died, he wanted to have a stupa made for him, and placed in such a way that the two stupas would be facing each other."

Before Mheme Amji died in the early 1990s he constructed a chhorten close to his home and dedicated it to his next life. After he died, the community built a small chhorten in his honor, next to the one he had built. The two structures stand on a hilltop a few hundred yards away from the stupa made in honor of Karma's father, in clear sight of the other. Two friends sustain a loving, mutual visual contact with one another beyond their corporeal lives.

The use of stupas, relics, and figurines points to the ways in which material remainders and reminders of a dead person are transformed in time. The deceased's identity undergoes a comprehensive transmutation as well. What occurs is a ritually geared movement from more personalized and concrete physical marks of the deceased (a corpse, a charred bone, a resting place, an effigy, a name card, clothes, a written name) to more depersonalized, abstract and collective ones (figurines, relics, shrines). Step by ritual step, image after image, the deceased comes to be perceived in more remote, subtle, nameless, unworldly terms. With this "systematic rarefaction" of the deceased's presence, through time the images become less vivid, less life-like and personalized.[8] The trajectory of re-presentation embedded in the funeral rites as a whole moves toward greater abstraction, subtlety, and anonymity.[9]

Other transitions arise as well. The dangerous impurity and coarseness generated by the corpse alters into the purity and transcendent otherworldliness associated with figurines and relics. Whereas corpses, effigies, and name cards are but fleeting images, the qualities central to figurines, relics, and shrines point to objects which can last for years, generations even. Images of the deceased thus shift from the world of the living and the dying, from painful cycles of samsara and suffering, to realms removed from this world, stepping toward the timeless and the painless. As the Tibetan sage Milarepa put it at the end of his life, "Now that my time has come, my earthly body has been transformed into a more subtle form, dissolved into a totally awakened state of emptiness."[10]

The Enigma of Mourning

Consider the ways in which the funeral rites work on the consciousness of the bereaved, how they relate to the painful rupture of death, to sentiments of grief, to ritual repetitions, to the play of image and remembrance within the flow of life.

Sigmund Freud once spoke of the "great enigma" of mourning, "one of those phenomena which cannot themselves be explained but to which other obscurities can be traced back."[11] Why is it, he pondered, that it's such a painful process for people to relinquish their bonds to lost loved ones and fashion new ties in life?

For several years now I have been consumed by a comparable enigma of mourning among Hyolmo people. This riddle has several, interrelated strands, tied to the ways in which the funeral rites proceed in time: why is it that the rites so incessantly invoke images of the deceased, one after another, only to dissolve many of those same images within the next ritual moment? Why is it that these images move so securely from imageries of tangibility, distinctiveness, and graphicness to ones of relative abstraction, anonymity, and otherworldliness? And in what ways, if any, do these funeral processes work to assuage or transform the grief of those mourning a loss? How, in brief, does mourning proceed in a Buddhist world?

I have been hooked on these questions, much as a person gets snagged on certain mysteries of life. I have dreamed about them, in a vague, inchoate way, especially in the years when I wasn't working on this book, only to wake with ghostly visitations at hand. To say that I've been gently haunted by these questions, and that the current text entails an attempted exorcism of that haunting, would be valid. My mind has wanted to come back to the enigmas, to figure them out or to gain at least an informed sense of what is involved in Hyolmo engagements with a death.[12]

There's no single answer to be had, however. In giving thought to what is at work here I can offer only a bundle of different readings that suggest plausible explanations, though I'm not sure of any of it. An air of uncertainty and undecidability runs through what can be said about all of this—is it all folded within an epistemology of *khoi?* Perhaps the most lasting truth lies in the broader pattern of thought that might emerge out of such a bundle of interpretations. These assessments, which run from what could be called the historical-genealogical and cultural to the psychological and phenomenological, speak to the workings of longing, memory, and imaginative forms in Hyolmo lives and deaths.

1. *The funeral rites reflect cultural and ritual formations of death in many societies.* In many communities mourners perform funerary rituals in which subsequent images of a dead person are invoked and then taken away. These images can involve quite tangible, life-like images of the deceased or more symbolic enactments of that person's "corpse." Debbora Battaglia, for instance, observes the ways in which mortuary rites among the Sabarl of Papua New Guinea enact and attend to six different "corpses" of the deceased.[13] And in his classic study on "the collective representation of death," Robert Hertz wrote of the ways in which "second bodies" of a deceased person are constructed in rituals in a number of societies, often long after the first body has been buried or cremated or transmuted into another state.[14] Hyolmo people know of similarly repeating images of the deceased—a third body, a fourth body, and so on—in ways that parallel what results from a death in other places.

Why do such multiple imaginings of the dead occur time and again in so many societies throughout the world? We cannot really say, but it's likely that there is more than principles of "cultural diffusion" at work here. There is something in the composition of human beings which leads them to respond to close deaths in ways that call for repeated—and changing—images of the person and body that has been lost to them while mourners engage in rituals which, in time, transform the gist of those simulations. The human mind, in combination with the world, in conversation with other minds, appears to promote a changing arena of images.

2. *The incessant invocation then dis-appearance of images of the deceased reflects the nature of temporal form in Hyolmo society.* The underpinnings of Hyolmo lives consist of a (richly Buddhist) play of forms and forces in the world. Presence, then absence, then presence again; changing involutions of form and image, of self and consciousness; names and emptiness; echoes reverberating and changing form in time: this is how the world works for Hyolmo people. Composite forms—bodies, persons, families, communities—arise, abide, then cease to exist. This is life's constant carnival, as Hyolmo people

know it. It is to be expected, then, that these are the structural and temporal forms by which the funeral rites proceed: one image after another, one image dissolving into another, forms echoing in time in a structured dream play of images and simulations, empty names. The deceased's recurring presence is an "echo," a *bhaja*, which becomes fainter, more subtle, through time.[15]

3. *The imagery advanced by the funeral rites serves as an object lesson in the ways of life.* The rites teach the living and the dead that living forms exist, then cease to exit. The funeral rites offer a weeks-long meditation on *chhiwa mita-kpa*, "death, impermanence." Much as family members might place a sacred text on the forehead of a dying person and ask him to consider the nature of death and impermanence, so the funeral rites generate a similar kind of contemplation. The rituals touch close to the heartminds of mourners. Form slides into emptiness, and emptiness into form. The recurrent, successive body-images model the life and death process in a temporally abrupt, accelerated form: arising, abiding, ceasing. Something is assembled, and then disassembled. "The great lesson of Buddhism," scholar John Strong rightly points out, "is not that of impermanence, if, by impermanence is simply meant 'nothing lasts forever.' It is rather that of process—that things, beings, buddhas come into existence due to certain causes and go out of existence due to certain causes."[16] The funeral rites convey just this lesson on process. A Buddhist philosophy of life and death is conveyed, but through ritual practice rather than explicit statement or textual exegesis.[17] These ritual invocations presumably inform the consciousnesses of the living and the dead alike. They teach people how to live, how to die, and how to engage with the changing tides of life and death.

4. *The funeral rites are a guide and ritual practicum for the deceased.* They "show the way" to the Pure Land or to a good rebirth. They serve as an explanation to the dead person, instructing him as to how to best proceed now that he is no longer alive and advising him on how to achieve a good rebirth. In this regard, the subsequent re-presentations of the deceased's post-life forms work to signal his changing form and status as the process of death unfolds. The funeral rites thus parallel a central aim of the *Liberation upon Hearing*, the Buddhist text which is read to the dying and the recently deceased: to provide a detailed pathmap into death. "Because if you look at the *Bardo Thedol*, it's just instruction," Karma told me when we spoke about this. "And the rituals are also helping them to go through this structure." The altering images of the deceased's form, combined with the many explanations and ritual enactments, offer signposts of the terrain involved and all changes afoot.

5. *The rites offer a model of transcendence.* The recursive, changing images, moving from the sorrowful body of the deceased to the subtle form found in figurines and stupas, speak to the ways in which a person can achieve liberation from the samsaric cycle of suffering that brings so much coarse suffering to people's lives. That model applies both to the idea of an individual life, in which rebirth in the Pure Land is achieved, and to the construct of a linked series of lives, deaths, and rebirths, with enlightenment and liberation being achieved once a consciousness has acquired sufficient wisdom, spiritual purity, and karmic merit. This is the model of a process in a clear and systematic form. What does it say about a lived world in which the processes at work in a person's death are equal to a process of transcendence?

6. *The funeral rites involve a circuit of mastery play through ritual.* Those affected by a loss are trying to manage the strains of death through ritual means. Hyolmo people, like many other peoples in the world, draw on cultural institutions which enable them to feel they have a significant hand in the procedures of death rather than being totally at the mercy of it.[18]

A paradigmatic example of mastery play comes from the writings of Sigmund Freud. In *Beyond the Pleasure Principle*, Freud describes how a one-and-a-half-year-old child would attend to anxiety and uncertainty in his life by manipulating objects within his reach. This young boy, who happened to be Freud's grandson, had the reputation for behaving "properly."

> Occasionally, however, this well-behaved child evinced the troublesome habit of flinging into the corner of the room or under the bed all the little things he could lay his hands on, so that to gather up his toys was often no light task. He accompanied this by an expression of interest and gratification, emitting a loud, long-drawn-out "O-o-o-oh" which in the judgment of the mother (one that coincided with my own) was not an interjection but meant "go away" (*fort*). I saw at last that this was a game, and that the child used all his toys only to play "being gone" (*fortsein*) with them. One day I made an observation that confirmed my view. The child had a wooden reel with a piece of string wound round it. It never occurred to him, for example, to drag this after him on the floor and so play horse and cart with it, but he kept throwing it with considerable skill, held by the string, over the side of his little draped cot, so that the reel disappeared into it, then said his significant "O-o-o-oh" and drew the reel by the string out of the cot again, greeting its reappearance with a joyful "*Da*" (there). This was therefore the complete game, disappearance and return. [19]

As Freud understood it, the child's solitary play of "fort-da" corresponded to the fact that his mother would leave in the morning and return at night, with the mother's recurring absence causing the boy some distress. By making something disappear and then come back, the boy could imagine that he was master of his life situation as well. Significantly, he used symbolic means to do so. "The meaning of this game was then not far to seek," Freud went on to say. "It was connected with the child's remarkable cultural achievement—the foregoing of the satisfaction of an instinct—as the result of which he could let his mother go away without making any fuss. He made it right with himself, so to speak, by dramatizing the same disappearance and return with the objects he had at hand."[20]

Hyolmo people engage in a similar kind of ritual play. When it comes to the funeral rites, however, the complete game is more a case of "da-fort," here-gone ("*āmā, khoi?*"). The mourners make the semblance of the deceased re-appear and then dissolve into emptiness again. Return and disappearance: this is mastery play with a Buddhist twist, consistent with a religious sensibility founded on ideas of emptiness. The funeral rituals attend to the play between life and death, presence and absence, as well as the faint and fluid differences between them. Is it that the rites are constantly trying to master absence without ever being fully successful in that effort? Do the rites simulate a recurrent scene of failed completion?

7. *The rites entail a culturally arranged brand of "repetition compulsion."* That is, the funeral rites tie into the need to re-enact painful experiences in words, acts, or dreams. As psychologists know it, this sort of compulsive recurrence is evident in people who talk incessantly about a painful event, or in trauma-tized individuals who repeatedly re-experience an original trauma through their dreams. In such cases, psychologist Erik Erikson suggests, "the individual unconsciously arranges for variations of an original theme which he has not learned either to overcome or to live with: he tries to master a situation which in its original form had been too much for him by meeting it repeatedly and of his own accord."[21] Something similar is in play with Hyolmo funeral rites, though here the repeating variations take on a cultural form within a ritual system that kicks in after a death. It's more like the ritual system rather than any individual persons is involved in the spiral of repetitions, as though the collectivity of the culture itself is trying to retrace and rework an earlier pain. In any event, when mourners attend to the invocation-then-dismantling of the deceased's semblance, they revisit the death and the emotions involved. This leads them to engage repeatedly with the loss and their responses to it.

And yet the rites involve constructive repetitions rather than any com-pulsive, same-bound ones, in the sense that the rituals do not simply keep re-peating the same actual moment of death but, rather, turn that moment into something different, more distant, transformative, and transcendent. Conceiv-ably, the mourners are not in the same place at the end of this spiraling, ever-turning ritual process as they were in the harsh hours of the death.[22] Do the repetitions change something in the bodies and consciousnesses which con-template them?

8. *The funeral rites entail a template of grieving, of, specifically, the diminu-tion of grief.* Grief at first is sharp, coarse, terribly raw, and dangerous. In time, it tends to become more diffuse, remote, abstract, and "subtle." Though it never expires completely, grief can come back to haunt a person or family in the quick of a word or image. The succeeding images of the deceased, first the coarse and impure tangibility of the corpse, and then the ghostly and emotion-producing specter of the effigy, and then finally any figurines, relics, and shrines that result, parallel a hard-traveled transition from acute grief to a remoter and subtler sense of loss. The rites offer an oblique guide for the bereaved, suggesting ways that their grief can turn into forms less sharp and painful. The altering images point to the infinite attenuation of grief in people's lives, in which sorrow, while never completely banished, diminishes in strength as time passes and life takes on new forms.

9. *The funeral rites entail a work of mourning.* The rituals can help people to recover, in at least some ways, from their grief. For one, by being able to view the successive constitution and deconstitution of the deceased's form, the be-reaved are aided in their efforts to come to terms with the death. Engaging with the different iterations of the deceased is like "holding" the body of the dead person in extended, ritually recurrent form. It's useful and valid to con-sider the various images of the deceased — effigy, bone, mirror image, name card, figurines — as "corpses," in a sense (or: part corpse; part living, remem-bered person). People take in the death sensorially and viscerally through a seven-week period. The ontologization of death, in which the loss is given concrete, tangible form, prompts a realization of death for both the living and the dead. The fact that people recognize these semblances as representations of a dead person, rather than those of a living one, underscores that percep-tion, as does the fact that many of the images first appear and then disappear. "Yes, it's death," people come to realize. Any potential denial of the reality of death is countered with palpable visual evidence. As Derrida averred, "Noth-ing could be worse, for the work of mourning, than confusion or doubt."[23]

10. *The rituals prompt transformations in memory and relation.* A series of
substitutions leads to changes in people's relations to the deceased. Through
time the deceased's persona changes; it becomes less life-like, less person-like
and personified, more divine and otherworldly. This reconfiguration of form
contributes to an altered sense of the deceased's status and a family's relation
to the loved one. Relations, perceptions, and emotions are different by the end
of the funeral rites, and this helps people to tend to their loss.

An instructive parallel can be drawn with the mortuary rites among the
Jivaro people of eastern Ecuador, as chronicled by anthropologist Anne Christine Taylor.[24] Taylor relates that among the Jivaro, in order for the dead to
transform into spirits, they must realize that they are dead, and the living
must "disremember" them by forgetting their existential individuality. A set
of mourning chants work to depersonalize the dead by stressing the separation
of the living and the dead, as well as the gradual loss of identity of the dead,
"as they become bereft of social relations, name, mutual vision and speech."[25]
The chants also speak to the decomposition of the body; the dead person's
"physical appearance is gradually ground into oblivion, through an obsessive
and very graphic description of the rotting of the flesh and particularly the
face."[26] The chants, Taylor contends, entail the "deliberate erasure of visual
memory effected through a verbal mimesis of bodily decomposition."[27] The
gist of the mourning chants rubs out the deceased's appearance in time and
blurs the memory of the individual himself.

Hyolmo funeral rites engage in a comparable kind of "remembering to
forget."[28] Here, though, the existential individuality is effaced through a visual
mimesis of bodily abstraction. Memories of the deceased as a subtle body,
transcended from a world of suffering, supplant more viscerally tangible (and
painful) memories of the deceased as a distinct being in the world of the living. For those grieving the loss of a loved one, initial memories of the death
often center on the jolting presence of the corpse, the shock of the burning
body, and the stark finality of the cremated remains. Subsequent invocations
of the deceased move toward increasingly more refined and subtle images of
the lost one until there is not so much distinct memories left but "the surface
of remembering," as Faulkner once put it.[29]

I introduced this line of thinking to Karma one wintry afternoon in December 2009 as we conversed in his home in Queens, New York, a light
snow falling outside. In the course of discussing a number of themes related
to Hyolmo mourning practices, I took out a pen and sketched out a chart
that diagrammed the increasingly abstract representations of the deceased

through the course of the funeral rites. "This also relates to how memories change through time, as well," I suggested at one point. "So at first these things are very distinct, and graphic and concrete. And then through time memories become more abstract."

"More subtle," Karma said.

"More subtle?"

"Yes."

"Okay, that's a good way to put it," I said, noting Karma's phrasing.

"Yes, these are the graphic things that bring more memories," Karma continued. "That's a good way to put it, that the memories are slowly getting more and more abstract, more subtle. Even when you get to this point, there's a memory, but the memory is not the same as when you were really—"

"It's not as intense."

"It's not intense. And now it's very subtle. It's more religious, or more spiritual."

"More transcendent?"

"*More transcendent.* As if now, the memories are already out of this world."

"It's beyond normal, everyday life."

"Yes, yes. They're out of this world now."

"And the deceased has taken on a different form now," I added.

"A different form now, yes. And this then is what reminds us of the deceased—the chhorten. Which is the most divine."

A death is often an abrupt, ruptured end to a life. A lifeless, distorted corpse and the subsequent cremated "heap" are often visually and psychically wounding. By prompting a series of subsequent and changing images of the deceased, the funeral rites enact semblances of the lost loved one that become increasingly more abstract and refined, less raw and graphic. New visual images replace more wounding ones. This changing imagery can help to drive away certain remembrances and take the edge off the loss.

The flow of images can also help to attenuate and alter the mourners' sense of attachment to the deceased. If creating images and rituals helps to sustain relations, then there has to be a modification of this in time. The diminishing images of the deceased simulate and prompt a gradual, compassionate waning of the relations between the living and the dead. "This is how you can relate to this person now."

11. *The recurrent focus on emptiness and impermanence works to assuage the grief of mourners.* It's all a dream, an illusion, the rites appear to be saying, so why be invested in the loss of something that is forever ephemeral and in-

substantial? In *The Life of Marpa the Translator*, a spiritual biography of the eleventh-century Tibetan scholar and teacher, it's told of how Marpa once tried to lessen the grief of an old man and woman whose only son had died by explaining Buddhist teachings to them. "If you dreamt that you had a son who died, you would feel grief," he tells them. "You would feel suffering for the death of someone who had not been born. Your suffering for your present son is not different from this. Think of all this as a dream, as an illusion, and don't be upset."[30]

When Marpa's own son Tarma Dode dies later on, his wife Dagmema is extremely grief-stricken. To "clear away" her grief, Marpa sings her a song, each stanza of which ends with the phrase, "O Dagmema, clear away your grief for our son."[31] "There is no one to grieve for," he sings at one point. And elsewhere:

> With the realization that appearances are empty,
> one cannot find anyone to care for. . . .
>
> With the realization of this land as illusory appearance-emptiness,
> grasping and clinging to it are futile.
> O Dagmema, cast off grasping and clinging to castles.
> O Dagmema, clear away your grief for our son. . . .
>
> Thus Marpa sang.
> The grief of Dagmema and all the others there was cleared away, and
>   their realization was heightened.[32]

In invoking then dismantling a series of wispy semblances of the deceased and advancing more generally a creed of emptiness, the funeral rites spur the cognition that appearances are empty of inherent existence, that clinging to lost illusions is pointless—that, in the end, there is no one to grieve for. There is no form, no self, no loss. Life itself is built of an oneiric structure, as is mourning and ritual. The poeisis of life is altogether dreamlike.

Such sentiments can help people to come to terms with the change in their relationship with the deceased. The relationship is now one of emptiness only. Marpa sings to his wife:

> In general, it is characteristic of all composite things
> That ultimately they are never permanent.

In particular, the connection and relationship
Between ourselves and Tarma Dode has ended.[33]

The rites strike at the end of the tangible connection between the living and the dead, either through specific ritual acts of disengagement, of "cutting" and dis-connection, or through the broader messages conveyed. Can a sense of emptiness lighten grief?

12. *The funeral rites serve, at times, as an anti-trauma device.* A sudden or tragic death can be wounding for family members, much as witnessing the burning of a loved one's body can be. The formality and temporality of the rites is soothing, as is the direction of that temporality. The funeral rites establish a temporal order that helps people to deal with the grief and trauma that so often comes with a death. If "trauma destroys time," in the sense that a traumatic event can shatter a person's sense of a secure and reliable continuity in time and in life, then the funeral rites can re-instantiate a sense of continuous, coherent time through the days and years after a death.[34] New images replace earlier, more painful ones, the graphic visions of the death are erased, and the world calendars on again. At the same time, the ethics of care upheld by mourners is itself comforting and reassuring, which is to say counter to wounding.

These ideas came into consideration when talking with Karma that same December day about the "shock" and "trauma" that family members face when seeing loved ones being cremated. "And so," I asked, "if actually seeing the person that way can be traumatic, then these other images of the person are less and less traumatic, right?"

"Yes. Like I said, at first things are very graphic," Karma said. "And then later on there's just the rhiba, there's just remnants now, it's just slowly dying away. And then, at these later stages you can still remember the death, but it's not traumatic any more. You've done the best you can do, and probably it has helped the deceased."

"So, is the ritual process itself reassuring?" I went on to ask. "What I mean is that one could make the argument that, if someone dies, there is this moment of anxiety and even trauma, and grief, and by having the ritual process, it gives a kind of order for people, something that is situated in time, and they know that things are going to progress in a certain way. Is that soothing for people, and comforting?"

"It is. It is. We have a common saying, for instance when someone dies, 'You shouldn't cry so much. That will just confuse the deceased.' What you said makes sense. Doing the rituals helps to smooth out and pacify all the confusions."

Nothing could be worse, for the recently dead, than confusion and doubt.

13. *The rites establish an ordered continuum of memories.* They set up a patterned scaffold of memories that moves people away from recalling the deceased in dangerously disruptive ways. Karma, again: "I think the funeral rites, like you said, work as a system. Even the memories are done in a nice sequence. That's what all the rituals are for, I think. If the memories are frenzied memories, then it could be very dangerous. But these are really the more structured ones."

"So the funeral rites give a kind of order to the memories?" I asked.

"Yes, it relates them to the different, important stages. You are not just remembering the bad times. It's really remembering them, but in a patterned way, relating them to the different stages."

"So the rituals are showing people how to use the memories."

"Yes."

"And they're saying this is the way you should remember the person, and not these more frenzied memories?"

"That's how you benefit the deceased, you know."

"As well."

"Yes, remembering them in this way helps the deceased to go through these stages."

Enacting ritual remembrances of the deceased after the death benefits both the living and the dead. The living come to remember a lost loved one in less-disturbing, "frenzied" ways, and those active recollections, conveyed through concrete and tangible images—a name card, an effigy—serve as clarifying statements to the deceased as it makes its way in the intermediate between. Is the dead person able to sense the new forms he is becoming?

14. *The imaginative operations involved in the funeral rites are a reflection of a particular kind of memory work undertaken by the grief-stricken.* Many memories of the death and lost loved one are painful and dangerous. Images of the deceased recur in the lives and dreams of the bereaved. People regard these images warily, as they know of their power to hurt and unsettle. It's best not to dwell on these memories or welcome them wholeheartedly. They can't stay around unless they linger in a more purified and remote way. The memories must be dissolved, transformed, driven away—exorcised, as it were. The recurrent appearance-then-dissolution of semblances of the deceased during the funeral rites parallels the churn of memories faced by the bereaved. *You're*

here, again. You have to go, you can't stick around. The funeral rites reflect how mourners often deal with memories of the deceased. They provide a model for that ambiguous, ambivalent process.

15. *The changing, recurrent re-presentations of the deceased involve a play of ambivalence.* Mourners want to hold on to their lost loved one, to preserve their ties to the deceased, to keep them alive and present in their lives and thoughts, as though they were not really dead. But they also concede that it's best to sever attachments and help the dead person wean itself from its present life and move on to its next. *Stay, don't go. You must go.* In line with this tug-of-war of competing desires, presences of the deceased are invoked and engaged with, and then undermined, in the same ritual breath. Care for a corpse, but eliminate it. Call the consciousness back to the house, only to tell it that it must leave. Construct and talk to an effigy, and then dismantle it. Preserve the charred bones and ashes and mold them into earthen figurines. Hold onto something singular and body-burnt of the deceased, yet transform those remains into something anonymous and collective. Retain, yet relinquish. The rites tender a theatre of ambivalence. They gird this wavering ambivalence, make a theme of it, play it out. People touch on conflicting desires and responsibilities within the imaginative folds of the rituals, with their ambivalence taking on more diffuse forms as the rites proceed.

16. *The rituals are in, and of, and about, time.* The funeral rites mark the progression and passing of time, both through the weeks-long expansiveness of the rites and by route of the churning transformations and temporal density of so many ritual moments. As such, the rites show how the passing of time inevitably involves difference and change.[35] Here, time itself is a force of change. That pressing sense of time as change and difference might help mourners to grasp how the forms of their loss might come to be altered. Do the rites help the grief-stricken to move along in life?

Or so go some nonbinding currents of interpretation, as overlapping as the rites themselves. Time and again, I am struck by the inherent beauty and the wisdom imbued within the funeral rites. It's unclear where this wisdom comes from, or who its "author" is, if any. There is no single creator at hand; the means and ends of the rites go beyond any given self or consciousness or community. There is a beauty in that wisdom. This is much like the wisdom evident within the folds of a flower, or the organic depths of a forest, or the ways in which a cut into the flesh of a body slowly heals, in time.

When I conveyed this bundle of interpretations to Karma that wintry afternoon in Queens, he said they made sense to him. But he also cautioned that the chief purpose of the rites is to transmit the deceased person's "soul" or consciousness to a buddha field or to help the person to achieve a good rebirth. Any explanation of the rites' purposes had to include that fact. Karma then added, "But when you put what you've said together with the focus on the soul, then it's going to make perfect sense. The rituals are doing two things at once. They are helping the mourners to realize what is going on, and they are doing these things for the deceased."

There is solace only. However effective the rites might be in altering certain perceptions and feelings among the bereaved—if that is even the case—it's clear that the severity of grief is, at best, lessened only some. In watching the video of the passing of Sange's father that September in Nepal, it struck me that Sange's mother did not appear especially distressed in the hours before her husband's passing. A few days later I asked Pemba, this woman's daughter-in-law, if that was in fact the case. "She was upset and sad," Pemba answered.

> But it was internal. She didn't show [her sadness] on her face. Sometimes when she is alone she remembers her husband and weeps. But another reason is that, as she is also old, she will also die, and death is a natural process. One who comes on this earth has to die. I think she thought in this way. Many lamas told her not to cry or weep, otherwise her husband's consciousness might not be able to go away and she might have semjha. She did what she was told. But despite all of these things, she cries when she is alone because it is very difficult for one to forget one's partner, the one with whom she has spent her life. She was upset and saddened by his death.

For many, the sting of an irrevocable absence lies just below the surface of everyday relations. When I visited with a family in the Hyolmo region in the summer of 2011, a woman and I got to reminiscing about my previous stay there, in the 1980s. We talked about some travels by foot I once undertook, which led me through the village where the woman grew up with her parents and sisters, a day's walk from where she now lived.

"I must have met your father when I was there," I told her. "I'm almost sure I met him when I was in your village and stayed in your family's home."

Mention of her father brought tears to her eyes. A pained look crept into her face. Troubled by her apparent distress, I mentioned another topic and we moved on to other reminiscences.

No rituals, no life-like simulations or transformations of consciousness, no soothing texts or prayers, no searing beauty, no suggestions to take life as a dream or an illusion can solve the cold actual stab of a loss.

The grief is seared into a person's life: it becomes the language she hears. The name of another carries a lasting emptiness. A lost love exceeds the processual logic of rituals. It's too much for any spiritual counsel. Love is the deepest cut.

Staring into the Sun

Engage with death in order to know it better, to better grasp what it means to be alive. Be careful not to stare at death for too long at a stretch, lest life itself become a form of dying. Recognize the emergence of new turns of life in places where loved ones have died.

"When are you going to see the bombo?" people asked me soon after I arrived. It had been some fifteen years since I had last seen him. Dupsang Bombo had been my *guru,* my teacher, in the late 1980s, when I was studying healing practices among Hyolmo people. I wanted to pay my respects twenty years after those lessons ended. In those first heady months of fieldwork I tagged along when he went to his clients' homes and sat by his side as he played the drum to exorcise evil ghosts or retrieve lost spirits. I stayed at his home some nights, dined with him and his family, and slept, like them, on the floor, close to a smoldering fire. He taught me his curative work. Bonds like this between a teacher and his student are singular in spirit and often entail lifelong commitments.

"When are you going to see the bombo?" a few asked me. He was still living in Dhupchugang, an hour's walk from Thodong, where I was staying. Having almost ninety years, he was old now and he could not walk about much. "His legs are skinny and he has no teeth," one woman told us. She hunched her back and sucked in her teeth to mime his posture. The bombo had stopped performing the healing rites. His son had taken on the bulk of that work.

To see the bombo would be to see his face again, and to see it, perhaps, for the last time.

I had returned to the villages in July of 2011, in the wet damp of the monsoon. The rains kept us from setting off for several days, but when the skies suggested drier hours one afternoon we set off for Dhupchugang. Pasang and Sange, sons of Dawa Lama, joined me as we climbed up to the trail that curved east around the shoulder past Thodong. We passed grass-green pastures, feeding cows, and water buffalo sucked by leeches. A misty rain fell. We traveled

Figure 32. The author, with Dupsang Bombo. Gulphubanjang, 1986.

along the new road, clear and expansive. I had traveled the old route countless times before in walking to and from the bombo's house, alone or with companions. Heading to his home on days when healing ceremonies had been arranged, I would walk alone and in apprehension of what might take place. I would then return the next morning, alone again, strung out from fatigue but invigorated by the ecstasies of healing and all that I was taking in. I remembered passing through dense, quiet woods where often the only sounds to be heard were forest birds and far-off youths chopping limbs for firewood and singing winsome *tser-lu*, songs of heartache. Now the road was clear of overhanging branches and craggy roots in the soil and we did not have to worry about leeches dropping down onto coats or shoes.

We descended into the narrow, cavernous path that zigzagged into the village. The trail was wet with rain and we labored to find good stones and roots to place the soles of our feet. We came to a set of two-story houses set close to the new road that passed through the area. Word of our arrival brought Rinzin, the bombo's second son, outside a well-kept house. I hadn't seen him in fifteen years. . He said his father was upstairs. I asked if I could see and talk with him.

"Sure," he said. "*Āunus.*" "Please come."

Mheme, "grandfather," was settled on the veranda that ran along the face of the second floor, surrounded by blankets and clothes. He wore the same large necklace he owned years ago. He was resting. We came close and his son helped him to sit upright. He knew who I was, right off. Perhaps he had heard I was around and would be coming to see him. He was thinner and more fragile than I had known him to be.

"He can't hear well," his son said.

Mheme pointed toward his mouth and said, "I have no teeth."

"*Hajur*," I said. Yes sir.

"He is at the time of dying," the son said in a quiet voice.

He had been so strong before, I thought. Energized by the spirits, this healer could perform a night's length of healing rites, starting in early evening and going till dawn while I collapsed from fatigue around three in the morning and curled up on a mat in a corner, into a jolty, restless sleep filled with drumming, the smoke of the fire, shadowy spirits. Through a night-long ceremony of sustained drumming and chanting, he worked to reestablish a sense of attentive, connected being in persons or households plagued by "spirit loss" or malevolent forces. He summoned deities and banished demons. He labored to retrieve lost spirits, "awaken life forces," ward off malevolent forces, rethread social bonds, and instill a vital sense of presence among his frail charges.[36] Whereas the death rites are geared toward the dissolution of a self and social relations, a bombo's healing ceremonies work to recompose selves and families.

I placed my knee on the floor and knelt close. It was good to be there with him and to have this opportunity to see him—and this despite of, or because of, the differences between us.

Difference had always been a feature of my days in Nepal, but not all differences are alienating. Dupsang was a good forty years older than me. From an early age he had undertaken a nightdark comprehension of deities, demons, witches, and lost spirits that set him apart from most men and women. When I stayed overnight with him and his family in his home, I found myself surrounded by habits distinct from those found in Thodong. I'm not sure Dupsang ever understood that I was conducting research on healing as part of my academic training; "When you play the drum back in your country," he would tell me, "make sure you play it like this." I told him that I would be writing a book on the subject, but the only books he knew of then were the lama texts and children's schoolbooks.

Philosophers speak of relations between people as necessarily entailing encounters with "the other," with these encounters often involving existentially disturbing, quietly disruptive effects on those involved. But difference alone, or any such "traumatism of the other," as Levinas put it, does not necessarily

Figure 33. Dupsang Bombo. Dhupchugang, 1998.

bring enmity or isolation.[37] Despite the fact that we came from quite different worlds, Dupsang and I got along well in an unspoken, mutually awkward way, within the frame of the "happy traumatism" that we found in relating to each other.[38] In fact, I believe the old man got a kick out of teaching and spending time with someone unlike himself, as did I, and he knew that others thought well of this unprecedented arrangement.

And here we were again, unlike one another but each appreciative of the other, as the elder's presence was fading in ways that neither of us could do much about.

"He smokes cigarettes constantly," said his son.

Rinzin lit a cigarette held in his father's hand. The older man wheezed in a breath and made an off-kilter sighing sound when he released that breath.

"I have no teeth. I can't see well."

"*Hajur*, Mheme."

"I can't walk."

"*Hajur*."

Yes, sir.

I felt rushed, uncertain. I wanted to come to his aid but there was nothing that could be done.

The son invited us into the adjacent room to have some tea. It was odd for me to leave Dupsang out on the porch alone, but others did not seem to mind. He was between the intimacies of life and the exteriority that lay beyond. Children curious about the visit joined us inside and sat together, close to the door. Pasang, Sange, and I sat on a cushioned bench that lined the outer wall. My companions kept shy and reserved and spoke when spoken to. Pasang reached into his backpack and took out a plastic bag filled with flattened rice. "This is from my parents," he said in handing the bag to Rinzin, who passed it to his wife, seated by the fire.

I took some photographs of the children who had gathered and told them I would send copies along.

"*Asti ko paisā siddiyo*," the son said to me.

"Yes," I said, uncertain.

He repeated his sentence: "The money from before has finished."

At first I wasn't sure what money he was referring to, but then I recalled that I had sent some cash his father's way some ten years earlier. Since our work together in the 1980s I had tried to transfer some money to his father whenever I visited or knew someone who would be visiting. It's customary for a bombo's student to pay lasting homage in this way, and it felt right to share the modest proceeds from the book.

"Yes," I answered. "It's been a while since then."

We drank tea and told stories from the past. Rinzin asked his wife to search among some articles close to the wall by her side. She located a photograph and handed it to him. He looked at the image for a moment and then turned it so I could see. The image was of Rinzin standing at the edge of a clearing, corn stalks grazing his back, a boy by his side.

"You took this photograph," he said. "Do you remember?"

He handed the photo to me. I held it in my hands. I had forgotten the after-noon we had composed the picture down the path from his house. Here now was the visual artifact of that singular, lasting instant.

"Yes, now I remember," I said. I smiled.

A young man walked into the room minutes later and greeted us.

"This is the boy in the photograph, my first son," said Rinzin. "He's now grown up. He's married and has a son of his own."

Time eddied before me.

"I'd like to give some money to your father," I told Rinzin.

He nodded yes and I followed him outside, to the covered porch. We came close to his father. I took out my wallet and pulled out a set of hundred-rupee notes that I had kept in reserve. Rinzin told me to put the money in his hands. I did so. The bills fell from our hands to the blankets and landed within the folds of the blankets.

"This is *paisā*," the son told his father, in a tone to be heard. "So you can buy more cigarettes. Keep it in your hands."

We took some photographs. I handed the camera to Sange and asked if he could take some photos. He nodded and stepped back to frame a double por-trait. I sat next to my teacher. We looked to the camera.

In the four photos that Sange took of us our hands are clasped together. The bombo is wearing a deep-blue shirt, a maroon knit cap over the top of his head. In one of the images I am looking at my teacher with something like sadness in my eyes.

"It's interesting that he's the one looking straight into the camera," a friend said later. "It's like you're the one who is dying."

Dying, yes, I was dying just then. Still now I am dying. Life itself is rife with moments of dying, when we are sick, a cough in our lungs or worn down, devas-tated, thrown by a loss, wasting away, or wrecked with confusion or absence, saying goodbye. Still I am dying. He had always been stronger than me, spiritually vital, as potent as the moon, and here in this brief moment of the photograph he has sum-moned the energies on which he could always draw, one last time, for the camera, a teacher and his student.

"Should we take some photos of you and your father?" I asked Rinzin.

The son agreed to this idea and sat to his father's left. I took several photo-graphs. In the images that resulted the son is looking straight and somber into the lens while his father's vision trails off to the side and downward.

He is looking away, toward some distant point to the side and lower down, below, as though he has been overwhelmed by the son's ascendency; the lunar vi-

brancy cannot sustain its powers forever, the son has the vital presence to continue on in life, the father is now the one who is dying.

I took four photographs of Mheme alone. I leaned close. He looked into the camera. I felt trusted but rushed and conscious of being watched. It was hard to find my footing in the close confines of the porch. I didn't think well about a good shutter speed. In the low light the photos came out blurred.

The camera pictured his face and retained it for later viewings. When I look at these few photographs now, I see an honest, weakened man who knows that soon he is going to die.

The rains had started again and I could tell that Sange and Pasang wanted to head back home. Rinzin asked if I would like to stay the night, but I said I needed to get back to Thodong. I snapped a couple of photos of Rinzin and his son standing by tall flowers close to the road. We took the road curving west toward Thodong, umbrellas keeping our clothes and skin dry. We found shelter with Pasang and Sange's aunt Mingmar in the main area of her house and warmed to tea and fried potatoes. Late that afternoon, rain dripping from the rooftops, I sat in the dry confines of my room. I wrote about the day's visit.

Out on the porch, with the old man. A sense of connection, like old friends, or teacher and student. This link is more valued than I would have thought.

Sad, profound, moving, unsettling.

He was a man aware of his own fading being and life, of his own growing decrepitude. The body has its own methods, reasons.

He's staying outside, close to the elements (like other bombo; not so comfortable inside the house, perhaps).

The interval of dying. Interminable, right now.

The sense that his powers, his śakti, had carried him for so many years, but then they fireballed out. Sad—that this is what is. The cruel radiance of what is, indeed.

Dupsang Bombo died in the spring of 2012. *Nyingjua.* I was unable to attend to attend the cremation and funeral rites performed on his behalf.

Some words of Michel de Montaigne, from his essay "That to philosophize is to learn to die," written in 1572–74:

so I have formed the habit of having death continually present, not merely in my imagination, but in my mouth. And there is nothing that I investigate so eagerly as the death of men: what words, what look, what bearing they main-

tained at the time. . . . If I were a maker of books, I would make a register, with comments, of various deaths. He who would teach men to die would teach them to live.[39]

I have similarly formed the habit of having death present, not just in my imagination, or in life more generally, but in my mouth. Hyolmo funeral rituals are of and about time. The efforts that have gone into this book, this register of various deaths, are also rooted in time, its many conversations, journeys, jotted notes, questions, and partial, imperfect drafts. I have observed changes in the composition of life and death for Hyolmo people in Nepal and elsewhere through the span of four decades now, and for several generations of families; the lives and losses involved are as much a part of me as the lines creased into my right hand.[40] Some journal entries, kept through the years:

June, 1988. On Tuesday, the 14th, a 60-year-old man died in the southern Sherpa village. The younger men from that village came down to Gulph. in the evening to call the lama; they went back up, carrying the lama drum, a horn, and something to use to cremate the body. At night, flashlights could be seen descending the northern hillside, probably heading up to the dead person's home.

Mrs. Lama seemed very distressed over the death. Very tense, talking very quickly, smoking many cigarettes. When I came to the doorway, she asked if I had tea, I said yes, and then she said "someone died above." She repeated this, and seemed like she was going to cry, and then whispered "om mani padme hum."

September, 2001. Kathmandu. I've been finding it difficult to talk with Hyolmo people about experiences of grief and mourning. Most of those I've been conversing with appear comfortable talking about conceptions of death and ways of dying, but whenever the conversation veers toward actual situations of loss and grief it's like touching a raw nerve. The upshot of this is that neither they nor I want to delve much into the pain of grief. I need more data on this stuff, but I'm wary of pressing the matter.

October, 2010. Cambridge. While asleep Sunday night, toward the morning hours, I dreamt I was working on some writing related to the ongoing book project and conversing with friends, vaguely identified, as I went about that effort. Someone pointed out that I was inserting the word "death" into every sentence I wrote. When I looked at the page of text before me I could see what this person meant: the word appeared in a muted way in each sentence on the page, or hovered just above it, whether or not that noun was relevant to the sentence or the insertion was grammatical.

November, 2010. Cambridge. A colleague sent me an email yesterday, asking "Do you know about this?" In the body of the email is a link to a new list-serve called "H-Death," a network on the history of death and dying. I have yet to check out the link. I'm not so fond of having death show up in my email inbox each morning.

March, 2011. New York. A student in my course on Engagements with Death and Mourning tells me that she sometimes finds it's difficult to do the assigned readings in one go. "I'm not used to thinking about death so much," she says. "When I'm reading about it, I often have to go lie down for a while and then come back to it." I know what she means.

July, 2011. Kathmandu. For me, just now: this new project on photography in Nepal is all about life and continuity. I haven't thought much about death this summer—"the death book"—but, rather, the thrill and jive of life. This project is densely grounded in life, smitten with it.

November, 2012. New York. Today I looked at the pages of the book on death for the first time in over a year. It's closer to being done than I had remembered. I really should try to finish it soon, despite not wanting to tread in these dark waters any longer.

December, 2014. Back to the death book, two years since last working on. It needs to be finished. The one chapter that is still missing, that needs to be there, is the one on grief. Getting close to it, again, delving into its forms, and then pushing it away, again.

September, 2015. The wound of the book, its absent center, is loss, grief.

This has not been an easy book to write. Its themes have weighed on my mind, a consciousness prone to identifying in an empathy of form with the phenomena it is contemplating. Grief is sensed; ritual forms, embodied. I started putting together my thoughts on the ethnographic data I had collected in Nepal once I returned to New York in late fall of 2001. I learned sadly via email in November that Kisang Omu had died. While teaching during the winter and spring that followed I tried to take my thoughts further. I fell into a surge of writing as soon as the school year ended and spelled out the first drafts of a number of sections. I wrote each day for seven weeks. Thinking about death all the time was getting to me. Death had become inserted into the moments of my life, and I was becoming proficient in the language of death, with my being increasingly tuned to its rhythms. I began to mull my own end. I began to think more about what a good death might entail for me and others and less about how to live my life. I had become, like the narrator of John Keats' *Ode to a Nightingale*, "half in love with easeful Death."[41]

One afternoon in early July of that year I swung my car into a parking space by my home after running some errands. As I stepped out of the car I found myself thinking, *That was a great parking job. If I could have a death like that, as neat and fluid and comfortable as the way my car slipped into that spot, then that would be a good death.* The perversity of this logic struck me, and I stood silent in the parking lot, car keys in hand. *What am I doing? I'm forty years old. I'm too young to be thinking about death all the time.*

I decided to take a break from the seductive aesthetics of death. An altogether different passion soon consumed my waking hours: an involvement, at once personal and anthropological, in the world of chess and chess players.[42] I found there a passionate intensity of life. As the next years became filled with queen and knight moves (and word was received, sadly, that Ghang Lama had died), the manuscripts on death collected dust on a bookshelf. I lost track of where my notebooks were. I did not give much thought to the project in those years and I wasn't sure if I would ever return to it. I dreamt about it, however, as one might a past experience or an unresolved love. The dreams touched most on the rituals involved, on the opaque sequence of images made and unmade during the funeral rites. The material had a generative force of its own. Something had remained unresolved, and my mind or something greater than my mind kept tinkering with it all, trying to figure it out. It had marked me. Hyolmo people might say I was "attached" to the subject, and the subject "hooked" on me, much as a ghost might cling to a person or household. An exorcism was required. I also came to wonder if my fascination with the material related to a compulsive repetition in my own life. Have I been working out some vague, obscure losses of my own in writing so intensively about loss and death? If so, I have no way to tell whether or not the repeated efforts have been constructive or bound to return me forever to the same forms of loss.

Only after I completed a book on the lifeworlds of chess players did I begin to think anew about returning to the project. By then Karma had settled into a life with his family in Queens, and Temba had married and was enjoying raising a son with his wife just a few blocks away. I felt compelled to return to the book, in part because so much work had already gone into it and it made sense to take it to completion and still the ghosts. I located the manuscript of first drafts, settled with six winters of dust, and tracked down the bulk of my field notes. I set to work again and sketched out new thoughts and observations. This time, I tried to keep the dark rhythms from taking hold of my life.

"Death, like the sun, cannot be looked at steadily," wrote the seventeenth-century author La Rochefoucauld.[43] That has been true in the current case, at least. If I gaze too steadily into that searing whiteness my spirit begins to wither. I came to adopt the existential equivalent of protective sunglasses: I cordoned off my work on the topic, filled my days with life otherwise, and often worked in cafes, in the company of others. I found myself sharing drafts with friends and colleagues, as though something like life could be infused into the sentences at hand. I discovered that writing could serve ritual purposes of its own. It helped me to make sense of death and loss, or connect anew, or steady the earth. Writing can entail a kind of dying, a slow dissolve into forces larger and unknown. Writing can also sustain a life.

I came to focus most on the existential themes involved. I have often felt that the material, so terrifically meaningful, fascinating even, the haunting interplay of the here and the not-here, gets at issues central not only to Hyolmo lives but to who we all are, as beings struggling to get along in life. Grief, like love, opens us, often in terribly vulnerable ways, to the most profound questions of connection and memory. Loss marks us. It defines who we are.

For these and other reasons this work has been far from being a scholarly project only. It has shaped how I engage in the world and relate to others. I cannot say whether or not I have learned how to die—this will be revealed some future day, I suppose. But all of this anthropologizing of death in Nepal has led, I believe, to a keener, sharper take on life, territories of death included. I have come to perceive life in ways at once unnerving and exhilarating, as consisting of so many "fields of apparitions," to use the Buddhist phrasing. If pressed, I would have to say that I now take the features of consciousness, yours or mine, to be spun out of such fields of apparition, ever-changing, ever-shifting, juiced with remarkable energies, tied to others, vexed at times, haunted, luminous in others, subject to countless forms and dissolutions.

Learn how to live, learn how to die, contemplate death, strive for a good and peaceful end, die at home if possible, reduce any attachments, comfort the dying, care for them, hear the dying man's last words, attend to the final hours, this life, moving beyond life, death-impermanence, transfer the consciousness, place coins in the mouth, see the face one last time, feed and nourish, soothe and calm, the rituals are at work now, transfer the body to the cremation grounds, show the way, make a Buddha out of the corpse, make the body beautiful, artful even, burn the body into grainy death, eliminate and dissolve, provide burnt offerings, the earthly body altered into a more subtle form, purify the burnt remains, sift through the remainders, retrieve a burnt bone, preserve any relics, reminders, formations of the sacred, construct a resting place, old clothes and a remnant bone, hook the consciousness, drag it home, talk to the deceased, explain that he is dead, diminish attachments and longing, provide a resting place, keep the consciousness there, offer foods, no longer living, it cannot stick around, tell it to leave, say there is no form, no taste, no texture, prepare a name card, image and text, perform prostrations, purify sins and impurities, remove any obstructions, write out the name, fill in the ellipses, so-and-so empty, the body now gone, wash away impurities, talk to the dead man, explain that he is dead, seek out a good rebirth, seek out your enlightenment, have family members speak to the deceased, set the name card on fire, the consciousness sent to a realm above and beyond, burn the dead name, eliminated, subtracted, emptiness only, transfer the conscious, there is no form, no sound, no smell, no taste, no texture, the name is empty, the

person, emptied, take away his name, generate merit, make an effigy, simulate
the corpse, the dead man once again, no body, no form, blank white, perform
prayers, voiced collectively, show the way to a good rebirth, send the dead
man off, away from his home, prayers and soaring *mani*, it's the last time to
talk, the last time to see his face, burn the name, dismantle the effigy, reduced
to a bundle of clothes, no face, no person, the name is lost, more impersonal
now, more abstract, collective, care for the dead, dissolve the dead, this compassionate violence, take away the deceased's clothes, drive away the remembrance, do not mourn too much, that love is dangerous, it's soon elsewhere,
ground the bone and burnt paper into powder, make nameless figures, warm
ash mixed with clay, made for forgetting, bless and purify them, place them
in a pure and sacred place, the pain of the grief now less, more subtle, further
away, the pain returns like a knife cut, do not say the names of the dead, efface
distinct identities, the dead have no need for names, no words, no consciousness, more subtle forms now, no grief, no mourning, a grief beyond mourning,
construct a memorial, diffuse memories, life edges on, the living survive the
living, new generations arise, new turns of life, the seasons keep turning, children, and then elders, grandchildren, now parents, parents now grandparents,
grandparents passed on, echoes in time, here-gone, life death, no names, no
perception, few remains, scant reminders, learn how to die, learn how to live,

And through all this come to form a better angle on life more generally.
Death is often taken to be the absolute other of life. Yet it can also be said that
the words "life" and "death" mark situations more complicated than that bi-
nary arrangement alone. Being alive is clearly different from not being alive;
there is a "difference of kind" between the two, not simply a difference of degree.[44] Yet the ever-changing flow of life and death, presence and absence, includes varying intensities and thresholds of existence, the circling of memories
plush with life, moments at once actual and virtual, ghosts as real as people
and people as vacant as ghosts. The end of one set of bonds leads to new
strands of connection. A life implies the imminent remove of that life, while
the loss of a life can bring a fullness of memories, feelings, and reverberations.
There can be a richness to loss, much as there can be a paucity to life, making
for nondualistic swirls of vitalities quick to alter. Moments of dying are found
in moments of living, and vice versa. An abiding theme in many a life is the
penchant for crafting new conditions and relations in life. And yet so often
people face continued hardships, the edge is rough, and there is a fine shaky
line between despair and renewal.

Much of this was evident in my recent visit to Nepal. I heard people speak of how Karma and his siblings have carried on the good name and creative brilliance of their father. I visited Temba's mother and brother in the family's new home in Boudhanath, a bright and roomy three-story structure gained through hard selfless work in Nepal and in foreign lands. I played word games with the granddaughters of Sange's father, radiant in their youth, days before they too left for the States. I glimpsed something of Ghang Lama in his grandson Pasang's emerging interest in Buddhist thought and in Sange's lanky gait and curly hair. I saw how the landscape had changed while retaining features of the past, and I sensed turns of life among the new generations toiling on sunlit lands once cultivated by Dupsang Bombo and his wife.

Curious are the ways of poiesis: a book on death has turned into a book about life.

Figure 37. Gulphubanjang, 2011.

Postscript:
Beyond Description

Try, in a time of disaster, to preserve life. Try to act without knowing how to act. Try, afterward, to perceive what has happened, while blocked from any clear and comprehensive perceptions. Attend to any deaths with the ritual and social and material means available just then. Mourn the losses collectively, and work, collectively, to rebuild a world.

A deadly earthquake shook Nepal on Saturday near its capital, Kathmandu, and set off avalanches around Mount Everest.

The earthquake, with a magnitude of 7.8, struck shortly before noon, and residents of Kathmandu ran into the streets and other open spaces as buildings fell, throwing up clouds of dust. Wide cracks opened on paved streets and in the walls of city buildings.[1]

The first glimmers of the devastation streamed through common media, newspapers in print or on the Internet, and cable television. That Saturday, April 25, 2015, the death toll in Nepal had reached 686, according to the Ministry of Home Affairs. It was clear that the count would go much higher.

Puffs, then billows, of dust rose from various parts of the city, within minutes shrouding the whole valley in a brown blanket. The historic town of Bhaktapur, at the eastern edge, looked like it was being swallowed by a sand storm. Katmandu disappeared.[2]

A video showed a man lying down in a hospital with red scrapes on his face and white gauze bandaged around his head and right eye. "It all started breaking and it all fell down," said the man. "I was lucky to survive and come out of the wreckage. But my eye has been damaged; I wished there were some friends to support me in this time." The video turned to scenes of Tibetan nuns praying outside their residences, chanting, crying.[3]

Witnesses described a chaotic rescue effort during the first hours after the quake as emergency workers and volunteers grabbed tools and bulldozers from construction sites, and dug with hacksaws, mangled reinforcing bars and their hands.[4]

It was difficult to contact Nepal with no electricity and few telephone lines functioning. Like countless others I sent e-mails to friends from Nepal, many of whom now lived in the United States. "I hope you and your family are doing okay," I wrote, "with the earthquake happening in Nepal, and all of the worry and sorrow that is coming of that." Karma and Temba and Pasang wrote back to say that their families were okay, but it seemed the whole Hyolmo region had been badly hit. They had heard some villages had all the houses and temples flattened to the ground. Several people had been killed, including some they knew. In Sermathang just a few houses were standing. Many houses had collapsed in other villages. "Helambu is destroyed," said one friend.

Just returned from Bhaktapur. Unimaginable situation there.[5]

"Unimaginable." "Unthinkable." "The condition of the affected people is beyond description." People used words like these for lack of possibly more accurate words or perceptions. The devastation went beyond what could be imagined or anticipated. It was too much for any single mind to take in. "It's all ruined. Lama what to do? The brain cannot work." A brain couldn't think on this. We shrunk stunned before it all, "dumbfounded." Some likened the situation to a "nightmare." I thought myself that the afterward was a bizarre sort of bardo, an off-kilter between in which everything was unstable, uncertain, with frightful apparitions flooding consciousness with chaotic images of distorted life and death.

We watched the televised reports from the twenty-four-hour cable news networks. Standing in line inside a local Citibank I caught the bright noisy sheen of the CNN reports on a flat-screen monitor bolted onto a wall. "Just describe to us the moment when the earthquake struck, how scared were you, what happened," said a reporter to a young woman taking shelter under a tent canopy. One news segment was followed by a commercial where yoga was the theme. A man voiced the word "Namaste." This juxtaposition of cash transactions, pop nirvana, and unattended visions of hardship was unsettling; I didn't know where to look or what to think; the world was confusingly multiple, a dizzying mix of different vectors of information, comfort, and pain, each playing its own reel of tape, simultaneously. No one else in the bank appeared to be watching the video box squawking chatter into the mundane errands of a Monday morning. No one in line seemed to know any families there, nor could they quite discern what the devastation might mean for thousands living in the villages, homes and livelihoods destroyed.

Friends and family wrote, asking sympathetically about people in Nepal. "Have you heard how the people you know in Nepal are doing?" It was good to know they cared for people I cared for, in a continent removed from their daily concerns. They did not know the families and individuals involved. Their concerns remained at a level of abstraction, distant perception, much as my own did when a tsunami wrecked Sri Lanka.

"Have you thought of writing an editorial for the *Times?*" a colleague asked me. "You could talk about what it's like in the villages, and how precarious the conditions of people's lives are." He then added, "But you'd have to do it sometime in the next few days"—before the collective media had turned its spotlight elsewhere.

By nightfall the breaking news had shifted to turmoil in Baltimore. Police brutality, political unrest, protestors defying a city-wide curfew, a standoff in the streets, media cameras zooming into the actions. Attorneys for the convicted Boston marathon bomber began their defense of their client in the sentencing phase of the trial. Welcome to "the constant carnival of cruelty," in which sightings of cruelty are not isolated events or limited to distinct arenas of life, like the carnivals of medieval Europe, but, rather, spill over "into the mainstream of daily experience."[6]

In Kathmandu, people sought open lands, open ground, where structures could not collapse around them. Gardens. A military parade ground. The middle of streets. School playgrounds. The open air meant safety. Anything built of stone, wood, and mud or steel and concrete risked collapsing from shaking caused by any new quakes or tremors.

By the end of May some 240 aftershocks troubled those living in Nepal, including a magnitude 7.3 earthquake that occurred on May 12. It was impossible to know when the tremors were coming, or their intensity, or when they would end.

"After Nepal earthquake, funeral rites." "Much lost, many to mourn." "Survivors bury the dead after last Saturday's earthquake in Kathmandu, Nepal." "After the other family members came in the morning, we started the funeral rites," said one man. In Kathmandu, many bodies were cremated by the Bagmati River, at Pashupatinath or other sites along the sacred river. Newspaper photos showed the fires lit by the dark shiny waters of the river. Young men were cremating the bodies, in rites that had the look of being expedient, exhausted, with no great formality.

Can a good death occur during a time of disaster? What happens to the dead in devastation, when survivors do not have the time or resources with which to conduct the funeral rites in a patient, careful, devoted manner? When do responses to a death become exhausted? What responsibilities for the care of the dead hold secure, and which are relinquished, when a number of deaths occur at once, in a village or within a family?

The images and words produced at this moment of crisis came quickly; soon there was a torrent of images. The pictures of dead bodies and cremation rites held surfaces only, lacking the depth of ritual. The images had no weight; they flitted by in a matter of seconds, to be consumed alongside a quick breakfast or an evening's beer.[7] Unlike the imagery and language of ritual, there was no sustained interrogation of life and death; no gradual, painstaking transformations of life into death through an intensity of time. Thinly virtual images provided no space for contemplation, or any means to relate to the dead until such relations could no longer occur. We did not know these individuals who had died; any sense of grief for them and their families was abstract, tentative, anonymous. Mourning was conjecture, and thus unreal. For those far away, there were no actual dead bodies to touch and behold, no corpses to be burnt; no name cards; no mani prayers; no summoning of a consciousness, no explanations to the dead, no tantric transfers of the soul to a world beyond, and the possibility of rebirth. Any media images of grief did not include the kind of imagery that would enable people to grieve.

Each time I saw an image of someone from Nepal, woman, man, or child, head bandaged, or heard someone speaking, dazed, I pictured someone I knew struggling with the same hardships. I did not know these particular persons and families portrayed in the news and yet their bodily forms, their speech and gestures, were so familiar my heart went out to them and those absent from the screen facing similar troubles. In a kind of lateral empathy I stood alongside them, listening, paralyzed.

I felt helpless, mired in a land without power, unable to act or perceive or help in any significant way. All of Nepal seemed to be a land without power. "We feel we are helpless," said one man, a pilot who wandered through his neighborhood darkened by a power blackout. "We can do nothing."[8]

Even if I could get there, I reasoned, I wouldn't be of much help. I'd just be in the way, another body to be fed. I could, at least, send money from New York.

A few quick rolling scenes in one video startled me because I thought I saw the son of a friend of mine who lives in Kathmandu, participating in a procession to a cremation ground. The video showed this young man, in his early twenties, sporting a dark coat and bushy black hair, helping with others to carry a corpse to a cremation ground, the body wrapped in a white cloth. I froze the video and looked carefully at the screen and tried to recognize the image of this man. The streaming video played again; they brought the body to a river. The man's jacket bore the word Adidas. From this angle I thought I saw the fleeting image of my friend's first son, helping to carry the corpse. I concluded that these young men only resembled people I knew, that they were apparitions of the familiar.

In the first days after the earthquake the state of life in the mountainous terrains beyond Kathmandu was said to be a "black hole," "inaccessible." Landslides were blocking roads. The highways were unusable. The phone and Internet systems had been knocked out, and no satellite images were possible in the first days due to a dense covering of rain clouds. There were no means of visibility or contact that could inform anyone outside those regions of the extent of the damage, the number of deaths, or what people had to contend with. An entire region went unperceived. No easy access, no lucidity; all was frightfully obscure. This lack of perceptual means was at odds with the presumed aura of immediate and easy knowing suggested by modern forms of technology.

I kept trying to conceive what was happening in the Hyolmo region. Those imaginings never got far. My mind could not picture anything beyond a vague uncertain sense of destruction, houses in ruins, people taking shelter in tents or crowding beneath strands of tin roofs. While drifting to sleep at night I saw myself trying to walk to the villages, along the old route, now that the roads were cut off from landslides and boulder debris. I would climb up the steep mountain ridge above Sundarijal and walk through the forest, hike past Patibhanyang and Chipling, and try to make my way to the villages. I could never get there. I could never make much progress or reach anything tangible or specific. In this liminal space between reality and imagination any details were beyond picturing, beyond description. (Much as death is beyond picturing.)

Describe while failing to describe. I found myself wanting to compose a mourning song, a lament, of sorts, that spoke to the deaths and hardships. Language became a means of response. A feeble response, language only, bits of meaning, a few words nonetheless. I felt the need to respond, to act in a formal way, not unlike how mourners respond to a death with rituals of mourning and transformation. *It's the only thing that you can do.*

Stunning was the rapid employment of numerous technologies of perception and communication. Cell phones, social media, Internet connections, instant messaging systems, cameras, satellites, drones, sensors, sonar pulsations, seismographs, heartbeat sensors, and any number of apps entailed the techne of detection and transmission. Google's "Person Finder" helped people to determine whether friends and family were safe or not, as did Facebook's "Safety Check." The efforts involved forms of perception and agency that were multiple, dispersed, collective, combining different perspectives and cyborg-like assemblages of body, machine, and relay. Contact or not knowing; dead, injured, or physically well; safety, alarm; worry and relief; secure or fearful; stillness, reverberation—these points of tension marked the affective forces involved.

Videos showed aerial footage of damage to Kathmandu, taken by unmanned drones. The drones circled like hawks above neighborhoods in Kathmandu or in nearby towns. People could be seen walking along streets, standing on shaken rooftops, or sitting on top of the rubble where their houses used to be. The footage showed damaged temples, cracked roads, collapsed buildings, and one of the camps where people were living in tents. The films were eerily silent, with no words heard, no sounds except a slight static buzz that continued throughout the footage, possibly the whirring of an engine. Any suffering, any *duḥkha*, was viewed remotely.

Maps showed the landscape of temporary shelters, the epicenter of the earthquake, and its aftershocks. The USGS presented a Shake Map that detailed the M 7.8 quake at 06:11:26 UTC, with a depth of 15.0 km. The perceived shaking ran from "Not felt" to "Very strong" to "Extreme." One map showed how much the earth rose, or fell, in various parts of the Himalayas. Charts diagrammed the transmission of aid from different nation-states to Nepal. Other maps showed the deaths reported in different districts, each a precise tabulated count, which changed each day. The numbers were abstract, removed from the sorrow and hardship of any actual deaths within a family or ruined household. No biographies. An amalgam of singularities. Statistical death.

Mapping itself became an activity, something to do, either to make counts of death and injuries or to coordinate relief efforts. Like others, I began to map reports, miscellaneous perspectives and discourses. I collected articles, clippings, bookmarks, videos, photographs, like so many field notes. In this way I thought I might begin to comprehend the range and depth of the devastation and the different forms of injury, hardship, and response at hand. It was largely a matter of approximation, of getting close to what was going on for people by picking up clues, disparate signs, and tracing the flow of a few perceptions. A distant anthropology emerged out of these thoughts and actions. I had begun to conduct ethnography from afar, tracking the dispersal of words and actions in spare moments during busy weeks of work and teaching. No sense at all of being there. No direct participant observation.

Exterior to any immediate engagements in Nepal, I was at best a seismographer, tracking reverberations in a distant land after pronounced trembling.

Newspaper photographs and videos showed people being rescued after being trapped under rubble; of lifting a concrete wall off a woman trapped in rubble; of relatives mourning the death of a woman as she was cremated; of a young girl waiting on a school bus, despondent and exhausted; of a man being consoled as a body of a relative was removed from the ruins of his home, soldiers standing about him, wearing army fatigues, light blue masks. There were photos of a rubble-littered alley; of people seated in chairs on a street made of bricks with damaged buildings seen in the background, a dog lying nearby. A video steadied on a young woman looking dazed, stunned, her eyes seemingly far off, a cut lip and bruised cheek and eye, a gauze bandage wound about her head. The cameraman must have crept close, waiting for the right moment, the proper composition, asking permission, or not. Photographs showed bright colors and a rich dynamic energy in the center of the image, visual elements radiating out from there. These energies stood as if in affinity with the force of the earthquake and its aftershocks rumbling from a central wound.

Other photos showed people lying on the ground, passive, carried or cared for by others. Pictures showed people digging, carrying, standing around others; agents and patients, rescuers and survivors. Members of a rescue team retrieved the body of an earthquake victim from the ruins of his home in Bhaktapur. Drenched in mud, the body was covered with a bright purple-blue shawl, a hand evident, gloved hands of others reaching out toward the body, a shovel close by. Life was upright action. Death was horizontal, flat, inert. Each picture carried a cosmology.

Piles of debris. A pair of socks. Pages of a book. A padlock. Old photographs.

One video showed a group of women, men, and children standing apprehensively by a river bank north of Kathmandu. They had walked two hours from their wrecked villages in search of provisions but had yet to encounter anyone who could help. *Pani chaina. Bhat chaina.* These words recurred on homemade videos and television reports. "There is no water." "There is no food." No tents. No help yet from outside. The residents of the devastated areas wanted to communicate their urgent need for food, water, medicines, and safe structures but there were few means to do so.

Different lines of image and language filled the airways, which held multiple formations of death and mourning, and frayed translations. A BBC video reported on a family from Chautara who had lost a grandmother in the first earthquake and then a father in the second earthquake.[9] The man had gone into town to collect relief funds for his family and was killed when the second earthquake struck. The video held images of the shaved heads of the man's sons; and of their mother, wearing white. "You see a lot of shaved heads here in Nepal. Like the white clothes, they are symbols of mourning," said the reporter. The sons were shown seated, looking down, forlorn, waiting, the light streaming into the room. This portrait of mourning appeared at once intimate and altogether distant from the lives involved. Death should not be this way.

The man's wife, now a widow, spoke of how her former husband of twenty-two years was a good man. "The world is gone. The world is gone," she could be heard saying in Nepali through the crevices of the reporter's commentary. "What the house stands on is no longer there. So isn't the house gone itself? So, if what the house stands on isn't there, the world has just died."

The translation into English, spoken by an unseen woman with an Indian accent (a multinational broadcast in a trans-global world) sounded as, "My world has been destroyed. I am like a house without a foundation. I don't think I'll ever feel safe again." This gloss missed the stark poetry of the woman's remarks. The woman spoke, metaphorically, of a house. The house of her life had just been destroyed because what it stood on, an intact family, the marriage with her husband, a sustainable life, was no longer there. Her world was gone.

With a death, a world can die. The foundation gives way. There is nothing there, nothing for a life to stand on. In Nepal, a house can be like a self, with a soul, a spirit. The house requires support, nourishment, care, respect. It can get sick, in need of healing. If shattered or destroyed, or left unattended, the house can die.

It proved difficult to perceive and translate the losses of others. I began to follow Pasang's Facebook page, to watch for any photos or updates he posted or shared. Early postings by him and others spoke of desperate pleas for information on the welfare of family and friends in Nepal, especially in

the villages of Gulphubanjang and Thodong, where his family had lived for
several generations (and where I myself resided in the late 1980s, and had
often visited since that time). Pasang, residing in Queens, had helped to raise
funds which were used to provide urgently needed foods in Gulphubanjang,
Thodong, and other neighboring villages. I did not recognize many of these
youths who were posting in Facebook; apparently the children of men and
women I had known for some time, they were members of a new generation,
highly capable of action. It was easy to discern when the earthquake struck
without looking at the dates of postings: the carefree normality of selfies and
pics of social gatherings was interrupted when a state of emergency took
hold of the minds and digital electronics of those reporting the news from
Nepal.

"Now Gulphubanjang" ran the caption alongside one photograph, posted by
a young man from Gulphubanjang currently working and residing in South
Korea. Visually misty around the edges, as if the aura of a dream, the photo
showed the main road through the village caved in with a calamity of rocks,
dirt, contorted wood and metal. The density of stone could now be seen,
not purely imagined. Some houses slanted precariously toward earth. The
crowded non-space looked terribly unlike the street known to run through
those paired rows of houses, a thoroughfare usually wide and clean and free
of dirt debris. In shambles were the tailor's place, where he sewed garments
and made clothes; the general store, the wood posts and walls painted a rich
bright blue; the teashop; the lodges and restaurants for passing trekkers and
NGO workers; the homes of families carrying the name Gurung, Tamang,
Lama, or Hyolmo. We've been that way before, present in that street, standing, sitting, talking, welcoming, and now that space had collapsed into itself.
So many stones and debris were impossibly there in that ruined village.

This was all incomprehensible, much as a sudden death is at first beyond
comprehension, difficult to take in. There are limits to knowing the mon-
strous reach of a disaster such as this. An earthquake, like a death, is disas-
trous, mired in irreality.

Writing about a disaster risks giving a sensible form and meaning to something that has no form, no meaning. A disaster, unruly, overwhelming, un-
tamable, carries an absence of meaning; it cannot be perceived through co-

herent images or commentary. "The danger that the disaster acquire meaning instead of body."[10] We wanted to ascribe meaning, but there was a danger in giving easy form to something which had no form, and tore at the body.

Buried under the rubble of the damaged structures, if not demolished altogether, were implements of life, likely including (to draw from memory, a structure itself prone to erosion) dharma books, family altars, ritual instruments, prayer flags, katha scarves, *chemi* lamps; *thangku* paintings; paintings and posters of deities; grains of rice, potatoes, corn flour, wheat flour, millet grains; dried meats; salts, spices, honey, sugar; teas; jars of instant coffee; medicines, herbal or pharmacological; amulets; tobaccos; tin boxes of snuff; cooking utensils, pots, pans, plates, cups, glasses; stoves; farming equipment, seeds; saws, hammers; identification cards, passports; gold, money; school books, textbooks, dictionaries, notebooks; household accounts, address books; cherished photographs and letters; bank books and statements; land and property deeds; cell phones; radios; laptops; DVDs; music CDs; clothes, blankets, pillows, winter coats, rain coats; flashlights; umbrellas; knives, axes; furniture, wood carvings; artwork; playing cards, games; calculators, calendars; sandals, boots and shoes; for starters. These materials enabled the residents of these homes to get along in life, cultivate the land, take nourishment and sustain livelihoods, protect themselves from the elements and unwanted forces, perchance prosper financially, communicate with others, value memories, enjoy hours of leisure, sleep well, be well, travel, and, not least, support their efforts toward spiritual transcendence. Nothing had any form any longer. Little remained that was built clearly, little that was solid, well kept, clear or pure or substantial. So much had come unworked. There is much that constitutes a household, and it's a strange, unworldly event to realize that years of work, of generative fashioning in households, the rich poiesis of families, can come crashing down within the shaking of forty seconds.

In the photograph, the home of Pasang's family stood to the far left, apparently still intact, disturbed. A blue placard pointed absently to the Himalayan Lodge. Signs lost their referents. No glimpse of Pasang's parents, their welfare or whereabouts, or of his brother.

A few days later other photos appeared. A group of young men had driven in jeeps up to the region transporting bags of rice, lentils, and medicines. The men looked alert and energetic, awash in nervous adrenaline. I could see Lhatul Lama standing by a pile of bags of rice. He looked tired, not sleeping well, older than I remembered him to be, still with his usual fortitude and awareness. His hand was touching the top of the stacks of rice as if to acknowledge receipt of them and to take responsibility for the oversight of its distribution. It was good to see him there, with his usual presence of mind, capable of being in charge. I trusted that his wife was well, that her absence in the photographs simply meant she was busy elsewhere.

People stood in the remnants of the street, trying to begin the task of sorting through the debris and salvaging anything worth keeping. I recognized a few of them, including some who I had photographed during my last visit there, a girl in a bright red coat. Women and men received bags of rice and carried them to wherever they now counted as home.

Photographs of the pages of a notebook showed inscriptions that documented the distribution of foods and supplies, village by village. Reading through the lists, written in English, I recognized a number of names, denoting representatives of different households and "team leaders." I knew then, at least, that the persons referred to were alive and free of severe bodily injury. Their names had not been burnt. Other names were not pictured. Alive, or dead? This was the first question of existence in those days.

A video posted on Facebook, shot from the northern side of Gulphubanjang, showed the destruction wrought on numerous homes. During its one-minute span some men could be heard reflecting on the damage in a mix of Nepali and Tamang. If we had been sitting there, outside, here, what would have happened? Everything would have been ash. It wasn't our time to die.

Kharānī: ash. *kharānī hunu*: to be utterly destroyed, wiped out, be reduced to ashes. *kharānī bhayo*: wiped out. These men had come close to being wiped out, reduced to ashes—much as a body, when cremated, turns to cinders.

It wasn't their destined time to die, apparently. It wasn't their *kāl*. For others, it was written on their foreheads, perhaps. People must have sought reasons for why some died while others went unharmed. It's difficult to live without explanations.

The camera panned about and showed the long tangled strewn street. A few persons, children perhaps, unclear figures, could be seen at the far end, looking on, reluctant to step into the rubble. Within its frame the camera included three men, one of whom I knew from the village. The men looked about, stunned, unable to take in the destruction. They were alive.

Fifty-six photos, taken by a young man from Gulphubanjang after the earthquake struck, chronicled the journey of a small group of people traveling from Kathmandu to the villages of their families—they probably traveled the first leg of the journey by jeep and then walked the rest of the route. This was the same route I had backpacked countless times before, the one I had imagined moving along nights before when I haplessly sought to reach the village and could not picture anything. This trickle of images showed elements of that terrain. The photos were a disturbance. I did not know these travelers. The places looked different than how I remembered them. So much had been brought down by the earthquake.

The first photos were of Chiso Pani, once a minor crossroad of footpaths on a rolling hillside that grew into a crowded settlement when a road circling the mountain north of Kathmandu was built and there was suddenly a demand for food and lodging. Several buildings there had collapsed from the earthquake, one an ornate and narrow four-story structure bearing the name Hotel Annapurna Mountain View and Restaurant. Next appeared photographs of Patibhanyang, another rest stop for travelers, a steep slope down from Chiso Pani; we used to pause for tea and *chow chow* noodle lunches when walking to the Kathmandu Valley. Some nights I slept in a meager hotel, tired out, while on my way to Gulphubanjang. The older houses were devastated. The path through the village was strewn with rocks and shards of lumber. The travelers walked on from Patibhanyang and arrived in Chipling, up along the bluff that led to the forested mountain ridge south of Thodong and Gulphubanjang. The white walls of a schoolhouse were cracked. The travelers must have taken the extent of this damage as a portent for what awaited them in Thodong and Gulphubanjang.

The interiors of a tent, on the outskirts of Golphubanyang, held people sleeping under a red canvas, close together, beneath an array of blankets. One man, lying down, his head resting, eyes open, looked apprehensive. One woman was seating upright, looking to her left. Their faces were familiar.

Photos of Gulphubanjang depicted collapsed and damaged homes, roofs caved in. A motorbike lay amidst the rubble. The *mani* shrine looked intact. The schoolhouse was damaged. Men were digging out a collapsed home, pulling rocks away. Where could one even begin? The strand of photographs then led to something unexpected on the pages of Facebook: a photo showed a deceased child, nearly buried, her head, arms, and torso covered by rocks and loose dirt, merged with the earth. Her first name was Nyima, "sun." She was being retrieved from the ground, her body delicately extracted, several men standing about her. Each of her hands lay clutched, as though the girl strove to grasp something. She was wearing a red pullover shirt with the image of a cartoon figure on the front. Her body was battered, the poor child, rocks and debris must have fallen with a crushing weight. Her face was swollen, around her eyes and mouth. There were remnants of blood by her nose and mouth. Her body was lifted and placed on a clean white sheet, enclosed within, and the blanket tied. The body was still, silent, unknowing of its present condition and its absence within a flow of time. A final photograph, taken from a distance, suggested where they had recovered her body.

The girl might have been playing when the earthquake struck, or she was seated within her home, eating. A wall might have collapsed on her. Her vital efforts were arrested in those few moments. May she not have felt pain or fear.

I came across these photographs late one night when I was not sleeping well. I logged into Facebook to check for any updates on the situation in Nepal and happened upon this posting. Once I saw the photos of the dead girl I could not get the image of her out of my mind. I tried to sleep but kept sensing the death of her body, and my own strained living fragile form, curled up in bed, blanketed by a few sheets, dying a little. My mind kept thinking on how the girl had died and what her final moments of living consciousness were like. Perhaps because of these empty considerations—my thoughts hit on nothing concrete, only vacant imaginings—I did not perceive her as being fully dead. I still do not. She is dead. She is not yet dead, and she keeps on dying. She is there in the photographs, in the moments before and after her death.

Each death is multiple, recurrent, unsettled. It shifts here and there. The disaster inhabits the shadows between clear forms. We carry the bodies of others with us. There is a trace of her dying within me. We perceive life and death through images. I wondered if the child was in any of the photographs I had taken while visiting in Gulphubanjang a few years back. She would have been four or five years old then. I could not tell much from the current photographs. Her face was estranged in death. I might have heard her laugh, or speak, or watched her play. One thought I had was that I could gather up the photographs I took that summer, bring them to Queens, and show them to Pasang, to see if he recognized the girl in any of them. He would know who she was. I wanted to comprehend who she had been while alive, who her grieving parents were, if she had brothers or sisters, and pay my respects in any slight and silent way.

Further photographs showed more relief provisions being distributed, in a location I could not recognize. Pasang's brother Sangye could be seen unloading sacks of rice in a crowd of people. He looked physically well, his face tired and concerned. In Thodong, a man stood in a field next to a ruined house, his wife and child behind him. In one photograph I could see Lhatul Lama's home in the distance, settled on a bluff (where his father, Ghang Lama, once lived). It was difficult to gauge how badly those structures had been damaged.

Two blurred photos showed men scouring an area in Gulphubanjang littered by stones and debris. The next revealed the body of a man who had died. This man, who came from the Terai region of Nepal, taught mathematics at the local school. He had lived in Gulphubanjang for some fifteen years, ran a wholesale shop. His head and face had been crushed by a heavy, dense weight. The man's life, devoted to teaching children, had been cut down. The existence of any life is fragile, precarious.

It's possible that the photographer posted the pictures of the dead man and child in order to convey the fact of the deaths to others, especially those living in foreign lands. The photos could enable mourners to see the faces of the deceased one last time, as well as their devastated homes and communities. It was jarring to view these images of death alongside sponsored ads and friend requests, amid a running spool of dancing cat videos and smiling babies. There was a kaleidoscope of strands of life in play here, some amiable, some deadly serious, different ways of knowing and relating in direct collision; "a heap of broken images."[11] This phantasmagoric slide show risked making the pictures of hard, brutal death seem like images only, fading away like so many pics skimming the surface of virtual posts. A body buried in earth rested uncomfortably within an empty shimmer of "likes" and selfies. If death becomes unreal, then doesn't life as well? It's true that Buddhist teachings also invoke words like "empty" and "unreal." But some forms of emptiness are more profound, more transcendent, than others.

A posting on Facebook showed the photographic images of two women from a Hyolmo community, accompanied by a text in Nepali. "We would like to express our heartfelt condolences to the departed souls and their families. . . . Those trapped in the destructive earthquake have been sent to heaven." The photographs showed a group of men and women bringing the deceased bodies, wrapped in cloths and adorned with white and gold kathas, up a hill, to a cremation site, and setting them on bundles of damp wood serving as cremation pyres. Those present looked exhausted, worn-out. Much of the infrastructure of funeral rites—sacred texts, ritual implements and instruments—was probably buried in collapsed homes and temples, other needs were pressing, yet these mourners were determined to eliminate the bodies in a good and respectful way. "To pay our respects, we would like to provide a glimpse of the photos," read the text.

In posting the photographs, and responding to those posts, people who knew the deceased were able to pay their respects to the deceased and give consolation to their families. Those commenting on the images were residing in a number of countries, Nepal, for one, but also places like Singapore, Cyprus, Israel, Ontario, Turkey, Korea, and Dubai, United Arab Emirates. Alongside the photographs they had posted words like "RIP" and "om mani peme hung." Several displayed images of lit *chemi* candles in support and honor of the deceased. A couple of followers posted pictures of girls crying—self-images, apparently, of their grief. A few others posted emoji-like images of a tearful face. One comment read, "Why did fate have to punish us with so much harshness?" A viewer asked, "Is this a dream or reality?"

These modalities of mourning were different than the ones evident in the Hyolmo region in the 1980s and 1990s. Any word of a death was now being transmitted though cell phones and Internet connections as much as word of mouth, and emojis were more common than effigies. And yet the sentiments involved appeared to be similar: heartfelt grief for lost loved ones and the need to share that grief with others, within a community of mourners. The Internet was serving as a forum for collective forms of grief, linking people in their sorrow, though they were thousands of miles apart. Social media websites provided a means to "show the face" of the deceased, and they enabled any number of people to witness the cremation and funeral rites. And yet, how well could these people communicate their grief, and share in their sorrow, if they were living in apartments in remote cities in Asia, Europe, and North America, with just a few friends and family nearby? There were few if any ways that people could come together and participate, in an embodied, face-to-face, intensely social way, in a series of rituals, held one week after another, starting with the cremation and ending with the final funeral rites, weeks later. What did these new, virtual forms of mourning entail for the cessation of a life and the slow hard work of mourning? Without an actual, touchable body to mourn and to burn, without full participation in a set of funeral rites, would the specter of a death remain suspended, for some, in a virtual realm between dream and reality?

How does disaster change the experience of mourning? Will grief remain incomplete? This probably depends on how extensive the funeral rites were with any particular loss, and how fully any mourners participated in the process of ritual. But given how much was on the line for days and weeks after the earthquake, with many struggling to obtain food, shelter, and life for their family, it's difficult to imagine that any funeral rites performed in the aftermath of the earthquake would have involved concentrations of thought, emotion, and ritual transformation common to funeral rites in noncatastrophic times. It could be that, while any cremation and first rites after a death were done in an expedient, hard-pressed manner, later funeral rites, conducted weeks or months afterward, would enable mourners to attend in depth to rituals of loss and transformation. It's an open question how people will mourn the deaths after the time of the earthquake.

Each death carries memories with it. My sense is that people will come to associate the deaths of those who died in the earthquake with the time of the earthquake. The history of that death will be intertwined with the event, the mark, of the disaster.

One of the more remarkable aspects of the human response to the earthquake was the efforts of young people and grass-roots organizations in Nepal to provide food, money, medicines, and temporary housing to those harmed by the earthquake. Interconnected through digital technologies and global telecommunications, men and women living in Nepal and abroad raised significant funds within days of the earthquake and brought supplies to their home villages. Skirting the bureaucracy and logistical log jams (and, some say, corruption and ineffectiveness) that hindered initiatives of the Nepalese government and other agencies, they provided invaluable relief to those hurt or displaced by the earthquake. Pasang, Temba, alongside many others, saved lives.

I met with Temba and Pasang in Queens one afternoon late in May. While enjoying a lunch of momos and dal bhāt at a Nepali restaurant in Jackson Heights (we sensed the dissonance of those pleasures with the hardships far away) we talked about the earthquake and the situation in Nepal. "There's affection and love for the villages and the people there," Pasang said. "And so one wants to help as much as possible." Pasang was troubled by the loss of livelihoods of those living in Gulphubanjang and other villages. "When someone doesn't have a home, and other people don't have homes, and everything is ruined and not functioning like it normally does, then you can't make a living," he said. "The situation is so dire."

Temba had heard that in a few remote villages in the northern reaches of the Hyolmo region the residents gave up on their livelihoods there. They released their surviving animals into the woods, left their farmlands and damaged houses, and walked off in the direction of Kathmandu.

I had meant to bring my laptop to Queens, so that I could use it to show Pasang some of the photographs I had taken in Gulphubanjang in 2011. I had forgotten the laptop at home, and so at the restaurant I took out my cell phone and tapped with a finger until I found the photos. "Do you think you could take a look at a few pictures, to see if the girl who had died is in any of them?" I asked Pasang. "Sure," he answered. Imposing this grim procedure on him, I showed him the images, one by one. Each time he shook his head no. "She would have been very little." "I don't think I know who she was, then," I said in putting the smart phone away. In a way, I felt relieved that I did not have any pictures of the girl when she was alive. Having known her in life would have added to the sorrow for her death. I felt for the grief of her parents.

Temba and Pasang said that they thought the people in Nepal had been "traumatized" by the earthquake and the constant tremors since that terrible event. The tremors were continuing, fraying people's nerves and making life highly unpredictable. Some in Nepal had started to joke that the tremors were like a medicine you had to take each day: one before breakfast, and one at night, before going to bed. Some had started to despair. "I spoke with a relative the other day," Temba said, "and he sounded very down — so different from how he usually talks. I told him not to give up hope, that things would be better soon, and the homes in the villages could be rebuilt."

"I was thinking that the days after the earthquake were like a bardo," I said, tentatively. "Well, the current situation is like a bardo," Temba explained. "Everything keeps changing. Nothing stays the same. Each day it changes." "Everything is impermanent," Pasang said. "There are so many uncertainties." "Right," said Temba. "And the thing is, usually a disaster has a single event. It has a clear moment in time, and then there is life after that. With the earthquakes and tremors in Nepal, you can't think that the disaster has ended."

Those in Nepal were in the midst of an uncertain, intermediate stretch of time in which the fallout from the earthquake kept continuing, with no end point in sight. So much was uncertain, impermanent, neither stable nor lasting. The time of the earthquake was open-ended, with no sense of actions that had come to completion. One couldn't think that the earthquake had ended. Life itself stood uncertainly, unhealed, a fresh wound still exposed.

People were traumatized, they said. If this was in fact the case, and there is no reason to think it was not, then it's possible that two orders of trauma were involved. One related to the psychological trauma of facing the death, injuries, destruction, and unrelenting tremors in Nepal, day after day, with no end in sight. The second related to a kind of trauma of perception: a consciousness could not perceive what was involved, the brain could not think on the devastation; that experience of broken, failed perceptions could be disturbing, wounding. (The modern English word trauma drives from the Greek *trauma*, "a wound, a hurt; a defeat.") In looking back at the unsteady stream of perceptions after the earthquake, with its sequences of distressing events, blocked knowledge, shocks of perception, ruptured assumptions, arrested time, and frozen memories, it can be said that the language of perception here was consonant with the language of trauma. There was a catastrophe of perception, a collapse of the means of recognition and comprehension.

A month after the earthquake, those living in the villages had enough food and supplies to sustain themselves. New photographs posted on Facebook showed scores of corrugated iron sheets arriving in the village, to be used to make rooftops. Temporary houses were being made in a number of villages, simple structures built out of a few walls and sheets of iron. People were planning to live in those temporary residences through the monsoon season, braving months of heavy rains and winds, and then work to rebuild their homes in the villages once the weather cleared in the fall and the earth dried. This time around, they would make plans for the design of villages and establish building codes for the construction of any new structures. People were trying to hold onto the idea that this was an opportunity for rebuilding and making something new and fruitful out of the ashes.

The imagery emerging here was one marking the end of a life, the collapse of a household or village or a nation; an intermediate period of despair, mourning, and uncertainty; and then signs of rebirth, rebuilding, and collective, generative making. True to a spirit of poiesis, new forms of life were appearing in place of damaged vitalities. Arising, abiding, ceasing, arising.

The night before I met Temba and Pasang in Queens I sat at my computer at home and scrolled through the many digital photographs I had taken in Gulphubanjang in the summer of 2011. In looking at these images, I kept noticing the built structures within which people lived in the village, the doorways, walls, window frames, hallways, stairways, and rooftops that provided necessary shelter. These structures, apparently quite solid, looked terribly fragile, and the people standing within buildings, or just outside them, beneath the span of their reach, were precarious in their existence in time and space. Considering these photographs that night helped me to under-

Figure 38. Repairing an electric cable connection. Gulphubanjang, 2011.

stand Eduardo Cadava's observation that "there can be no image that is not about destruction and survival, and this is especially the case in the image of ruin. We might even say that the image of ruin tells us what is true of every image: that it bears witness to the enigmatic relation between death and survival, loss and life, destruction and preservation, mourning and memory."[12] Each image is an image of potential ruin, as are all moments in life. In the words of Jacques Derrida, "the ruin does not supervene like an accident upon a monument that was intact only yesterday. In the beginning there is ruin. Ruin is that which happens to the image from the moment of the first gaze. . . . The ruin is not in front of us. . . . It is experience itself."[13] Each perception is a ruin. And yet each perception, each experience, is also an image of potentiality and creation.

Another image recurs. This is a photograph taken on April 26 by Prakash Mathema, an Agence France-Presse photographer based in Kathmandu.[14] A man can be seen trapped in a crevice remaining between two flattened floors of a building, beside a dead friend. The top floor of a three-story house in Swayambu, a neighborhood to the west of Kathmandu, had collapsed, trapping the two men side-by-side for more than eighteen hours. The eyes of the

Figure 39. Gulphubanjang, 2011.

dead man are closed, as though he is sleeping. His body could at first glance
be mistaken for a mannequin, or an effigy. An injury marks the left side of
the face, which is swollen. His body has become lifeless, adjacent to the
matter surrounding it, keeping strange company. The other man is looking
out toward members of a search-and-rescue team. A pillow, placed beneath
this man's head, covers a craggy surface of sharp-edged concrete, stones,
and metal rods. Four men are kneeling close to the small rough crevice from
which they are trying to extract the living man. They must have chiseled this
opening wide enough to pull the two bodies from the collapsed chamber.
A second photograph shows the living man, his face in pain, his body taut
with tension, being wrenched out of the cramped opening. Beside him lies
the body of the dead man, his face quiet and unsensing. The scene suggests a
cauldron of energy, life and death, as though this then were the shape of the
world.

New York, May 2015

Acknowledgments

This book is the product of a collaborative effort from the first pages to the last. In Nepal, many people contributed their time and efforts to the research endeavors at hand, when I was conducting ethnographic research in the Hyolmo region and in Kathmandu in 1986, 1988–89, 1997, 1998, 2000, 2001, 2002, and 2011. Special thanks go to Binod Lama Hyolmo, Pramod Hyolmo, Nogapu Prakash Sherpa Hyolmo, Lhatul Lama, Mingmar Lama, Dawa Lama, Norki Lama, Pasang Norbu Lama Hyolmo, Sange Lama, Norbu Wangchuk Hyolmo, Tashi Lama, Kunsang Lama, Goser Lama, Kānchā Lama, Lama Sonam Tshering, Dawa Jyaba Hyolmo, Pemba Dolma Lama, Tshering Lama, and Sangye Omu Hyolmo. Ghang Lama and Kisang Omu Lama are fondly remembered for their remarkable wisdom and generous presence in life. Residents of Gulphubanjang, Thodong, Boudhanath, and the Hyolmo region more generally welcomed me into their homes in impressively kind and understanding ways. Temba Dongba Hyolmo has been a great friend and colleague since we began working together in the year 2000, and this project has been greatly informed by his selfless efforts and perceptive thinking—and his poetry, to be found in these pages. Karma Gyaltsen Lama has offered invaluable advice and ideas to this work since we first met in 1989. I greatly appreciate his friendship, his unending, creative contributions, and his wise, astute sense of the matters at hand.

Many colleagues and friends have contributed in rich ways to the thought involved. My heartfelt thanks go to Maria Elena Garcia, Sarah Pinto, Sarah Willen, Anne Lovell, Lisa Stevenson, Eduardo Kohn, Byron Good, Mary-Jo

Delvechio Good, Arthur Kleinman, Lisa Stevenson, Anand Pandian, Bhrigupati Singh, Clara Han, Brian Goldstone, Tyler Zoanni, Todd Meyers, João Biehl, Stephanie Spray, Lydie Fialová, Jarrett Zigon, Elizabeth Monson, and Dominic Sur. Veena Das and Jason Throop gave highly insightful and expansive readings of the manuscript, ones which helped me to sharpen several lines of thought. Yael Shinar lent her fine editorial skills to many of the narrative sections of the book. Susan Lloyd McGarry contributed to the formation of key statements. Tracy McGarry contributed in countless ways to the ideas and modes of attentiveness found in the book, and I greatly appreciate her support and friendship.

My colleagues at Sarah Lawrence College have enriched the work immensely. I would especially like to thank Bella Brodzki, Barbara Schecter, David Hollander, Eduardo Lago, Nick Mills, Deanna Barenboim, Aurora Donzelli, Mary Porter, Elke Zuern, Shahnaz Rouse, David Peritz, and Charles Zerner. The Alice Ilchman Chair in Comparative and International Studies, and research funding from the Ziesing Fund for Social Science Research, helped me to conduct anthropological research in Nepal. Students in a range of courses have been a great boon to the ideas considered there. Gemma de Choisy drew on her considerable talents in writing to help get an early version of the manuscript into readable shape. Aidan Seale-Feldman, first as a student and now as an anthropological colleague, has contributed a number of fine reflections to the project. Pragyan Thapa Ghimire helped me to understand the events and aftermath of the earthquake in Nepal in April, 2015, in important ways. Mary Kairidi's keen sense of the languages of life has been invaluable. The staff at the college's library provided valuable assistance, and Jennifer Bianca Hook assisted in highly skilled ways in the production of the photographs in the book.

Several aspects of the book were presented to audiences at Harvard University, Princeton University, McGill University, and the University of Chicago. The feedback I received during these engagements was highly beneficial. Marsha Hurst's invitations to Karma Gyaltsen Lama and me to discuss the book manuscript with her students in her seminars on "Narrative of Death, Living and Caring at the end of Life" at Columbia University have enabled me to further my understanding of processes of dying and death. Fellowships from the John Simon Guggenheim Memorial Foundation and the George A. and Eliza Gardner Howard Foundation, as well as a grant from the American Philosophical Society, enabled me to conduct research in Nepal in the late 1990s and early 2000s.

A visiting research fellowship in 2010 at the Center for the Study of World Religions at the Harvard Divinity School provided a wonderfully stimulating environment within which to think and to write. Conversations there with Janet Gyatso, Charles Hallisey, Anne Monius, and Francis X. Clooney helped me to take my thinking further in several key dimensions. Co-teaching a course with Michael D. Jackson on "Existential and Phenomenological Anthropology" enabled me to develop many of the book's ideas and forms of analysis. Michael's friendship, and his endless willingness to discuss a wide range of thought relevant to anthropological and philosophical inquiry, has added in immense ways to the life of this project.

I also want to thank Priya Nelson, editor at the University of Chicago Press, for her encouragement of this project and her knowing reflections on it. Her invaluable advice on important aspects of the text came at just the right time. Jo Ann Kiser skillfully helped to edit the text and get the language right.

To all involved: thank you for the generous, creative spirit of your lives and work.

Notes

Prelude

1. Thanks to Sangye Omu Lama for her help on the glosses and pragmatic import of the utterance. Sangye tells me that, in most cases, the Nepali phrase "*Āmā khoi?*" is accompanied by other sentences, such as "*Āmā khoi? Timrō āmā kata gayo?*" This would mean, "Where is your mother? Where did she go?" In turn, "*Āmā khoi? Ke bhayo? Katā gayo?*" would mean, "What has happened to your mother? What happened? Where did she go?" Finally, "*Āmā khoi? Timrō āmā gayo*" would mean, "Where is your mother? Your mother left you."

2. For a brief discussion of the phrase and concept "form of no form," see Kasulis, 1981:14.

3. Deleuze, 1994:70.

4. I take the term "spectral subject" from Boulter, 2008.

5. See, for instance, Heidegger, 1982; Arendt, 1958. Michael Lambek writes of how certain anthropological accounts of religion place emphasis "on world construction, entailing an imaginative poiesis by means of symbols, tropes, and performative rituals, and on locating and identifying people as subjects and agents within such worlds" (2008:10).

6. Hayles, 1999:138. See also Handelman, 2005:1–31.

7. Lambek, 2002:15–16.

8. While there is no direct equivalent of the term poiesis in the Hyolmo language, there are two often-voiced verb structures that cover a similar semantic and pragmatic range. The first is *zhoi*, which means "to make, to construct, to build"; the word implies activities creative or constructive. A person makes or constructs a painting, a house, a block print, or a poem. The second is *bheken*. Cognate with the Tibetan written verb *byed-pa*, *bheken* can mean "to make, fabricate," "to do," "to cause, to effect," "to produce, procure, provide," "to commit, perform, execute," "to act, proceed, intend, affect," or "to take, to assume, to count" (cf. Jäschke, 1995:378–79). The verb *bheken* connotes agents doing, making, producing, and fabricating. *Le bheken*, for instance, is to do or undertake some kind of work,

while *ro bheken* is to build a friendship or to come to someone's aid. *Shyarchen bheken*, in turn, means "to arise, to bloom, to blossom." The semantic range of these verb structures convey something of the cultural poiesis at play in how Hyolmo people go about their lives. A strong inclination toward creative fashioning recurs in many domains of life in Hyolmo communities, from the inventive industriousness often displayed by individuals and families to the "skilled means" employed by Buddhist adepts to the diligent attempts to generative positive karmic merit for oneself and others. The focus on self-transformation central to Tibetan Buddhist religious practices similarly involves motifs of overt and active fashioning (see Gyatso, 2002:183). For many who identify as Hyolmo there is an inclination to do things well, to undertake actions in a skillful way, to enjoy aesthetic endeavors, to relate to others in a gracefully respectful way, and to live personally and as a family in ways that speak well to these inclinations (see Desjarlais, 1992). A number of aesthetic sensibilities— evolving around such themes as fullness, presence, balance, and harmony—are evident in the everyday lives of Hyolmo people. A focus on learning skills shapes many a childhood. Health is largely a matter of personal and familial balance, harmony, and presence. Bottles filled with colorful waters stand on display on the shelves of homes in the Hyolmo region, while pots and plates, richly apparent as well, appear immaculately cleansed and polished. Peony is used as a polish for floors, such that a good glow and scent lingers. In many collective gatherings, including the New Year, people delight in singing folk songs and dancing to them. People find pleasure in generating forms, from artwork to conversations to folk songs, on their own or with others. These diffuse, usually unmentioned sensibilities go hand in hand with the processes of making, fashioning, and refashioning.

9. See, for instance, Spinoza, 1985; Deleuze, 2001; Stewart, 2005; Ingold, 2010, 2013; Jackson, 2011.

10. Or so says the narrator of Samuel Beckett's *The Unnameable* (1994:339).

11. Sartre, 1963:xii.

12. FitzGerald, 2011:15.

13. Sterne, 2003:375.

14. Rabinow, 1996:13.

15. Ricoeur, 1990:110–11.

16. Proust, 1993:689.

17. Sylvester, 1993:79–80.

18. Critchley, 2009:xv–xiv.

Part I

1. Our conversation ended when a friend who lived down the street telephoned to say that cable television programs were reporting that two planes had crashed into buildings in New York City.

2. Blanchot, 1989:47.

3. Blanchot, 1989:48.

4. "With the Photograph, we enter into *flat death*. One day, leaving one of my classes, someone said to me with disdain: 'You talk about Death very flatly.'—As if the horror of Death were not precisely its platitude! The horror is this: nothing to say about the death of one whom I love most, nothing to say about her photograph, which I contemplate without

ever being able to get to the heart of it, to transform it.' 'I have no other resource than this *irony*; to speak of the 'nothing to say''' (Barthes, 2010:92–93).

5. Patrul Rinpoche, 1998:85.

6. Patrul Rinpoche, 1998:85.

7. This observation comes directly from the work of anthropologist Michael D. Jackson. See, for instance, Jackson, 2011.

8. Deleuze, 1988:42.

9. "If death is inevitable, this is not at all because death is internal to the existing mode; on the contrary, it is because the existing mode is necessarily open to the exterior, because it necessarily experiences passions, because it necessarily encounters other existing modes capable of endangering one of its vital relations, because the extensive parts belonging to it under its complex relation do not cease to be determined and affected from without" (Deleuze, 1988:100).

10. Kaufman, 2006:4.

11. Kaufman, 2006:98.

12. Lock, 2002.

13. Green, 2008:47.

14. Sedgwick, 2003:175.

15. Sedgwick, 2003:174–75.

16. Sedgwick, 2003:174.

17. Fialová, 2009.

18. On the concept of "phenomenological modification" see Husserl, 1962; and Throop, 2010.

19. It may be that many people throughout the world engage in a similar kind of release of the ego into the larger flows of the world while dying. Charles Hallisey, a scholar of Buddhist religions and ethics, has related to me an observation made by a woman who has worked extensively in hospices, caring for the dying. "All people die Buddhists," she told him.

20. See Green, 2008:11.

21. Patrul Rinpoche. 1998:84.

22. Gilles Deleuze: "What is immanence? A life. . . . No one has described what *a* life is better than Charles Dickens, if we take the indefinite article as an index of the transcendental. A disreputable man, a rogue, held in contempt by everyone, is found as he lies dying. Suddenly, those taking care of him manifest an eagerness, respect, even love, for his slightest sign of life. Everybody bustles about to save him, to the point where, in his deepest coma, this wicked man himself senses soft and sweet penetrating him. But to the degree that he comes back to life, his saviors turn colder, and he becomes once again mean and crude. Between his life and his death, there is a moment that is only that of *a* life playing with death" (2001:28).

23. An American friend has told me of a death by drowning that she witnessed while vacationing along the Pacific Shoreline in Mexico. "A whole world stopped," she said, in speaking of the minutes when someone was trying, unsuccessfully, to resuscitate the person who had drowned. "And it stayed like that for several hours." The day after my own father died in 1993, a mentor of mine, some twenty years older than me, approached me and sat

down by my side. "You will never forget this day," he said. At the time, I took this be a cold and aloof statement, in response to the distress I was feeling. But it has since proven to be true.

24. Paul Ricoeur: "The internal grace that distinguishes the dying person consists in the emergence of the Essential within the very framework of the time of agony. . . . The Essential, in one sense . . . is the religious; it is, if I dare to put it this way, that which is common to every religion and what, at the threshold of death, transgresses the consubstantial limitations of confessing and confessed religion. . . . But because dying is transcultural, it is transconfessional, transreligious in this sense: and this insofar as the Essential breaks through the filter of reading 'languages' of reading. This is perhaps the only situation where one can speak of religious experience. Moreover, I am wary of the immediate, the fusional, the intuitive, the mystical. There is one exception, in the grace of a certain dying" (2009:13–16).

25. Blanchot, 1989:19.

26. Cavell, 1999:418–19. Talal Asad (2007:65–92) draws on Cavell's thought here in writing about the horror involved, as a felt "state of being," in responses to the dissolution of the human body that occurs with suicide bombings, as well as the erosion of bodies perceived in life more generally

27. Mullin, 1988:221.

28. Levinas, 2002:112.

29. Levinas, 2002:128.

30. Jill Robbins uses this term in her book *Altered Reading: Levinas and Literature* (1999) in speaking of the ethicofigural aspects of Emmanuel Levinas's philosophy— encountering the "face" of the other, "substituting" one's own concerns for another, for instance.

31. Ricoeur, 2009:17–20.

32. Ricoeur, 2009:20.

33. Much the same sentiment is evident in certain Tibetan Buddhist societies, dating back several centuries now. The fifteenth-century *Life of Milarepa*, for instance, recounts the way in which Milarepa's devoted student Retchung learns of his master's death. Retchung undertakes a journey and arrives at the cave where Milarepa's corpse lies, surrounded by great disciples, monks, and lay worshippers. Not knowing who Retchung is, some new monks prevent him from coming close to the body. Saddened by this, Retchung sings in an aggrieved tone a song of devotion. Announcing his wish to dedicate the virtues of his religious efforts to his master's intentions, he sings:

> May I realize the result of this dedication, and
> May I see your face.
> I, whom you first treated with compassion,
> Am now being prevented from seeing your body.
> Unfortunate am I, not to see the living Master;
> Yet may I behold your face in death,
> And after seeing your face
> May I receive directly or through visions your most valuable instruction for
>   overcoming obstacles in the two higher stages of meditation (Lhalungpa,
>   1992:180).

In Tibetan Buddhist circles, seeing the face of a dying or deceased loved one can involve the transmission of values or a darśan-like encounter with a divine presence.

34. See Jhala, 1997; as well as Desjarlais, 2003:58, 61. Sarah Pinto traces out similar themes in her account of the daily lives of rural women in the Sitapur district of Uttar Pradesh: "Where seeing threatens, it also involves shared emotion. It acknowledges the new—newcomers, those with a new status—and punctuates change. . . . People advised me, on different occasions, that I should go to the home of a person (often people I have never met) recently returned from hospital because 'everyone will be going to see,' or to a home where someone had died in order to 'see' a corpse. Such acknowledgement is also part of the socialities of emotion, a way to 'share' or 'divide' the grief. Mandates or desires to 'see'—the new, the visitor, the transformed, the resplendent, the bride, the groom, the sick, the injured, the dead—are based in a mode of communion in which visual witnessing does not objectify or efface the subject, but rather shares an essence or emotion and facilitates transformation." (2008:153).

35. As quoted in Difruscia, 2010.

36. See, for instance, Desjarlais, 2003:54–101.

37. Dorje, 2005:219.

38. Thurman, 1994:xxi.

39. Dorje, 2005:267.

40. Dorje, 2005:280.

41. Dorje, 2005:136.

42. Ricoeur, 1992:162.

43. Jeffery Hopkins notes that *"dharma*—the basic Sanskrit word that can be taken as meaning "religion," and that is built from the verbal root *dhr* (to hold)—is etymologized as referring to doctrines (or practices) that hold a practitioner back from fright, specifically frights (1) of being reborn in a bad transmigration; (2) of being trapped in the round of suffering, whether in a good or bad transmigration; (3) of all sentient beings being limited by obstructions preventing full development; and (4) of ordinary appearances and the conception of ordinariness" (1992:226).

44. I am drawing here from anthropological writings which speak of the ways in which ritualized chants and utterances can take a person out of the immediacy of his or her suffering while offering the sense of a broader mythic placement of that suffering. See, for instance, Throop, 2010:182, and Lévi-Strauss, 1963. The word "encompassing" here derives from Karl Jasper's existential phenomenology.

45. On spirit-calling rites among Hyolmo people see Desjarlais, 1992, 1997.

46. Dorje, 2005:221.

47. See, for instance, Burge, 2008.

48. Quoted in Blanchot, 1995:5.

49. Levinas, 1989:133.

50. Bataille, 1988:71.

51. On the phenomenon of neurogenesis after a stroke, see, for instance, Greenberg, 2007.

Part II

1. Karma went on to speak of the cremation and funeral rites performed on his father's behalf. His narration of these events led to a conversation about the importance of his father's life for Hyolmo communities.

2. A buddha field is a "pure realm" manifested by a buddha or a great bodhisattva. Arriving in a buddha field after death is understood to be highly auspicious, for beings born into a buddha field may travel the path toward enlightenment without falling back into the lower realms. Sukhavati—Dewa Chen in Tibetan and Hyolmo—is the blissful buddha field of Amitābha.

3. Soldev is spelled as *son dev* in Tibetan script.

4. Das, 2007:193.

5. Maurice Blanchot: "One ought perhaps to speak of a *subjectivity without any subject*: the wounded space, the hurt of the dying, the already dead body which no one could ever own, the already dead body which no one could ever own, or ever say of it, *I, my body*." (Blanchot, 1995:30). Jonathan Boulter (2008:129) makes compelling use of Blanchot's concept in his discussion of the "posthuman condition" depicted in Beckett's *The Unnameable*: "In some sense the unnamable has become merely a series of impulses, a reflex action of a language that dictates his movement, his thoughts. He has not fully left behind the materiality of the body (he speaks of his tears, hands, knees), but we never feel his body cohere. He is, to borrow once more and finally, from Blanchot, a *subjectivity without subject*: he is a free-floating consciousness attached to no particular body or agency but at times exhibits a kind of compromised interiority (he does, we cannot forget, actively meditate on the condition of being spoken)."

6. Dorje, 2005:274.

7. Corlin, 1998:71.

8. Thurman, 1994:44.

9. Dorje, 2005:313.

10. Dorje, 2005:112, 114, and 167, respectively.

11. Dorje, 2005:281.

12. Dorje, 2005:278.

13. See Dorje, 2005:291–92.

14. It's true that the deceased's absent presence has the potential to leave ghostly reverberations within the world of the living, but that is an altogether different kind of influence.

15. Joan Didion: "People who have recently lost someone have a certain look, recognizable maybe only by those who have seen that look on their own faces. I have noticed it on my face and I notice it now on others. The look is one of extreme vulnerability, nakedness, openness. . . . These people who have lost someone look naked because they think themselves invisible. I myself felt invisible for a period of time, incorporeal" (2005:74–75).

16. The phrase "exact fantasy" comes from Adorno, 1977:131.

17. Suárez-Orozco, 1990:368.

18. Sarah Pinto puts it well when she observes of the use of similar images in Hindu India, "Such things become replicable with the aid of the camera lens, as experience, emotion, and communion remain as traces in the image. Photography may solidify the object of

gaze into a static image, may 'capture' beauty and tragedy, but more importantly, it enables continued socialities, ongoing participation in the weight—or levity—of the moment" (2008:153).

19. Blanchot, 1989:256–7.

20. Blanchot, 1981:52.

21. Blanchot, 1989:256.

22. Vernant, 1991:68.

23. The words are pronounced in the Hyolmo language as, respectively, *ku, sung, thu, yenden, thilen.*

24. Dorje, 2005:379.

25. Dorje, 2005:345.

26. *Rig* literally means "species, kind, class, lineage, family," while *nga* means "five." For a detailed explanation see Trungpa, 1995:216.

27. Lacan, 1992:55.

28. *Doyen ngogen* is spelled in Tibetan as '*dod yon bsngo ba.*

29. See Jäschke, 1995:290, 576.

30. One text read early on is known as *dhemen* (*mdo-man* in Tibetan). An acronym of the words *dewa chen gi melum*, dhemen consists of a set of sutras that give information pertaining to *dewa chen gi shing kham*. This text describes the qualities of Dewa Chen, a blissful buddha field "where only pleasures and happiness exist," as well as of Amitābha, the Buddha associated with that Pure Land of Bliss. The main purpose of reciting the dhemen is to inform the deceased person about *dewa chen gi shing kham*, to offer guidance in getting there, and to depict the various deities that must be prayed to in order to arrive there. Yet many Hyolmo people also understand that those who recite the dhemen are helping, and giving support to, the deceased. The more times the text is recited, the more it benefits the deceased.

31. The mani prayers performed during Hyolmo funeral rites compare in significant ways to laments and ritual wailing undertaken in a number of societies when members of a community die, in which people "lodge the work of mourning in poetics" (Briggs, 2014:315; for exemplary accounts of laments in specific societies, see, for instance, Urban, 1988; Seremetakis, 1991; Wilce, 2003, 2008; and Briggs, 1992, 1993, 2014). One point of distinction is that, unlike many of these laments, which often attend to specific aspects of the deceased's biography and the mourners' relations to the deceased in life or the possible causes and implications of a death, the mani prayers do not specify individual aspects of the death at hand. The prayers are voiced in much the same way at all cremation and funeral rites—and their indistinctiveness, general prayers that go beyond the specifics of a particular human life, speaks to the processes of cessation, transformation, and de-individualization at work during the rites.

32. In the processions that I have attended, when mourners brought the corpse to the cremation ground or carried an effigy of the deceased to the scene of the final funeral rites, I noticed tears lining the faces of many mourners as they accompanied the deceased and sang mani prayers. I have also been affected by the tenor of these moods, even though I was observing them from a place not immediate to the grief involved. Some have told me that participating in the prayers has brought to mind for them people they have lost themselves—a

father, a husband, a daughter. Because of this, some women and men are apprehensive about participating in the mani prayers, especially during the cremation and funeral processions; they join in on them because it is right and proper to do so. The prayers are intensely echoic of previous deaths, of other marked losses. Any tears shed are not necessarily due to the parting at hand.

33. On this see Desjarlais, 1997.

34. G. M. Hopkins, 2011:54.

35. Deleuze and Guattari, 1987:299.

36. From the poem "Reuben, Reuben" by Michael S. Harper, 1970:64.

Part III

1. Blanchot, 1989:257.

2. See, for instance, Jäschke, 1995:405.

3. There are also several days in the month that, customarily, a body is not cremated: the eighth day after a new moon, the eighteenth day, and the second day before a new moon. Most cremations take place on the second or third day after the day of the death, although some bodies are cremated the day after the death. An exception to this are rites held for the bodies of people who died by suicide or at the hands of others, since it is a law that the police must inspect such bodies before they can be disposed of. Poorer families in particular will often try to cremate the body of a relative sooner than later, since they cannot afford the cost of keeping the body in their household and hosting visitors who help to perform the mani rites. Wealthier families are generally able to earn more karmic merit for the deceased in the days prior to a cremation, as they can afford to sponsor the rites which accrue such merit. Wealth begets good karma, which can ripen into subsequent wealth in any future lives.

4. See Becker-Ritterspach, 1994.

5. When a single dadar flag is used, it also signifies the five directions.

6. See Jäschke, 1995:405, 584.

7. Karma, in turn, said that, in contrast to the strong effect that touching a corpse has had on him, corpse impurity did not really bother him. "That really doesn't bother me," he said. "I don't know why. People are so concerned, but I don't care so much about that. I cleanse myself [after I return from the cremation site], of course. But I'm not really concerned about it."

8. Derrida, 1987.

9. *Thi* is spelled as *Krus* in written Tibetan.

10. *Rhiko* is the Hyolmo word for "bone" in general. *Rhiba* refers specifically to burnt bones. The transformation in form and quality apparently calls for a distinct name.

11. Jaspers, 1932:178–9. See also Jackson, 2009:xii.

Part IV

1. Sharf, 2005:257.

2. Thanks to Charles Hallisey for raising these ideas and questions to me.

3. Handelman and Lindquist, 2005.

4. Kapferer, 2006:672.

5. Kapferer, 2006:672.

6. Cabezón, 2009.

7. Cabezón, 2009.

8. Rappaport, 1999.

9. Sacks, 1985:19.

10. Gyatso, n.d.

11. The paper is also sometimes called a *mhin jhang*, "name purification."

12. Berger, 1972:4.

13. Derrida, 1994:9.

14. Goser Lama explained the process as such: "While performing the visualization, the lama hooking the consciousness should make the image visualized in a good way, so as to hook not only the consciousness but all the features of the deceased, such as his bodily structure, his voice, and so forth. Everything should be established in this way."

15. See, for instance, Jäschke, 1995:129, 337.

16. Goser Lama's words gave the flavor of some of these instructions:

The lama should inform the deceased that he is already dead and has no connection or relation with any living human beings. Taking this in mind, the dead person has to realize that he is no more like the living person, and that he has to make his way either to the Pure Land or to the next life, as determined by his actions as a living being on earth.

The lama also advises the consciousness that there will appear innumerable, familiar voices, saying, "I am your parents, come with me," or "I am your beloved, come with me." If the consciousness follows these voices, the dead one will find no way to go and has to keep roaming in the between. "These voices are the result of the bad deeds and sins committed in your lifetime, and they've appeared to confuse you and keep you roaming in the between. You should not follow them, but listen carefully to these words and do as instructed by the lama."

17. Lopez, 1998:9.

18. Robinson and Johnson, 1997:89.

19. The name card and stand do in fact resemble an arrow. In some Tibetan societies a parallel kind of print block is fixed on an actual arrow.

20. My thinking and language here is influenced by some words of Derrida: "We are already specters of the 'televised.' In the nocturnal space in which this image of us, this picture we are in the process of having 'taken,' is described, it is already night. Furthermore, because we know that, once it has been taken, captured, this image will be reproducible in our absence, because we know this already, we are already haunted by this future, which brings our death. Our disappearance is already here" (Derrida and Stiegler, 2002:131).

21. Freud, 1916.

22. See, for instance, Hertz, 1960; and Metcalf and Huntington, 1991.

23. The centrality of these exchanges at a ghewa is underscored by the fact that ghewa are not held for young children (before the age of eight or nine) who have died. What is done instead is a small, brief rite called *torma tange*, "sending/giving torma," in which lamas

prepare several *torma* (figures made mostly of rice, flour, and butter and used in Tibetan Buddhist ritual practices) and a milky water, then offer these foods to the dead child while reciting certain mantras: the offerings satiate the child's hunger and thirst. As many Hyolmo people understand it, since young children have not lived long enough to accrue any significant debts to others, the distribution of foods at a ghewa would have no beneficial effect. Some in fact feel that, if a ghewa were performed on a child's behalf, it would be a burden to her; it would complicate the processes of her death and rebirth, and the child could be forced to remain roaming in the between. Another reason that ghewa are not held for young children is that, since they are rather innocent and pure, it's not necessary to engage in the ritual actions of eliminating sins and impurities from their consciousness, as is the case with older people. Others in turn feel that, since so many members of a community offer their assistance to the bereaved family when a ghewa is being performed, the dead person owes a debt to them for this assistance and support; while any older person who dies would have had occasion to assist in similar ways before his death, the burden of that debt is balanced out. But if a ghewa were to be held for a young child, who by definition never had a chance to help others out, the assistance and support paid to her at the ghewa would constitute a "load" or "burden" for the child that could never be paid back. That burden would detract from the child's karmic merit and trouble its passage in the bardo.

24. When lamas lead the effigy from the house to the temple, they are "transferring it from this to the otherworld," as anthropologist David Holmberg reports on a similar process among Tamang people of north-central Nepal. Holmberg goes on to note that this movement of the effigy parallels the movement of the consciousness "from the world of the living to the authority of the Buddha" (1989:208).

25. See, especially, Derrida, 1974.

26. It could be argued, in the spirit of a deconstruction of presumed origins and essentials, that the lama texts are, in themselves, a supplement to the word of the Buddha and the originary knowledge, enlightenment, and transcendence associated with that speech. The texts, a written substitution, copies upon copies, entail potent sets of linguistic signs. They are a necessary supplement.

27. Objects of this sort, sometimes referred to as *ketak*, are customarily made in the name of a recently deceased person. Soon after the death a lama will perform *tsi*, "calculation," to determine what object should be made, be it a thangku scroll painting, a statue, or a new copy of a set of sacred texts (in performing the tsi, the birth year of the person and his or her time of death are taken into consideration).

28. Some often choose on their own to observe certain restraints for a year after the death.

29. Along with other rites and prayers, a ne par is performed in which the consciousness is summoned, established on the name card, and then sent to the Pure Land. In Kathmandu in recent years, however, Buddhist lamas esteemed for their knowledge and spiritual powers (who mostly happen to be of Tibetan descent) are often asked to perform these rites. The reason for this is that, while local lineage lamas might well have transferred the consciousness to the Pure Land during any earlier funeral rites held, it's possible that they might not have been successful in this endeavor. More powerful lamas are therefore asked

to perform the rite. The arrow-shot rite performed on this day also serves as a kind of "re-confirmation" that the consciousness is being sent to the best place possible.

Part V

1. Jäschke defines *tsha-tsha* as "little images of the Buddha, and conical figures, molded of clay and used at sacrifices" (1995:443).

2. Corlin, 1998:73.

3. Malamoud, 1982:448.

4. See Jäschke, 1995:529.

5. Jäschke, 1995:529.

6. These concerns and practices say as much about the means and implications of sensory engagement as they do about the need to keep bodies uncontaminated.

7. See Robinson and Johnson, 1997:80.

8. Mills, 2003:226–7.

9. As Claes Corlin observed of a similar mortuary process among Tibetan Buddhist peoples, "Thus there is a process of transformation from the most tangible evidence of death (the corpse) to a fully abstract and general symbol" (1998:73).

10. Lhalungpa, 1977:163.

11. Freud, 1916:306.

12. To draw from Freud: "In an analysis . . . a thing which has not been understood inevitably reappears: like an unlaid ghost, it cannot rest until the mystery has been solved and the spell broken" (1909:122).

13. Battaglia, 1992.

14. Hertz, 1960.

15. For a detailed inquiry into the concept of bhaja or "echo" in Hyolmo Buddhist lives, see Desjarlais, 2000 and 2003.

16. Strong, 2004:6.

17. Hyolmo funeral rites are "paratexts of elementary tenets of Buddhist doctrine," to borrow the words of anthropologist David Holmberg. "Death feasts are Buddhist rituals," Holmberg notes of the mortuary rites of Tamang peoples of north-central Nepal. "Elementary notions of karma, suffering, desire, and disjunctions between this and otherworlds all unfold in a ritual rather than a textual idiom" (1989:205).

18. For an exemplary account of the significance of mastery play in the lives of peoples, see Jackson, 2005.

19. Freud, 1990:12.

20. Freud, 1990:13.

21. Erikson, 1995:189.

22. This possibility compares to Dominick Lacapra's contention, building on Freud, that mourning might be considered as a form of "working through" whereas melancholy is a form of "acting out." In this perspective, melancholia is characteristic of an arrested process. Mourning, in contrast, "brings the possibility of engaging trauma and achieving a reinvestment in, or recathexis of, life which allows one to begin again" (2001:66). Lacapra finds this distinction important among survivors of the Holocaust, for some were able to "work

through" what happened to them in forms of mourning, whereas others remained stuck in a form of melancholia, characterized as an arrested process "in which the depressed, self-berating, and traumatized self, locked in compulsive repetition, is possessed by the past, faces a future of impasses, and remains narcissitically identified with the lost object" (2001:65–66). The constructive, transformative repetition evident in Hyolmo funeral rites is geared more toward mourning as a form of working through. As such, it perhaps works against any potential impasse of compulsive, static repetition of loss and trauma.

23. Derrida, 1994:9.

24. Taylor, 1993.

25. Taylor, 1993:664.

26. Taylor, 1993:665.

27. Taylor, 1993:665.

28. Taylor, 1993.

29. Faulkner, 1990:144.

30. Heruka, 1995:173–74.

31. Heruka, 1995:178–81.

32. Heruka, 1995:178–81.

33. Heruka, 1995:180.

34. Stolorow, 2007:17.

35. This observation relates to Henri Bergson's idea that time—and life more generally—implies processes of differentiation and novelty, as evident in his claim that "time is the invention of the new, or is nothing at all" (Bergson 1998:340). On this see also Marrati, 2011:48.

36. See Desjarlais 1992, 1997.

37. On the phrase "traumatism of the other," see, for instance, Levinas, 2000.

38. Jacques Derrida (1999:11) uses the phrase "happy traumatism" in speaking of an important contribution from the philosopher Emmanuel Levinas, who spoke of the "traumatism of the other."

39. Montaigne, 1958:62.

40. For an incisive account of the experience and implications of time in anthropological research and thought, see Pandian, 2012.

41. John Keats, *Ode to a Nightingale*:

> Darkling I listen; and, for many a time
> I have been half in love with easeful Death,
> Call'd him soft names in many a mused rhyme,
> To take into the air my quiet breath.

42. This immersion led, once I surfaced from it, to a book of mine entitled *Counterplay: An Anthropologist at the Chessboard* (Desjarlais, 2011).

43. *Le soleil ni la mort ne se peuvent regarder fixement.* François de La Rochefoucauld, Maxim 26. A more direct translation of this maxim would be: "The sun nor death can be looked at directly."

44. To use terms of Gilles Deleuze, 1994:4.

Postscript: Beyond Description

1. Barry, 2015.

2. Dixit, 2015.

3. Bhandari and Archdeacon, 2015.

4. Barry, 2015.

5. *Twitter*. @Salokya. Umesh Shrestha. April 27, 2015.

6. As Zygmunt Bauman (1995:149) puts it.

7. The writer Karl Ove Knausgaard touches on similar observations in the opening pages of his expansive novel *My Struggle: Book 1*:

> A father and his child are killed as the father attempts to pull the child out of the line of fire in a town somewhere in the Middle East, and the image of them huddled together as the bullets thud into flesh, causing their bodies to shudder, as it were, is caught on camera, transmitted to one of the thousands of satellites orbiting the Earth and broadcast on TV sets around the world, from where it slips into our consciousness as yet another picture of death or dying. These images have no weight, no depth, no time, and no place, nor do they have any connection to the bodies that spawned them. They are nowhere and everywhere. Most of them just pass through us and are gone; for diverse reasons some linger and live on in the dark recesses of the brain (Knausgaard, 2012:7).

8. Fuller and Buckley, 2015.

9. "Nepal quake survivor: 'I'll never feel safe again.'" BBC News. 13 May 2015. http://www.bbc.com/news/world-asia-32729286.

10. Blanchot, 1995:41.

11. To draw from T. S. Eliot's *The Wasteland:*

> What are the roots that clutch, what branches grow
> Out of this stony rubbish? Son of man,
> You cannot say, or guess, for you know only
> A heap of broken images, where the sun beats,
> And the dead tree gives no shelter, the cricket no relief,
> And the dry stone no sound of water.

12. Cadava, 2001:35.

13. Derrida, 1993:68–69.

14. One place that this photograph can be seen is: Olivier Laurent, "Life and Death in One Picture after Quake Hits Nepal," Times Lightbox, April 26, 2015. http://time.com/3835915/earthquake-nepal-kathmandu-trapped/?xid=tcoshare.

References

Adorno, Theodor. 1977. "The Actuality of Philosophy." *Telos* 131:120–33.

Arendt, Hannah. 1958. *The Human Condition*. Chicago: University of Chicago Press.

Asad, Talal. 2007. *On Suicide Bombing*. New York: Columbia University Press.

Barry, Ellen. 2015. "Earthquake Devastates Nepal, Killing More than 1,900." *New York Times*. April 25.

Barthes, Roland. 2010 [1981]. *Camera Lucida*. New York: Hill & Wang.

Battaglia, Debora. 1992. "The Body in the Gift: Memory and Forgetting in Sabarl Mortuary Exchange." *American Ethnologist* 19:3–18.

Bataille, Georges. 1988. *Inner Experience*. Buffalo: State University of New York Press.

Bauman, Zygmont. 1995. *Life in Fragments: Essays in Postmodern Morality*. New York: Blackwell.

Becker-Ritterspach, R. O. A. 1994. "Two Nepalese Shrines of the Śāha-period with Eclectic Characteristics," *Artibus Asiae* 54:156–93.

Beckett, Samuel. 1994. *Three Novels: Molloy, Malone Dies, The Unnameable*. New York: Grove Press.

Berger, John. 1972. *Ways of Seeing*. New York: Penguin.

Bergson, Henri. 1998 [1907]. *Creative Evolution*. New York: Dover.

Bhandari, Rajneesh, and Colin Archdeacon. 2015. "Devastation in Katmandu." Times Video. *New York Times*, April 25; http://www.nytimes.com/video/world/asia/100000003649768/devastation-in-katmandu.html?src=vidm

Blanchot, Maurice. 1981. *The Gaze of Orpheus and Other Literary Essays*. Trans. Lydia Davis. Barrytown, NY: Station Hill Press.

———. 1989. *The Space of Literature*. Lincoln: University of Nebraska Press.

———. 1995. *The Writing of the Disaster*. Lincoln: University of Nebraska Press.

Boulter, Jonathan. 2008. *Beckett: A Guide for the Perplexed*. New York: Continuum.

Briggs, Charles. 1992. "'Since I Am a Woman, I Will Chastise My Relatives': Gender, Reported Speech, and the (Re)production of Social Relations in Warao Ritual Wailing." *American Ethnologist* 19:337–61.

———. 1993. "Personal Sentiments and Polyphonic Voices in Warao Women's Ritual Wailing: Music and Poetics in a Critical and Collective Discourse." *American Anthropologist* 95:929–57.

———. 2014. "Dear Dr. Freud." *Cultural Anthropology* 29:312–43.

Burge, Kathleen. 2008. "As life ebbs, healing music flows." *Boston Globe*, October 26.

Cabezón, José Ignacio. 2009. "Introduction." In *Tibetan Ritual*, ed. José Ignacio Cabezón, 1–34. Oxford: Oxford University Press.

Cadava, Eduardo. 2001. "*Lapsus Imaginis*: The Image in Ruins." *October* 96:35–60.

Cavell, Stanley. 1999. *The Claim of Reason*. Oxford: Oxford University Press.

Corlin, Claes. 1998. "The Journal through the Bardo: Notes on the Symbolism of Tibetan Mortuary Rites and the Tibetan Book of the Dead." In *On the Meaning of Death: Essays on Mortuary Rituals and Eschatological Beliefs*, ed. S. Cederroth, C. Corlin, and J. Lindström, 63–76. Uppsala: Almqvist & Wiksell International.

Critchley, Simon. 2009. *The Book of Dead Philosophers*. New York: Vintage.

Das, Veena. 2007. *Life and Words: Violence and the Descent into the Ordinary*. Berkeley: University of California Press.

Deleuze, Gilles. 1988. *Spinoza: Practical Philosophy*. San Francisco: City Light Books.

———. 1994. *Difference and Repetition*. New York: Columbia University Press.

———. 2001. *Pure Immanence: Essays on a Life*. Cambridge, MA: Zone Books.

Deleuze, Gilles, and Félix Guattari. 1987. *A Thousand Plateaus: Capitalism and Schizophrenia*. Trans. Brian Massumi. Minneapolis: University of Minnesota Press.

Derrida, Jacques. 1974. *Of Grammatology*. Baltimore: Johns Hopkins University Press.

———. 1987. "On Reading Heidegger," *Research in Phenomenology* 17:171–85.

———. 1993. *Memoirs of the Blind: The Self-Portrait and Other Ruins*. Chicago: University of Chicago Press.

———. 1994. *Specters of Marx*. New York: Routledge.

———. 1999. *Adieu to Emmanuel Levinas*. Stanford, CA: Stanford University Press.

Derrida, Jacques, and Bernard Stiegler. 2002. *Echographies of Television: Filmed Interviews*. Cambridge: Polity Press.

Desjarlais, Robert. 1992. *Body and Emotion: The Aesthetics of Illness and Healing in the Nepal Himalayas*, Philadelphia: University of Pennsylvania Press.

———. 1997. "Presence," In *The Performance of Healing*, ed. Carol Laderman and Marina Roseman, 143–64. New York: Routledge.

———. 1997. *Shelter Blues: Sanity and Selfhood among the Homeless*. Philadelphia: University of Pennsylvania Press.

———. 2000. "Echoes of a Yolmo Buddhist's Life, in Death." *Cultural Anthropology* 15:260–93.

———. 2003. *Sensory Biographies: Lives and Deaths among Nepal's Yolmo Buddhists*. Berkeley: University of California Press.

———. 2011. *Counterplay: An Anthropologist at the Chessboard*. Berkeley: University of California Press.

Didion, Joan. 2005. *The Year of Magical Thinking*. New York: Vintage.

Difruscia, Kim Turcot. 2010. "Listening to Voices. An Interview with Veena Das." *Altérités* 7:136–45.

Dixit, Kunda. 2015. "A View of Katmandu after the Earthquake." *New York Times*. April 26.

Dorje, Gyurme, trans., Graham Coleman with Thupten Jinpa, eds. 2005. *The Tibetan Book of the Dead: First Complete Translation.* New York: Penguin.

Erikson, Erik. 1995. *Childhood and Society.* New York: Random House.

FitzGerald, Edward. 2011 [1859]. *The Rubáiyát of Omar Khayyám.* New York: Dover.

Faulkner, William. 1990 [1932]. *Light in August.* New York: Vintage International.

Fialová, Lydie. 2009. "Medicine and the Nature of Hope." In *Hoffnung in Wissenschaft, Gesellschaft und Politik in Tschechien und Deutschland,* ed. Michal Andel, Detlev Brandes, and Jiri Pesek. Veröffentlichungen zur Kultur und Geschichte im östlichen Europa, Band 32.

Freud, Sigmund. 1909. "Analysis of a Phobia in a 5-year-old Boy." In *The Standard Edition of the Complete Psychological Works of Sigmund Freud, Volume X (1909): Two Case Histories,* ed. and trans. J. Strachey, 1–150. London: Hogarth Press and the Institute of Psycho-Analysis.

———. 1916. "On Transience." In *The Standard Edition of the Complete Psychological Works of Sigmund Freud, Volume XIV (1914–1916): On the History of the Psycho-Analytic Movement, Papers on Metapsychology and Other Works,* ed. and trans. J. Strachey, 303–7. London: Hogarth Press and the Institute of Psycho-Analysis.

———. 1990 [1920]. *Beyond the Pleasure Principle.* New York: Norton.

Fuller, Thomas, and Chris Buckley. 2015. "Earthquake Aftershocks Jolt Nepal as Death Toll Rises above 3,400." *New York Times,* April 26.

Green, James. 2008. *Beyond the Good Death: The Anthropology of Modern Dying.* Philadelphia: University of Pennsylvania Press.

Greenberg, D. A. 2007. "Neurogenesis and Stroke." *CNS Neurological Disorders Drug Targets.* 6(5):321–25.

Gyatso, Janet. 2002. "The Ins and Outs of Self-Transformation: Personal and Social Sides of Visionary Practice in Tibetan Buddhism." In *Self and Self-Transformation in the History of Religions,* ed. David Shulman and Guy Stroumsa, 183–94. New York: Oxford University Press.

———. n.d. "The Relic Text as Prophecy: The Semantic Drift of *Byang-bu* and Its Appropriation in the Treasure Tradition." Unpublished manuscript, Harvard University.

Handelman, Don. 2005. "Introduction: Why Ritual in Its Own Right? How So?" In *Ritual in Its Own Right: Exploring the Dynamics of Transformation,* ed. Don Handelman and Galina Lindquist, 1–34. New York: Berghahn Books.

Handelman, Don, and Galina Lindquist, eds. 2005. *Ritual in Its Own Right.* New York: Berghahn Books.

Harper, Michael S. 1970. *Dear John, Dear Coltrane.* Champaign: University of Illinois Press.

Hayles, Katherine Hayles. 1999. *How We Became Postmodern: Virtual Bodies in Cybernetics, Literature, and Infomatics.* Chicago: Chicago University Press.

Heidegger, Martin. 1982. *The Question Concerning Technology, and Other Essays.* New York: Harper Perennial.

Hertz, Robert. 1960. "A Contribution to the Study of the Collective Representation of

Death." In *Death; & the Right Hand*, trans. Rodney and Claudia Needham, 27–96. Glencoe, IL: Free Press.

Heruka, Tsang Nyön. 1995. *The Life of Marpa the Translator: Seeing Accomplishes All*. Boston: Shambala Publications.

Holmberg, David. 1989. *Order in Paradox: Myth, Ritual, and Exchange among Nepal's Tamang*. Ithaca, NY: Cornell University Press.

Hopkins, Jeffrey. 1992. "A Tibetan Perspective on the Nature of Spiritual Experience," In *Paths to Liberation: The Mārga and Its Transformations in Buddhist Thought*, ed. Robert Buswell and Robert Gimello, 225–64. Honolulu: University of Hawai'i Press.

Hopkins, Gerald Manley. 2011. *The Selected Poems of Gerald Manley Hopkins*. New York: Dover.

Husserl, Edmund. 1962. *Ideas: General Introduction to Pure Phenomenology*. New York: Collier Books.

Ingold, Tim. 2010. "The Textility of Making." *Cambridge Journal of Economics* 34:91–102.

———. 2013. *Making: Anthropology, Archaeology, Art and Architecture*. London and New York: Routledge.

Jackson, Michael. 2005. *Existential Anthropology*. New York: Berghahn Books.

———. 2009. *The Palm at the End of the Mind: Relatedness, Religiosity, and the Real*. Durham, NC: Duke University Press.

———. 2011. *Life within Limits: Well-being in a World of Want*. Durham, NC: Duke University Press.

Jäschke, H. A. 1995 [1881]. *A Tibetan-English Dictionary*. New Delhi: Motilal Banarsidass.

Jaspers, Karl. 1932. *Philosophie, Vol. 2, Existenzenhellung*. Berlin: Springer Verlag.

Jhala, Jayasinjji. 1997. "Some Speculations on the Concept of Indic Frontality Prompted by Questions on Portraiture." *Visual Anthropology* 9:2.

Kapferer, Bruce. 2006. "Virtuality." In *Theorizing Rituals: Classical Topics, Theoretical Approaches, Analytical Concepts*, ed. J. Kreinath, J. A. M. Snoek, M. Stausberg, 671–84. Leiden: Numen Book Series, Brill Academic Publishers.

Kasulis, T. P. 1981. *Zen Action, Zen Person*. Honolulu: University of Hawai'i Press.

Kaufman, Sharon. 2006. . . . *And a Time to Die: How American Hospitals Shape the End of Life*. Berkeley: University of California Press.

Knausgaard, Karl Ove. 2012. *My Struggle: Book One*. New York: Farrar, Straus & Giroux.

Lacan, Jacques. 1992. *The Seminar, Book VII, The Ethics of Psychoanalysis, 1959–60*. Trans. Dennis Porter. New York: Routledge.

Lacapra, Dominick. 2001. *Writing History, Writing Trauma*. Baltimore: Johns Hopkins University Press.

Lambek, Michael. 2002. *The Weight of the Past: Living with History in Mahajanga, Madagascar*. Hampshire: Palgrave.

———, ed. 2008. *A Reader in the Anthropology of Religion*. New York: Wiley-Blackwell.

Levinas, Emmanuelle. 1980. *Totality and Infinity: An Essay on Exteriority*. Berlin: Springer.

———. 1989. *The Levinas Reader*. Ed. Seán Hand. New York: Blackwell.

———. 2000. *God, Death, and Time*. Stanford, CA: Stanford University Press.

———. 2002. *Entre Nous*. New York: Columbia University Press.

Lévi-Strauss, Claude. 1963. "The Effectiveness of Symbols." In *Structural Anthropology*, 185–205. New York: Basic Books.

Lhalungpa, Lopsang P., trans. 1992. *The Life of Milarepa*. New York: Penguin.

Lock, Margaret. 2002. "Inventing a New Death and Making It Believable." *Anthropology and Medicine*, 9:97–115.

Lopez, Donald. 1998. *Elaborations on Emptiness*. Princeton, NJ: Princeton University Press.

Malamoud, Charles. 1982. "Mort sans visage." In *La mort, les morts dans les sociétés anciennes*, ed. G. Gnoli and J.-P. Vernant, 441–53. Paris: Cambridge University Press and Editions de la Maison des Sciences de l'Homme.

Marrati, Paola. 2011. "The Novelty of Life." *Constellations* 18:48–52.

Metcalf, Peter, and Richard Huntington. 1991. *Celebrations of Death: The Anthropology of Mortuary Ritual*. Cambridge: Cambridge University Press.

Mills, Martin. 2003. *Identity, Ritual and State in Tibetan Buddhism: The Foundations of Authority in Gelukpa Monasticism*. New York: Routledge.

Montaigne, Michel de. 1958 [1588]. *The Complete Essays of Montaigne*. Stanford, CA: Stanford University Press.

Mullin, Glen. 1988. *Death and Dying: The Tibetan Tradition*. New York: Penguin.

Pandian, Anand. 2012. "The Time of Anthropology: Notes from a Field of Contemporary Experience." *Cultural Anthropology* 27:547–71.

Patrul Rinpoche. 1998. *Words of My Perfect Teacher*. Boston: Shambala Publications.

Pinto, Sarah. 2008. *Where There Is No Midwife*. New York: Berghahn Books.

Proust, Marcel. 1993. *The Captive; The Fugitive*. Trans. K. Scott Moncrieff and Terence Kilmartin, revised, D. J. Enright. New York: Random House.

Rabinow, Paul. 1996. *Essays on the Anthropology of Reason*. Princeton, NJ: Princeton University Press.

Rappaport, Roy. 1999. *Ritual and Religion in the Making of Humanity*. Cambridge: Cambridge University Press.

Ricoeur, Paul. 1990. *Time and Narrative, Volume 1*. Chicago: University of Chicago Press.

———. 1992. *Oneself as Another*. Chicago: University of Chicago Press.

———. 2009. *Living up to Death*. Chicago: University of Chicago Press.

Robbins, Jill. 1999. *Altered Reading: Levinas and Literature*. Berkeley: University of California Press.

Robinson, Richard, and Willard Johnson. 1997. *The Buddhist Religion: A Historical Introduction*. 4th ed. Belmont, CA: Wadsworth.

Sacks, Peter. 1985. *The English Elegy: Studies in the Genre from Spenser to Yeats*. Baltimore: Johns Hopkins University Press.

Sartre, Jean-Paul. 1963. *Search for a Method*. Trans. Hazel Barnes. New York: Knopf.

Sedgwick, Eve. 2003. *Touching Feeling: Affect, Pedagogy, Performativity*. Durham, NC: Duke University Press.

Seremetakis, C. Nadia. 1991. *The Last Word: Women, Death, and Divination in Inner Mani*. Chicago: University of Chicago Press.

Sharf, Robert. 2005. "Ritual." In *Critical Terms for the Study of Buddhism*, ed. Donald S. Lopez Jr., 245–70. Chicago: University of Chicago Press.

Spinoza, Baruch. 1985. *The Collected Works of Spinoza, Volume I*. Ed. and trans. Edwin Curley. Princeton, NJ: Princeton University Press.

Sterne, Laurence. 2003. *The Life and Opinions of Tristram Shandy, Gentleman*. New York: Penguin.

Stewart, Kathleen. 2005. "Cultural Poesis: The Generativity of Emergent Things." In *Handbook of Qualitative Research*. 3rd ed., ed. Norman Denzin and Yvonna Lincoln, 1027–42. New York: Sage Publications.

Stolorow, Robert. 2007. *Trauma and Human Existence: Autobiographical, Psychoanalytic, and Philosophical Reflections*. New York: Routledge.

Strong, John. 2004. *Relics of the Buddha*. Princeton, NJ: Princeton University Press.

Suárez-Orozco, Marcelo. 1990. "Speaking of the Unspeakable: Toward a Psychosocial Understanding of Responses to Terror." *Ethos* 18:353–83.

Sylvester, David. 1993. *Interviews with Francis Bacon*. New York: Thames & Hudson.

Taylor, Anne Christine. 1993. "Remembering to Forget: Identity, Mourning, and Memory among the Jivaro." *Man*, n.s., 28:653–78.

Throop, Jason. 2010. *Suffering and Sentiment: Exploring the Vicissitudes of Suffering and Pain*. Berkeley: University of California Press.

Thurman, Robert, trans. and ed. 1994. *The Tibetan Book of the Dead*. New York: Random House.

Trungpa, Chogyam. 1995. *The Life of Marpa the Translator: Seeing Accomplishes All*. Boston: Shambala Publications.

Turner, Terrence. 1966 [1931]. *A Comparative and Etymological Dictionary of the Nepali Language*. Delhi: Allied Publishers.

Urban, Greg. 1988. "Ritual Wailing in Amerindian Brazil." *American Anthropologist* 90:385–400.

Vernant, Jean Pierre. 1991. *Mortals and Immortals: Collected Essays*. Princeton, NJ: Princeton University Press.

Wilce, James. 2003. *Eloquence in Trouble: The Poetics and Politics of Complaint in Rural Bangladesh*. Oxford: Oxford University Press.

———. 2008. *Crying Shame: Metaculture, Modernity, and the Exaggerated Death of Lament*. New York: Wiley-Blackwell.

Wylie, T.V. 1959. "A Standard System of Tibetan Transcription." *Harvard Journal of Asiatic Studies* 22:261–67.

Index